THE POEMS OF OSSIAN

JAMES MACPHERSON

Table of Contents

Table of Contents

THE POEMS OF OSSIAN

JAMES MACPHERSON

Kessinger Publishing reprints thousands of hard–to–find books!

- CATH–LODA — DUAN I.
- CATHLODA — DUAN II.
- CATH–LODA — DUAN III.
- COMALA, A DRAMATIC POEM
- CARRIC–THURA.
- CARTHON.
- OINA–MORUL.
- COLNA–DONA.
- OITHONA.
- CROMA.
- CALTHON AND COLMAL.
- THE WAR OF CAROS.
- CATHLIN OF CLUTHA.
- SUL–MALLA OF LUMON.
- THE WAR OF INIS–THONA
- THE SONGS OF SELMA.
- FINGAL — BOOK I.
- FINGAL — BOOK II.
- FINGAL — BOOK III
- FINGAL — BOOK IV.
- FINGAL — BOOK V.
- FINGAL — BOOK VI.
- LATHMON.
- DAR–THULA
- THE DEATH OF CUTHULLIN.
- THE BATTLE OF LORA.
- TEMORA.

CATH–LODA — DUAN I.

ARGUMENT

Fingal when very young, making a voyage to the Orkney Islands, was driven by stress of weather into a bay of Scandinavia, near the residence of Starno, king of Lochlin. Starno invites Fingal to a feast. Fingal, doubting the faith of the king, and mindful of a former breach of hospitality, refuses to go. — Starno gathers together his tribes; Fingal resolves to defend himself. — Night coming on, Duth–maruno proposes to Fingal to observe the motions of the enemy. — The king himself undertakes the watch. Advancing towards the enemy, he accidentally comes to the cave of Turthor, where Starno had confined Conban–Cargla, the captive daughter of a neighboring chief. — Her story is imperfect, a part of the original being lost. — Fingal comes to a place of worship, where Starno, and his son Swaran, consulted the spirit of Loda concerning the issue of the war. — The rencounter of Fingal and Swaran.— Duan first concludes with a description of the airy hall of Cruth–loda, supposed to be the Odin of Scandinavia.

The bards distinguished those compositions in which the narration is often interrupted by episodes and apostrophes, by the name of Duan.

A TALE of the times of old!

Why, thou wanderer unseen! thou bender of the thistle of Lora; why, thou breeze of the valley, hast thou left mine ear? I hear no distant roar of streams! No sound of the harp from the rock! Come, thou huntress of Lutha, Malvina, call back his soul to the bard. I look forward to Lochlin of lakes, to the dark billowy bay of U–thorno, where Fingal descends from ocean, from the roar of winds. Few are the heroes of Morven in a land unknown!

Starno sent a dweller of Loda to bid Fingal to the feast; but the king remembered the past, and all his rage arose. "Nor Gormal's mossy towers, nor Starno, shall Fingal behold. Deaths wander, like shadows, over his fiery soul! Do I forget that beam of light, the white–handed daughter of kings? Go, son of Loda; his words are wind to Fingal: wind, that, to and fro drives the thistle in autumn's dusky vale. Duth–maruno, arm of death! Cromma–glas, of Iron shields! Struthmor, dweller of battle's wing! Cromar, whose ships bound on seas, careless as the course of a meteor, on dark–rolling clouds! Arise around me, children of heroes, in a land unknown! Let each look on his shield like Trenmor, the ruler of wars." — "Come down," thus Trenmor said, "thou dweller between the harps! Thou shalt roll this stream away, or waste with me in earth."

Around the king they rise in wrath. No words come forth: they seize their spears. Each soul is rolled into itself. At length the sudden clang is waked on all their echoing shields. Each takes his hill by night; at intervals they darkly stand. Unequal bursts the hum of songs, between the roaring wind!

Broad over them rose the moon!

In his arms came tall Duth–maruno: he, from Croma of rocks, stern hunter of the boar! In his dark boat he rose on waves, when Crumthormo awaked its woods. In the chase he shone, among foes: No fear was thine, Duth–maruno!

'O Son of daring Comhal, shall my steps be forward through night? From this shield shall I view them, over their gleaming tribes? Starno, king of lakes, is before me, and Swaran, the foe of strangers. Their words are not in vain, by Loda's stone of power. Should Duth–maruno not return, his spouse is lonely at home, where meet two roaring streams on Crathmocraulo's plain. Around are hills, with echoing woods; the ocean is rolling near. My son looks on screaming sea–fowl, a young wanderer on the field. Give the head of a boar to Candona, tell him of his father's joy, when the bristly strength of U–thorno rolled on his lifted spear. Tell him of my deeds in war! Tell where his father fell!"

3

"Not forgetful of my fathers," said Fingal, "I have bounded over the seas. Theirs were the times of danger in the days of old. Nor settles darkness on me, before foes, though youthful in my locks. Chief of Crathmocraulo, the field of night is mine."

Fingal rushed, in all his arms, wide bounding over Turthor's stream, that sent its sullen roar, by night, through Gormal's misty vale. A moonbeam glittered on a rock; in the midst stood a stately form; a form with floating locks, like Lochlin's white-bosomed maids. Unequal are her steps, and short. She throws a broken song on wind. At times she tosses her white arms: for grief is dwelling in her soul.

"Torcal-torno, of aged locks," she said, "where now are thy steps, by Lulan? Thou hast failed at thine own dark streams, father of Conban-cargla! But I behold thee, chief of Lulan, sporting by Loda's hall, when the dark-skirted night is rolled along the sky. Thou sometimes hidest the moon with thy shield. I have seen her dim, in heaven. Thou kindlest thy hair into meteors, and sailest along the night. Why am I forgot, in my cave, king of shaggy boars? Look from the hall of Loda, on thy lonely daughter."

"Who art thou," said Fingal, "voice of night?"

She, trembling, turned away.

"Who art thou, in thy darkness?"

She shrunk into the cave.

The king loosed the thong from her hands. He asked about her fathers.

"Torcul-torno," she said, "once dwelt at Lulan's foamy stream: he dwelt—but now, in Loda's hall, he shakes the sounding shell. He met Starno of Lochlin in war; long fought the dark-eyed kings. My father fell, in his blood, blue-shielded Torcul-torno! By a rock, at Lulan's stream, I had pierced the bounding roe. My white hand gathered my hair from off the rushing winds. I heard a noise. Mine eyes were up. My soft breast rose on high. My step was forward, at Lulan, to meet thee, Torcul-torno. It was Starno, dreadful king! His red eyes rolled on me in love. Dark waved his shaggy brow, above his gathered smile. Where is my father, I said, he that was mighty in war! Thou art left alone among foes, O daughter of Torcul-torno! He took my hand. He raised the sail. In this cave he

4

placed me dark. At times he comes a gathered mist. He lifts before me my father's shield. But often passes a beam of youth far distant from my cave. The son of Starno moves in my sight. He dwells lonely in my soul."

"Maid of Lulan," said Fingal, "white–handed daughter of grief! a cloud, marked with streaks of fire, is rolled along my soul. Look not to that dark–robed moon; look not to those meteors of heaven. My gleaming steel is around thee, the terror of my foes! It is not the steel of the feeble, nor of the dark in soul! The maids are not shut in our caves of streams! They toss not their white arms alone. They bend fair within their locks, above the harps of Selma. Their voice is not in the desert wild. We melt along the pleasing sound!"

* * * * * * *

Fingal again advanced his steps, wide through the bosom of night, to where the trees of Loda shook amid squally winds. Three stones, with heads of moss, are there; a stream with foaming course: and dreadful, rolled around them, is the dark red cloud of Loda. High from its top looked forward a ghost, half formed of the shadowy stroke. He poured his voice, at times, amidst the roaring stream. Near, bending beneath a blasted tree, two heroes received his words: Swaran of lakes, and Starno, foe of strangers. On their dun shields they darkly leaned: their spears are forward through night. Shrill sounds the blast of darkness in Starno's floating beard.

They heard the tread of Fingal. The warriors rose in arms. "Swaran, lay that wanderer low," said Starno, in his pride. "Take the shield of thy father. It is a rock in war." Swaran threw his gleaming spear. It stood fixed in Loda's tree. Then came the foes forward with swords. They mixed their rattling steel. Through the thongs of Swaran's shield rushed the blade of Luno. The shield fell rolling on earth. Cleft, the helmet fell down. Fingal stopt the lifted steel. Wrathful stood Swaran, unarmed. He rolled his silent eyes; he threw his sword on earth. Then, slowly stalking over the stream, he whistled as he went.

Nor unseen of his father is Swaran. Starno turns away in wrath. His shaggy brows were dark above his gathered rage. He strikes Loda's tree with his spear. He raises the hum of songs. They come to the host of Lochlin, each in his own dark path; like two foam–covered streams from two rainy vales! To Turthor's plain Fingal returned. Fair rose the beam of the east. It shone on the spoils of Lochlin in the hand of the king. From her cave came forth, in her beauty, the daughter of Torcul– torno. She gathered her hair from wind. She wildly raised her song. The song of Lulan of shells, where once her father dwelt. She saw Starno's bloody shield. Gladness rose, a light. on her face. She saw the cleft helmet of Swaran She shrunk, darkened, from Fingal. "Art thou fallen by thy hundred streams, O love of the mournful maid?"

U–thorno that risest in waters! on whose side are the meteors of night? I behold the dark moon descending behind thy resounding woods. On thy top dwells the misty Loda: the house of the spirits of men! In the end of his cloudy hall bends forward Cruth–loda of swords. His form is dimly seen amid his wavy mist. His right hand is on his shield. In his left is the half viewless shell. The roof of his dreadful hall is marked with nightly fires!

The race of Cruth–loda advance, a ridge of formless shades. He reaches the sounding shell to those who shone in war. But between him and the feeble, his shield rises a darkened orb. He is a setting meteor to the weak in arms. Bright as a rainbow on streams, came Lulan's white–bosomed maid.

The white–handed daughter of kings: Agandecca, the daughter of Starno, whom her father killed, on account of her discovering to Fingal a plot laid against his life.

Crumthormoth: one of the Orkney or Shetland Islands

The blade of Luno: The sword of Fingal, so called from its maker, Luno of Lochlin

CATHLODA — DUAN II.

ARGUMENT

Fingal, returning with day, devolves the command on Duth– maruno, who engages the enemy, and drives them over the stream of Turthor. Having recalled his people, he congratulates Duth–maruno on his success, but discovers that that hero had been mortally wounded in the action — Duth–maruno dies. Ullin, the bard in honor of the dead, introduces the episode of Colgorm and Strina–dona, which concludes this duan.

"WHERE art thou, son of the king?" said darkhaired Duth– maruno. "Where hast thou

6

failed, young beam of Selma? He returns not from the bosom of night! Morning is spread on U– thorno. In his mist is the sun on his hill. Warriors, lift the shields in my presence. He must not fall like a fire from heaven, whose place is not marked on the ground. He comes like an eagle, from the skirt of his squally wind! in his hand are the spoil of foes. King of Selma, our souls were sad!"

"Near us are the foes, Duth–maruno. They come forward, like waves in mist, when their foamy tops are seen at times above the low–sailing vapor. The traveller shrinks on his journey; he knows not whither to fly. No trembling travellers are we! Sons of heroes call forth the steel. Shall the sword of Fingal arise, or shall a warrior lead?"

The deeds of old, said Duth–maruno, are like paths to our eyes, O Fingal! Broad–shielded Trenmor is still seen amidst his own dim years. Nor feeble was the soul of the king. There no dark deed wandered in secret. From their hundred streams came the tribes, to glassy Colglan–crona. Their chiefs were before them. Each strove to lead the war. Their swords were often half unsheathed. Red rolled their eyes of rage. Separate they stood, and hummed their surly songs. "Why should they yield to each other? their fathers were equal in war." Trenmor was there, with his people stately, in youthful locks. He saw the advancing foe. The grief of his soul arose. He bade the chiefs to lead by turns; they led, but they were rolled away. From his own mossy hill blue–shielded Trenmor came down. He led wide–skirted battle, and the strangers failed. Around him the dark–browed warriors came: they struck the shield of joy. Like a pleasant gale the words of power rushed forth from Selma of kings. But the chiefs led by turns, in war, till mighty danger rose: then was the hour of the king to conquer in the field.

"Not unknown," said Cromma–glas of shields, "are the deeds of our fathers. But who shall now lead the war before the race of kings? Mist settles on these four dark hills: within it let each warrior strike his shield. Spirits may descend in darkness, and mark us for the war." They went each to his hill of mist. Bards marked the sounds of the shields. Loudest rung thy boss Duth–maruno. Thou must lead in war!

Like the murmurs of waters the race of U–thorno came down. Starno led the battle, and Swaran of stormy isles. They looked forward from iron shields like Cruth–loda, fiery–eyed, when he looks from behind the darkened moon, and strews his signs on night. The foes met by Turthor's stream. They heaved like ridgy waves. Their echoing strokes are mixed. Shadowy death flies over the hosts. They were clouds of hail. with squally winds in their skirts. Their showers are roaring together. Below them swells the dark–rolling deep.

Strife of gloomy U–thorno, why should I mark thy wounds? Thou art with the years that are gone; thou fadest on my soul!

Starno brought forward his skirt of war, and Swaran his own dark wing. Nor a harmless fire is Duthmaruno's sword. Lochlin is rolled over her streams. The wrathful kings are lost in thought. They roll their silent eyes over the flight of their land. The horn of Fingal was heard; the sons of woody Albion returned. But many lay, by Turthor's stream, silent in their blood.

" Chief of Crathmo," said the king, " Duth–maruno, hunter of boars! not harmless returns my eagle from the field of foes! For this white–bosomed Lanul shall brighten at her streams; Candona shall rejoice as he wanders in Crathmo's fields."

" Colgorm," replied the chief, " was the first of my race in Albion; Colgorm, the rider of ocean; through Its watery vales. He slew his brother in I–thorno: he left the land of his fathers. He chose his place in silence, by rocky Crathmo–craulo. His race came forth in their years; they came forth to war, but they always fell. The wound of my fathers is mine, king of echoing isles!

He drew an arrow from his side! He fell pale in a land unknown. His soul came forth to his fathers, to their stormy isle. There they pursued boars of mist, along the skirts of winds. The chiefs stood silent around, as the stones of Loda, on their hill. The traveller sees them, through the twilight, from his lonely path. He thinks them the ghosts of the aged, forming future wars.

Night came down on U–thorno. Still stood the chiefs in their grief. The blast whistled, by turns, through every warrior's hair. Fingal, at length, broke forth from the thoughts of his soul. He called Ullin of harps, and bade the song to rise. "No falling fire, that is only seen, and then retires in night; no departing meteor was he that is laid so low. He was like the strong–beaming sun, long rejoicing on his hill, Call the names of his fathers from their dwellings old!'"

THE POEMS OF OSSIAN

I-thorno, said the bard, that risest midst ridgy seas! Why is thy head so gloomy in the ocean's mist? From thy vales came forth a race, fearless as thy strong winged eagles: the race of Colgorm of iron shields, dwellers of Loda's hall.

In Tormoth's resounding isle arose Lurthan, streamy hill. It bent its woody head over a silent vale. There, at foamy Cruruth's source, dwelt Rurmar, hunter of boars! His daughter was fair as a sunbeam, white-bosomed Strina-dona!

Many a king of heroes, and hero of iron shields; many a youth of heavy locks came to Rurmar's echoing hall. They came to woo the maid, the stately huntress of Tormoth wild. But thou lookest careless from thy steps, high-bosomed Strina-dona!

If on the heath she moved, her breast was whiter than the down of cana; If on the sea-beat shore, than the foam of the rolling ocean. Her eyes were two stars of light. Her face was heaven's bow in showers. Her dark hair flowed round it, like the streaming clouds. Thou wert the dweller of souls, white-handed Strina-dona!

Colgorm came in his ship, and Corcul-suran, king of shells. The brothers came from I-thorno to woo the sunbeam of Tormoth wild. She saw them in their echoing steel. Her soul was fixed on blue-eyed Colgorm. Ul-lochlin's nightly eye looked in, and saw the tossing arms of Strina-dona. . Wrathful the brothers frowned. Their flaming eyes in silence met. They turned away. They struck their shields. Their hands were trembling on their swords. They rushed into the strife of heroes for long haired Strina-dona.

Corcul-suran fell in blood. On his isle raged the strength of his father. He turned Colgorm from I-thorno, to wander on all the winds. In Crathmocraulo's rocky field he dwelt by a foreign stream. Nor darkened the king alone, that beam of light was near, the daughter of echoing Tormoth, white armed Strina-dona.

I-thorno: an island of Scandinavia.

The cana is a certain kind of grass, which grows plentifully in the heathy morasses of the north.

Ul-lochlin "the guide to Lochlin;" the name of a star

CATH–LODA — DUAN III.

ARGUMENT

Ossian, after some general reflections, describes the situation of Fingal, and the position of the army of Lochlin. — The conversation of Starno and Swaran. — The episode of Corman– trunar and Foina–bragal. — Starno, from his own example, recommends to Swaran to surprise Fingal, who had retired alone to a neighboring hill. Upon Swaran's refusal, Starno undertakes the enterprise himself, is overcome and taken prisoner by Fingal. He is dismissed after a severe reprimand for his cruelty.

WHENCE is the stream of years? Whither do they roll along? Where have they hid, in mist, their many colored sides.

I look unto the times of old, but they seem dim to Ossian's eyes, like reflected moonbeams on a distant lake. Here rise the red beams of war! There, silent dwells a feeble race! They mark no years with their deeds, as slow they pass along. Dweller between the shields! thou that awakest the failing soul! descend from thy wall, harp of Cona, with thy voices three! Come with that which kindles the past: rear the forms of old, on their own dark–brown years!

U–thorno, hill of storms, I behold my race on thy side. Fingal is bending in night over Duthmaruno's tomb. Near him are the steps of his heroes, hunters of the boar. By Turthor's stream the host of Lochlin is deep in shades. The wrathful kings stood on two hills: they looked forward on their bossy shields. They looked forward to the stars of night, red wandering in the west. Cruth– loda bends from high, like formless meteor in clouds. He sends abroad the winds and marks them with his signs. Starno foresaw that Morven's king was not to yield in war.

He twice struck the tree in wrath. He rushed before his son. He hummed a surly song, and heard his air in wind. Turned from one another, they stood like two oaks, which different winds had bent; each hangs over his own loud rill, and shakes his boughs in the course of blasts.

" Annir," said Starno of lakes, "was a fire that consumed of old. He poured death from his eyes along the striving fields. His joy was in the fall of men. Blood to him was a summer stream, that brings joy to the withered vales, from its own mossy rock. He came forth to the lake Luth–cormo, to meet the tall Corman– trunar, he from Urlor of streams, dweller of battle's wing."

The chief of Urlor had come to Gormal with his dark– bosomed ships. He saw the daughter of Annir, white–armed Foina-bragal. He saw her! Nor careless rolled her eyes on the rider of stormy waves. She fled to his ship in darkness, like a moonbeam through a nightly veil. Annir pursued along the deep; he called the winds of heaven. Nor alone was the king! Starno was by his side. Like U–thorno's young eagle, I turned my eyes on my father.

We rushed into roaring Urlor. With his people came tall Corman–trunar. We fought; but the foe prevailed. In his wrath my father stood. He lopped the young trees with his sword. His eyes rolled red in his rage. I marked the soul of the king, and I retired in night. From the field I took a broken helmet; a shield that was pierced with steel; pointless was the spear in my hand. I went to find the foe.

On a rock sat tall Corman–trunar beside his burning oak; and near him beneath a tree, sat deep–bosomed Foina–bragal. I threw my broken shield before her! I spoke the words of peace. "Beside his rolling sea lies Annir of many lakes. The king was pierced in battle; and Starno is to raise his tomb. Me, a son of Loda, he sends to white–handed Foina, to bid her send a lock from her hair, to rest with her father in earth. And thou, king of roaring Urlor, let the battle cease, till Annir receive the shell from fiery–eyed Cruth–loda."

Bursting into tears, she rose, and tore a lock from her hair; a lock, which wandered in the blast, along her heaving breast. Corman–trunar gave the shell, and bade me rejoice before him. I rested in the shade of night, and hid my face in my helmet deep. Sleep descended on the foe. I rose, like a stalking ghost. I pierced the side of Corman–trunar. Nor did Foina–bragal escape. She rolled her white bosom in blood.

Why, then, daughter of heroes, didst thou wake my rage?

Morning rose. The foe were fled, like the departure of mist. Annir struck his bossy shield. He called his dark–haired son. I came, streaked with wandering blood: thrice rose the

THE POEMS OF OSSIAN

shout of the king, like the bursting forth of a squall of wind from a cloud by night. We rejoiced three days above the dead, and called the hawks of heaven. They came from all their winds to feast on Annir's foes. Swaran, Fingal is alone in his hill of night. Let thy spear pierce the king in secret; like Annir, my soul shall rejoice.

"O Son of Annir," said Swaran, "I shall not slay in shades: I move forth in light: the hawks rush from all their winds. They are wont to trace my course: it is not harmless through war."

Burning rose the rage of the king. He thrice raised his gleaming spear. But, starting, he spared his son, and rushed into the night. By Turthor's stream, a cave is dark, the dwelling of Conban–carglas. There he laid the helmet of kings, and called the maid of Lulan; but she was distant far in Loda's resounding hall.

Swelling in his rage, he strode to where Fingal lay alone. The king was laid on his shield, on his own secret hill.

Stern hunter of shaggy boars! no feeble maid is laid before thee. No boy on his ferny bed, by Turthor's murmuring stream. Here is spread the couch of the mighty, from which they rise to deeds of death! Hunter of shaggy boars, awaken not the terrible!

Starno came murmuring on. Fingal arose in arms. "Who art thou, son of night!" Silent he threw the spear. They mixed their gloomy strife. The shield of Starno fell, cleft in twain. He is bound to an oak. The early beam arose. It was then Fingal beheld the king. He rolled awhile his silent eyes. He thought of other days, when white–bosomed Agandecca moved like the music of songs. He loosed the thong from his hands. Son of Annir, he said, retire. Retire to Gormal of shells; a beam that was set returns. I remember thy white–bosomed daughter; dreadful king, away! Go to thy troubled dwelling, cloudy foe of the lovely Let the stranger shun thee, thou gloomy in the hall"

A tale of the times of old!

COMALA, A DRAMATIC POEM

ARGUMENT.

THE POEMS OF OSSIAN

This poem. is valuable on account of the light it throws on the antiquity of Ossian's compositions. The Caracul mentioned here is the same with Caracalla, the son of Severus, who, in the year 211, commanded an expedition against the Caledonians. The variety of the measure shows that the poem was originally set to music, and perhaps presented before the chiefs upon solemn occasions. Tradition has handed down the story more complete than it is in the poem. "Comala, the daughter of Sarno, king of Inistore, or Orkney Islands, fell in love with Fingal, the son of Comhal, at a feast, to which her father had invited him [Fingal, B. III.] upon his return from Lochlin, after the death of Agandecca. Her passion was so violent, that she followed him, disguised like a youth, who wanted to be employed in his wars. She was soon discovered by Hidallan, the son of Lamor, one of Fingal's heroes, whose love she had slighted some time before. Her romantic passion and beauty recommended her so much to the king, that he had resolved to make her his wife; when news was brought him of Caracul's expedition. He marched to stop the progress of the enemy, and Comala attended him. He left her on a hill, within sight of Caracul's army, when he himself went to battle, having previously promised, if he survived, to return that night." The sequel of the story may be gathered from the poem itself.

The Persons.

```
FINGAL
COMALA
HIDALLAN
MELILCOMA        }Daughters
DERSAGRENA       }of Morni.
BARDS
```

Dersagrena. The chase is over. No noise on Erdven but the torrent's roar! Daughter of Morni, come from Crona's banks. Lay down the bow and take the harp. Let the night come on with songs; let our joy be great on Ardven.

Melilcoma. Night comes on apace, thou blue−eyed maid! gray night grows dim along the plain, I saw a deer at Crona's stream; a mossy bank he seemed through the gloom, but soon he bounded away. A meteor played round his branching horns; the awful faces of other times looked from the clouds of Crona.

Dersagrena. These are the signs of Fingal's death. The king of shields is fallen! and Caracul prevails. Rise, Comala, from thy rock; daughter of Sarno, rise in tears! the youth of thy love is low; his ghost is on our hills.

Melilcoma. There Comala sits forlorn! two gray dogs near shake their rough ears, and catch the flying breeze. Her red cheek rests upon her arm, the mountain wind is in her hair. She turns her blue eyes towards the fields of his promise. Where art thou, O Fingal? The night is gathering around.

Comala. O Carun of the streams! why do I behold thy waters rolling in blood? Has the noise of the battle been heard; and sleeps the king of Morven? Rise, moon, thou daughter of the sky! look from between thy clouds; rise, that I may behold the gleam of his steel on the field of his promise. Or rather let the meteor, that lights our fathers through the night, come with its red beam, to show me the way to my fallen hero. Who will defend me from sorrow? Who from the love of Hidallan? Long shall Comala look before she can behold Fingal in the midst of his host; bright as the coming forth of the morning in the cloud of an early shower.

Hidallan. Dwell, thou mist of gloomy Crona, dwell on the path of the king! Hide his steps from mine eyes, let me remember my friend no more. The bands of battle are scattered, no crowding tread round the noise of his steel. O Carun! roll thy streams of blood, the chief of the people is low.

Comala. Who fell on Carun's sounding banks, son of the cloudy night? Was he white as the snow of Ardven? Blooming as the bow of the shower? Was his hair like the mist of the hill, soft and curling in the day of the sun? Was he like the thunder of heaven in battle? Fleet as the roe of the desert?

Hidallan. O that I might behold his love, fair—leaning from her rock! Her red eye dim in tears, her blushing cheek half hid in her locks! Blow, O gentle breeze! lift thou the heavy locks of the maid, that I may behold her white arm, her lovely cheek in her grief.

Comala. And is the son of Comhal fallen, chief of the mournful tale! The thunder rolls on the hill! The lightning flies on wings of fire! They frighten not Comala; for Fingal is low. Say, chief of the mournful tale, fell the breaker of the shields?

Hidallan. The nations are scattered on their hills! they shall hear the voice of the king no more.

Comala. Confusion pursue thee over thy plains! Ruin overtake thee, thou king of the world! Few be thy steps to thy grave; and let one virgin mourn thee! Let her be like Comala, tearful in the days of her youth! Why hast thou told me, Hidallan, that my hero fell? I might have hoped a little while his return; I might have thought I saw him on the distant rock: a tree might have deceived me with his appearance; the wind of the hill might have been the sound of his horn in mine ear. O that I were on the banks or Carun; that my tears might be warm on his cheek.

Hidallan. He lies not on the banks of Carun: on Ardven heroes raise his tomb. Look on them, O moon! from thy clouds; be thy beam bright on his breast, that Comala may behold him in the light of his armor.

Comala. Stop, ye sons of the grave, till I behold lily love! He left me at the chase alone. I knew not that he went to war. He said he would return with the night; the king of Morven is returned! Why didst thou not tell me that he would fall, O trembling dweller of the rock? Thou sawest him in the blood of his youth; but thou didst not tell Comala.

Melilcoma. What sound is that on Ardven? Who is that bright in the vale? Who comes like the strength of rivers, when their crowded waters glitter to the moon?

Comala. Who is it but the foe of Comala, the son of the king of the world! Ghost of Fingal! do thou, from thy cloud, direct Comala's bow. Let him fall like the hart of the desert. It is Fingal in the crowd of his ghosts. Why dost thou come, my love, to frighten and please my soul?

Fingal. Raise, ye bards, the song; raise the wars of the streamy Carun! Caracul has fled from our arms along the field of his pride. He sets far distant like a meteor, that encloses a spirit of night, when the winds drive it over the heath, and the dark woods are gleaming around. I heard a voice, or was it the breeze of my hills? Is it the huntress of Ardven, the white–handed daughter of Sarno? Look from the rocks, my love; let me hear the voice of Comala!

Comala. Take me to the cave of thy rest, O lovely son of death

Fingal. Come to the cave of my rest. The storm is past, the sun is on our fields. Come to the cave of my rest, huntress of echoing Ardven!

Comala. He is returned with his fame! I feel the right hand of his wars! But I must rest beside the rock till my soul returns from my fear! O let the harp be near! raise the song, ye daughters of Morna.

Dersagrena. Comala has slain three deer on Ardven, the fire ascends on the rock; go to the feast of Comala, king of the woody Morven!

Fingal. Raise, ye sons of song, the wars of the streamy Carun; that my white−handed maid may rejoice: while I behold the feast of my love.

Bards. Roll, streamy Carun, roll in joy, the sons of battle are fled! the steed is not seen on our fields; the wings of their pride spread on other lands. The sun will now rise in peace, and the shadows descend in joy. The voice of the chase will be heard; the shields hang in the hall. Our delight will be in the war of the ocean, our hands shall grow red in the blood of Lochlin. Roll, streamy Carun, roll in joy, the sons of battle fled!

Melilcoma. Descend, ye light mists from high! Ye moonbeams, lift her soul! Pale lies the maid at the rock! Comala is no more!

Fingal. Is the daughter of Sarno dead; the white−bosomed maid of my love? Meet me, Comala, on my heaths, when I sit alone at the streams of my hills.

Hidallan. Ceased the voice of the huntress of Ardven? why did I trouble the soul of the maid? When shall I see thee, with joy, in the chase of the dark−brown hinds? Fingal. Youth of the gloomy brow! No more shalt thou feast in my halls! Thou shalt not pursue my chase, my foes shall not fall by thy sword. Lead me to the place of her rest, that I may behold her beauty. Pale she lies as the rock, the cold winds lift her hair. Her bow−string sounds in the blast, her arrow was broken in her fall. Raise the praise of the daughter of Sarno! give her name to the winds of heaven.

Bards. See! meteors gleam around the maid! See! moonbeams lift her soul! Around her, from their clouds, bend the awful faces of her father: Sarna of the gloomy brow! the red−rolling eyes of Hidallan! When shall thy white hand arise? When shall thy voice be heard on our rocks? The maids shall seek thee on the heath, but they shall not find thee. Thou shalt come, at times, to their dreams, to settle peace in their soul. Thy voice shall remain in their ears, they shall think with joy on the dreams of their rest. Meteors gleam around the maid, and moonbeams lift her soul!

By the " dweller of the rock" she means a Druid.

CARRIC–THURA.

ARGUMENT.

Fingal, returning from an expedition which he had made into the Roman province, resolved to visit Cathulla, king of Inistore, and brother to Comala, whose story is related at large in the preceding dramatic poem. Upon his coming in sight of Carric– thura, the palace of Cathulla, he observed a flame on its top, which, in those days, was a signal of distress. The wind drove him into a bay at some distance from Carric–thura, and he was obliged to pass the night on shore. Next day he attacked the army of Frothal, king of Sora, who had besieged Cathulla in his palace of Carric–thura, and took Frothal himself prisoner, after he had engaged him in a single combat. The deliverance of Carric–thura is the subject of the poem; but several other episodes are interwoven with it. It appears, from tradition, that this poem was addressed to a Culdee, or one of the first Christian missionaries, and that the story of the spirit of Loda, supposed to be the ancient Odin of Scandinavia, was introduced by Ossian in opposition to the Culdee's doctrine. Be this as it will, it lets us into Ossian's notions of a superior Being; and shows us that he was not addicted to the superstition which prevailed all the world over, before the introduction of Christianity.

HAST thou left thy blue course in heaven, golden–haired son of the sky! The west opened its gates; the bed of thy repose is there. The waves come to behold thy beauty. They lift their trembling heads. They see thee lovely in thy sleep; they shrink away with fear. Rest in thy shadowy cave, O sun! let thy return be in joy.

But let a thousand lights arise to the sound of the harps of Selma: let the beam spread in the hall, the king of shells is returned! The strife of Crona is past, like sounds that are no more. Raise the song, O bards! the king is returned with his fame!

THE POEMS OF OSSIAN

Such were the words of Ullin, when Fingal returned from war; when he returned in the fair blushing of youth with all his heavy locks. His blue arms were on the hero; like a light cloud on the sun, when he moves in his robes of mist, and shows but half his beams. His heroes followed the king: the feast of shells is spread. Fingal turns to his bards, and bids the song to rise.

Voices of echoing Cona! he said; O bards of other times! Ye, on whose souls the blue host of our fathers rise! strike the harp in my hall: and let me hear the song. Pleasant is the joy of grief; it is like the shower of spring when it softens the branch of the oak, and the young leaf rears its green head. Sing on, O bards! to- morrow we lift the sail. My blue course is through the ocean, to Carric-thura's walls; the mossy walls of Sarno, where Comala dwelt. There the noble Cathulla spreads the feast of shells. The boars of his woods are many; the sound of the chase shall arise!

Cronnan, son of the song! said Ullin; Minona, graceful at the harp! raise the tale of Shilric, to please the king of Morven. Let Vinvela come in her beauty, like the showery bow when it shows its lovely head on the lake, and the setting sun is bright. She comes, O Fingal! her voice is soft, but sad.

Vinvela. My love is a son of the hill. He pursues the flying deer. His gray dogs are panting around him; his bow-string sounds in the wind. Dost thou rest by the fount of the rock, or by the noise of the mountain stream? The rushes are nodding to the wind, the mist flies over the hill. I will approach my love unseen; I will behold him from the rock. Lovely I saw thee first by the aged oak of Branno; thou wert returning tall from the chase; the fairest among thy friends.

Shilric. What voice is that I hear? that voice like the summer wind! I sit not by the nodding rushes; I hear not the fount of the rock . Afar, Vinvela, afar, I go to the wars of Fingal. My dogs attend me no more. No more I tread the hill. No more from on high I see thee, fair moving by the stream of the plain; bright as the bow of heaven; as the moon on the western wave.

Vinvela. Then thou art gone, O Shilric! I am alone on the hill! The deer are seen on the brow: void of fear they graze along. No more they dread the wind; no more the rustling tree. The hunter is far removed, he is in the field of graves. Strangers! sons of the waves! spare my lovely Shilric!

Shilric. If fall I must in the field, raise high my grave, Vinvela. Gray stones, and heaped up earth, shall mark me to future times. When the hunter shall sit by the mound, and produce his food at noon, "some warrior rests here," he will say; and my fame shall live in his praise. Remember me, Vinvela, when low on earth I lie!

Vinvela. Yes! I will remember thee! alas! my Shilric will fall! What shall I do, my love, when thou art for ever gone? Through these hills I will go at noon: I will go through the silent heath. There I will see the place of thy rest, returning from the chase. Alas! my Shilric will fall; but I will remember Shilric.

And I remember the chief, said the king of woody Morven; he consumed the battle in his rage. But now my eyes behold him not. I met him one day on the hill; his cheek was pale: his brow was dark. The sigh was frequent in his breast: his steps were towards the desert. But now he is not in the crowd of my chiefs, when the sounds of my shields arise. Dwells he in the narrow house, the chief of high Carmora?

Cronnan! said Ullin of other times, raise the song of Shilric! when he returned to his hills, and Vinvela was no more. He leaned on her gray mossy stone he thought Vinvela lived. He saw her fair moving on the plain; but the bright form lasted not: the sunbeam fled from the field, and she was seen no more. Hear the song of Shilric; it is soft, but sad!

I sit by the mossy fountain; on the top of the hill of winds. One tree is rustling above me. Dark waves roll over the heath. The lake is troubled below. The deer descend from the hill. No hunter at a distance is seen. It is mid–day: but all is silent. Sad are my thoughts alone. Didst thou but appear, O my love? a wanderer on the heath? thy hair floating on the wind behind thee; thy bosom heaving on the sight; thine eyes full of tears for thy friends, whom the mists of the hill had concealed? Thee I would comfort, my love, and bring thee to thy father's house?

But is it she that there appears, like a beam of light on the heath? bright as the moon in autumn, as the sun in a summer storm, comest thou, O maid, over rocks, over mountains, to me? She speaks: but how weak her voice! like the breeze in the reeds of the lake.

"Returnest thou safe from the war? Where are thy friends, my love? I heard of thy death on the hill; I heard and mourned thee, Shilric! Yes, my fair, I return: but I alone of my race. Thou shalt see them no more; their graves I raised on the plain. But why art thou on the desert hill? Why on the heath alone?

" Alone I am, O Shilric! alone in the winter–house. With grief for thee I fell. Shilric, I am pale in the tomb."

She fleets, she sails away; as mist before the wind; and wilt thou not stay, Vinvela? Stay, and behold my tears! Fair thou appearest, Vinvela! fair thou wast, when alive!

By the mossy fountain I will sit; on the top of the hills of winds. When mid–day is silent around, O talk with me, Vinvela! come on the light–winged gale! on the breeze of the desert, come! Let me hear thy voice, as thou passest, when mid–day is silent around!

Such was the song of Cronnan, on the night of Selma's joy. But morning rose in the east; the blue waters rolled in light. Fingal bade his sails to rise; the winds came rustling from their hills. Inistore rose to sight, and Carric–thura's mossy towers! But the sign of distress was on their top: the warning flame edged with smoke. The king of Morven struck his breast: he assumed at once his spear. His darkened brow bends forward to the coast: he looks back to the lagging winds. His hair is disordered on his back. The silence of the king is terrible!

Night came down on the sea: Rotha's bay received the ship. A rock bends along the coast with all its echoing wood. On the top is the circle of Loda, the mossy stone of power! A narrow plain spreads beneath covered with grass and aged trees, which the midnight winds, in their wrath, had torn from their shaggy rock. The blue course of a stream is there! the lonely blast of ocean pursues the thistle's beard. The flame of three oaks arose: the feast is spread round; but the soul of the king is sad, for Carric– thura's chief distrest.

The wan cold moon rose in the east. Sleep descended on the youths! Their blue helmets glitter to the beam; the fading fire decays. But sleep did not rest on the king: he rose in the midst of his arms, and slowly ascended the hill, to behold the flame of Sarno's tower.

The flame was dim and distant; the moon hid her red face in the east. A blast came from the mountain, on its wings was the spirit of Loda. He came to his place in his terrors, and shook his dusky spear. His eyes appear like flames in his dark face; his voice is like distant thunder. Fingal advanced his spear in night, and raised his voice on high.

Son of night, retire; call thy winds, and fly! Why dost thou come to my presence, with thy shadowy arms? Do I fear thy gloomy form, spirit of dismal Loda! Weak is thy shield of clouds; feeble is that meteor, thy sword! The blast rolls them together; and thou thyself art lost. Fly from my presence, son of night; call thy winds, and fly!

Dost thou force me from my place? replied the hollow voice. The people bend before me. I turn the battle in the field of the brave. I look on the nations, and they vanish: my nostrils pour the blasts of death. I come abroad on the winds; the tempests are before my face. But my dwelling is calm, above the clouds; the fields of my rest are pleasant.

Dwell in thy pleasant fields, said the king: Let Comhal's son be forgot. Do my steps ascend from my hills into thy peaceful plains? Do I meet thee with a spear on thy cloud, spirit of dismal Loda? Why then dost thou frown on me? Why shake thine airy spear? Thou frownest in vain: I never fled from the mighty in war. And shall the Sons of the wind frighten the king of Morven? No! he knows the weakness of their arms!

Fly to thy land, replied the form: receive thy wind and fly? The blasts are in the hollow of my hand the course of the storm is mine. The king of Sora is my son, he bends at the stone of my power. His battle is around Carric—thura; and he will prevail! Fly to thy land, son of Comhal, or feel my flaming wrath.

He lifted high his shadowy spear! He bent forward his dreadful height. Fingal, advancing, drew his sword; the blade of dark—brown Luno. The gleaming path of the steel winds through the gloomy ghost. The form fell shapeless into the air, like a column of smoke, which the staff of the boy disturbs as it rises from the half—extinguished furnace.

The spirit of Loda shrieked, as, rolled into himself, he rose on the wind. Inistore shook at the sound. The waves heard it on the deep. They stopped in their course with fear; the friends of Fingal started at once, and took their heavy spears. They missed the king: they rose in rage; all their arms resound!

The moon came forth in the east. Fingal returned in the gleam of his arms. The joy of his youth was great, their souls settled, as a sea from a storm. Ullin raised the song of gladness. The hills of Inistore rejoiced. The flame of the oak arose; and the tales of heroes are told. But Frothal Sora's wrathful king sits in sadness beneath a tree. The host spreads around Carric—thura. He looks towards the walls with rage He longs for the blood of

Cathulla, who once overcame him in war. When Annir reigned in Sora, the father of sea–borne Frothal, a storm arose on the sea, and carried Frothal to Inistore. Three days he feasted in Sarno's halls, and saw the slow–rolling eyes of Comala. He loved her in the flame of youth, and rushed to seize the white–armed maid. Cathulla met the chief. The gloomy battle arose. Frothal was bound in the hall: three days he pined alone. On the forth, Sarno sent him to his ship, and he returned to his land. But wrath darkened in his soul against the noble Cathulla. When Annir's stone of fame arose, Frothal came in his strength. The battle burned round Carric– thura and Sarno's mossy walls.

Morning rose on Inistore. Frothal struck his dark brown shield. His chiefs started at the sound; they stood, but their eyes were turned to the sea. They saw Fingal coming in his strength; and first the noble Thubar spoke, "Who comes, like the stag oft he desert, with all his herd behind him? Frothal, it is a foe! I see his forward spear. Perhaps it is the king of Morven, Fingal the first of men. His deeds are well known in Lochlin! the blood of his foes is in Sarno's halls. Shall I ask the peace of kings? His sword is the bolt of heaven!"

Son of the feeble hand, said Frothal, shall my days begin in a cloud? Shall I yield before I have conquered, chief of streamy Tora? The people would say in Sora, Frothal flew forth like a meteor; but a darkness has met him, and his fame is no more. No, Thubar, I will never yield; my fame shall surround me like light. No: I will never yield, chief of streamy Tora!

He went forth with the stream of his people, but they met a rock; Fingal stood unmoved, broken they rolled back from his side. Nor did they safely fly; the spear of the king pursued their steps. The field is covered with heroes. A rising hill preserved the foe.

Frothal saw their flight. The rage of his bosom rose. He bent his eyes to the ground, and called the noble Thubar. Thubar! my people are fled. My fame has ceased to rise. I will fight the king; I feel my burning soul! Send a bard to demand the combat. Speak not against Frothal's words! But, Thubar! I love a maid; she dwells by Thano's stream, the white–bosomed daughter of Herman, Utha, with soft–rolling eyes. She feared the low–laid Comala; her secret sighs rose when I spread the sail. Tell to Utha of harps that my soul delighted in her.

Such were his words, resolved to fight. The soft sigh of Utha was near! She had followed her hero in the armor of a man. She rolled her eye on the youth, in secret, from beneath

22

her steel. She saw the bard as he went; the spear fell thrice from her hand! Her loose hair flew on the wind. Her white breast rose with sighs. She raised her eyes to the king. She would speak, but thrice she failed.

Fingal heard the words of the bard; he came in the strength of his steel. They mixed their deathful spears: they raised the gleam of their arms. But the sword of Fingal descended and cut Frothal's shield in twain. His fair side is exposed; half−bent, he foresees his death. Darkness gathered on Utha's soul. The fear rolled down her cheek. She rushed to cover the chief with her shield: but a fallen oak met her steps. She fell on her arm of snow; her shield, her helmet flew wide. Her white bosom heaved to the sigh; her dark−brown hair is spread on earth.

Fingal pitied the white−armed maid! he stayed the uplifted sword. The tear was in the eye of the king, as, bending forward, he spoke, "King of streamy Sora! fear not the sword of Fingal. it was never stained with the blood of the vanquished it never pierced a fallen foe. Let thy people rejoice by their native Streams. Let the maid of thy love be glad. Why shouldst thou fall in thy youth, king of streamy Sora?" Frothal heard the words of Fingal, and saw the rising maid: they stood in silence, in their beauty, like two young trees of the plain, when the shower of spring is on their leaves, and the loud winds are laid.

Daughter of Herman, said Frothal, didst thou come from streams? didst thou come in thy beauty to behold thy warrior low? But he was low before the mighty, maid of the slow−rolling eye! The feeble did not overcome the son of car−borne Annir! Terrible art thou, O king of Morven! in battles of the spear. But, in peace, thou art like the sun when he looks through a silent shower: the flowers lift their fair heads before him; the gales shake their rustling wings. O that thou wert in Sora! that my feast were spread! The future kings of Sora would see thy arms and rejoice. They would rejoice at the fame of their fathers, who beheld the mighty Fingal!

Son of Annir, replied the king, the fame of Sora's race shall be heard! When. chiefs are strong in war, then does the song arise! But if their swords are stretched over the feeble; if the blood of the weak has stained their arms; the bard shall forget them in the song, and their tombs shall not be known. The stranger shall come and build there, and remove the heaped−up earth. An half−worn sword shall rise before him; bending above it, he will say, "These are the arms of the chiefs of old, but their names are not in song." Come thou, O Frothal! to the feast of Inistore: let the maid of thy love be there; let our faces brighten with joy!

Fingal took his spear, moving in the steps of his might. The gates of Carric–thura are opened wide. The feast of shells is spread. The soft sound of music arose. Gladness brightened in the hall. The voice of Ullin was heard; the harp of Selma was strung. Utha rejoiced in his presence, and demanded the song of grief; the big tear hung in her eye when the soft Crimora spoke. Crimora, the daughter of Rinval, who dwelt at Lotha's roaring stream! The tale was long, but lovely; and pleased the blushing Utha.

Crimora. Who cometh from the hill, like a cloud tinged with the beam of the west? Whose voice is that, loud as the wind, but pleasant as the harp of Carril? It is my love in the light of steel; but sad is his darkened brow! Live the mighty race of Fingal? or what darkens Connal's soul?

Connal. They live. They return from the chase like a stream of light. The sun is on their shields. Like a ridge of fire they descend the hill. Loud is the voice of the youth! the war, my love, is near! To–morrow the dreadful Dargo comes to try the force of our race . The race of Fingal he defies; the race of battles and wounds!

Crimora. Connal, I saw his sails like gray mist on the dark– brown wave. They slowly came to land. Connal, many are the warriors of Dargo.

Connal. Bring me thy father's shield, the bossy iron shield of Rinval! that shield like the full–orbed moon, when she moves darkened through heaven.

Crimora. That shield I bring, O Connal! but it did not defend my father. By the spear of Gormar he fell. Thou mayst fall, O Connal!

Connal. Fall I may! but raise my tomb, Crimora! Gray stones, a mound of earth, shall send my name to other times. Bend thy red eye over my grave, beat thy mournful heaving breast. Though fair thou art, my love, as the light; more pleasant than the gale of the hill; yet I will not hear remain. Raise my tomb, Crimora!

Crimora. Then give me those arms that gleam; that sword and that spear of steel. I shall meet Dargo with Connal, and aid him in the fight. Farewell, ye rocks of Ardven! ye deer! and ye streams of the hill! We shall return no more! Our tombs are distant far!

"And did they return no more?" said Utha's bursting sigh." Fell the mighty in battle, and did Crimora live? Her steps were lonely; her soul was sad for Connal. Was he not young and lovely; like the beam of the setting sun? Ullin saw the virgin's tear, he took the softly trembling harp; the song was lovely, but sad, and silence was in Carric–thura.

Autumn is dark on the mountains; gray mist rests on the hills. The whirlwind is heard on the heath. Dark rolls the river through the narrow plain. A tree ands alone on the hill, and marks the slumbering Connal. The leaves whirl round with the wind, and strew the grave of the dead. At times are seen here the ghosts of the departed, when the musing hunter alone stalks slowly over the heath.

Who can reach the source of thy race, O Connal, who recount thy fathers? Thy family grew like an oak on the mountain, which meeteth the wind with its lofty head. But now it is torn from the earth. Who shall supply the place of Connal? Here was the din of arms; here the groans of the dying. Bloody are the wars of Fingal, O Connal! it was here thou didst fall. Thine arm was like a storm; thy sword a beam of the sky; thy height a rock on the plain; thine eyes a furnace of fire. Louder than a storm was thy voice, in the battles of thy steel. Warriors fell by thy sword, as the thistles by the staff of a boy. Dargo the mighty came on, darkened in his rage. His brows were gathered into wrath. His eyes like two caves in a rock. Bright rose their swords on each side; loud was the clang of their steel.

The daughter of Rinval was near; Crimora bright in the armor of man; her yellow hair is loose behind, her bow is in her hand. She followed the youth to the war, Connal her much– beloved. She drew the string on Dargo; but, erring, she pierced her Connal. He falls like an oak on the plain; like a rock from the shaggy hill. What shall she do. hapless maid? He bleeds; her Connal dies! All the night long she cries, and all the day, "O Connal, my love, and my friend!" With grief the sad mourner dies! Earth here encloses the loveliest pair on the hill. The grass grows between the stones of the tomb: I often sit in the mournful shade. The wind sighs through the grass; their memory rushes on my mind. Undisturbed you now sleep together; in the tomb of the mountain you rest alone!

And soft be their rest, said Utha, hapless children of dreamy Lotha! I will remember them with tears, and my secret song shall rise; when the wind is in the groves of Tora, when the stream is roaring near. Then shall they come on my soul, with all their lovely grief!

Three days feasted the kings: on the fourth their white sails arose. The winds of the north drove Fingal to Morven's woody land. But the spirit of Loda sat in his cloud behind the ships of Frothal. He hung forward with all his blasts, and spread the white–bosomed sails. The wounds of his form were not forgotten! he still feared the hand of the king!

The narrow house: The grave.

They: Frothal and Utha.

CARTHON.

ARGUMENT.

This poem is complete, and the subject of it, as of most of Ossian's compositions, tragical. In the time of Comhal, the son of Trathal, and father of the celebrated Fingal, Cless mmor, the son of Thaddu, and brother of Morna, Fingal's mother, was driven by a storm into the river Clyde, on the banks of which stood Balclutha, a town belonging to the Britons, between the walls. He was hospitably received by Reuth mir, the principal man in the place, who gave him Moina, his only daughter, in marriage. Reudo, the son of Cormo, a Briton, who was in love with Moina, came to Reuth mir's house, and behaved haughtily towards Cless mmor. A quarrel ensued, in which Reudo was killed; the Britons who attended him, pressed so hard on Cless mmor, that he was obliged to throw himself into the Clyde and swim to his ship. He hoisted sail, and the wind being favorable, bore him out to sea. He often endeavored to return, and carry off his beloved Moina by night; but the wind continuing contrary, he was forced to desist.

Moina, who had been left with child by her husband, brought forth a son, and died soon after. Reuth mir named the child Carthon, i. e., "the murmur of waves," from the storm which carried off Cless mmor his father, who was supposed to have been cast away. When Carthon was three years old, Comhal, the father of Fingal, in one of his expeditions against the Britons, took and burnt Balclutha. Reuth mir was killed in the attack; and Carthon was carried safe away by his nurse, who fled farther into the country of the Britons. Carthon, coming to man's estate, was resolved to revenge the fall of Balclutha on Comhal's posterity. He set sail from the Clyde, and falling on the coast of Morven, defeated two of Fingal's heroes, who came to oppose his progress. He was, at last, unwittingly killed by his father Cless mmor, in a single combat. This story is the foundation of the present poem, which opens on the night preceding the death of Carthon, so that what passed before is introduced by way of episode. The poem is addressed to Malvina, the daughter of Toscar.

A TALE of the times of old! The deeds of days of other years.

The murmur of thy streams, O Lora! brings back the memory of the past. The sound of thy woods, Garmaller, is lovely in mine ear. Dost thou not behold Malvina, a rock with its head of heath! Three aged pines bend from its face; green is the narrow plain at its feet; there the flower of the mountain grows, and shakes its white head in the breeze. The thistle is there alone, shedding its aged beard. Two stones, half sunk in the ground, show their heads of moss. The deer of the mountain avoids the place, for he beholds a dim ghost standing there. The mighty lie, O Malvina! in the narrow plain of the rock.

A tale of the times of old! The deeds of days of other years!

Who comes from the land of strangers, with his thousands around him? The sunbeam pours its bright stream before him; his hair meets the wind of his hills. His face is settled from war. He is calm as the evening beam that looks from the cloud of the west, on Cona's silent vale. Who is it but Comhal's son, the king of mighty deeds! He beholds the hills with joy, he bids a thousand voices rise. "Ye have fled over your fields, ye sons of the distant land! The king of the world sits in his hall, and hears of his people's flight. He lifts his red eye of pride; he takes his father's sword. Ye have fled over your fields, sons of the distant land!

Such were the words of the bards, when they came to Selma's halls. A thousand lights from the stranger's land rose in the midst of his people. The feast is spread around; the night passed away in joy. Where is the noble Cless mmor? said the fair-haired Fingal. Where is the brother of Morna, in the hour of my joy? Sullen and dark, he passes his days in the vale of echoing Lora: but, behold, he comes from the hill, like a steed in his strength, who finds his companions in the breeze, and tosses his bright mane in the wind. Blest be the soul of Cless mmor, why so long from Selma?

Returns the chief, said Cless mmor, in the midst of his fame? Such was the renown of Comhal in the battles of his youth. Often did we pass over Carun to the land of the strangers: our swords returned, not unstained with blood: nor did the kings of the world rejoice. Why do I remember the times of our war? My hair is mixed with gray. My hand forgets to bend the bow: I lift a lighter spear. O that my joy would return, as when I first beheld the maid; the white bosomed daughter of strangers, Moina, with the dark−blue eyes!

Tell, said the mighty Fingal, the tale of thy youthful days. Sorrow, like a cloud on the sun, shades the soul of Cless mmor. Mournful are thy thoughts, alone, on the banks of the roaring Lora. Let us hear the sorrow of thy youth and the darkness of thy days!

"It was in the days of peace," replied the great Cless mmor, "I came in my bounding ship to Balclutha's walls of towers. The winds had roared behind my sails, and Clutha's streams received my dark−bosomed ship. Three days I remained in Reuth mir's halls, and saw his daughter, that beam of light. The joy of the shell went round, and the aged hero gave the fair. Her breasts were like foam on the waves, and her eyes like stars of light; her hair was dark as the raven's wing: her soul was generous and mild. My love for Moina was great; my heart poured forth in joy.

"The son of a stranger came; a chief who loved the white− bosomed Moina. His words were mighty in the hall; he often half− unsheathed his sword. 'Where,' said he, 'is the mighty Comhal, the restless wanderer of the heath? Comes he, with his host, to Balclutha, since Cless mmor is so bold?' My soul, I replied, O warrior! burns in a light of its own. I stand without fear in the midst of thousands, though the valiant are distant far. Stranger! thy words are mighty, for Cless mmor is alone. But my sword trembles by my side, and longs to glitter in my hand. Speak no more of Comhal, son of the winding Clutha!

"The strength of his pride arose. We fought: he fell beneath my sword. The banks of Clutha heard his fall; a thousand spears glittered around. I fought: the strangers prevailed: I plunged into the stream of Clutha. My white sails rose over the waves, and I bounded on the dark−blue sea. Moina came to the shore, and rolled the red eye of her tears; her loose hair flew on the wind; and I heard her mournful, distant cries. Often did I turn my ship; but the winds of the east prevailed. Nor Clutha ever since have I seen, nor Moina of the dark−brown hair. She fell in Balclutha, for I have seen her ghost. I knew her as she came through the dusky night, along the murmur of Lora: she was like the new moon, seen through the gathered mist; when the sky pours down its flaky snow, and the world is silent and dark."

Raise, ye bards, said the mighty Fingal, the praise of unhappy Moina. Call her ghost, with your songs, to our hills, that she may rest with the fair of Morven, the sunbeams of other days, the delight of heroes of old. I have seen the walls of Balclutha, but they were desolate. The fire had resounded in the halls: and the voice of the people is heard no more. The stream of Clutha was removed from its place by the fall of the walls. The thistle shook there its lonely head: the moss whistled to the wind. The fox looked out from the windows, the rank grass of the wall waved round its head. Desolate is the dwelling of Moina, silence is in the house of her fathers. Raise the song of mourning, O bards, over the land of strangers. They have but fallen before us: for one day we must fall. Why dost thou build the hall, son of the winged days? Thou lookest from thy towers to−day: yet a few years, and the blast of the desert comes; it howls in thy empty court, and whistles round thy half−worn shield. And let the blast of the desert come! we shall be renowned in our day! The mark of my arm shall be in battle; my name in the song of bards. Raise the song, send round the shell: let joy be heard in my hall. When thou, sun of heaven! shalt fail; if thou shalt fail, thou mighty light! if thy brightness is for a season, like Fingal; our fame shall survive thy beams.

Such was the song of Fingal in the day of his joy. His thousand bards leaned forward from their seats, to hear the voice of the king. It was like the music of harps on the gale of the spring. Lovely were thy thoughts, O Fingal! why had not Ossian the strength of thy soul? But thou standest alone, my father! who can equal the king of Selma?

The night passed away in song; morning returned in joy. The mountains showed their gray heads; the blue face of ocean smiled. The white wave is seen tumbling round the distant rock; a mist rose slowly from the lake. It came, in the figure of an aged man, along the silent plain. Its large limbs did not move in steps, for a ghost supported it in mid air. It came towards Selma's hall, and dissolved in a shower of blood.

The king alone beheld the sight; he foresaw the death of the people. He came in silence to his hall, and took his father's spear. The mail rattled on his breast. The heroes rose around. They looked in silence on each other, marking the eyes of Fingal. They saw battle in his face; the death of armies on his spear. A thousand shields at once are placed on their arms; they drew a thousand swords. The hall of Selma brightened around. The clang of arms ascends. The gray dogs howl in their place. No word is among the mighty chiefs. Each marked the eyes of the king and half−assumed his spear.

Sons of Morven, began the king, this is no time to fill the shell; the battle darkens near us, death hovers over the land. Some ghost, the friend of Fingal, has forewarned us of the foe. The sons of the stranger come from the darkly rolling sea; for from the water came the sign of Morven's gloomy danger. Let each assume his heavy spear, each gird on his father's sword. Let the dark helmet rise on every head; the mail pour its lightning from every side. The battle gathers like a storm; soon shall ye hear the roar of death.

The hero moved on before his host, like a cloud before a ridge of green fire, when it pours on the sky of night, and mariners foresee a storm. On Cona's rising heath they stood: the white–bosomed maids beheld them above like a grove; they foresaw the death of the youth, and looked towards the sea with fear. The white wave deceived them for distant sails; the tear is on their cheek! The sun rose on the sea, and we beheld a distant fleet. Like the mist of ocean they came and poured their youth upon the coast. The chief was among them, like the stag in the midst of the herd. His shield is studded with gold; stately strode the king of spears. He moved towards Selma; his thousands moved behind.

Go, with a song of peace, said Fingal: go, Ullin, to the king of swords. Tell him that we are mighty in war; that the ghosts of our foes are many. But renowned are they who have feasted in my halls; show the arms of my fathers in a foreign land; the Sons of the strangers wonder, and bless the friends of Morven's race; for our names have been heard afar: the kings of the world shook in the midst of their host.

Ullin went with his song. Fingal rested on his spear: he saw the mighty foe in his armor: he blest the stranger's son. "How stately art thou, son of the sea!" said the king of woody Morven. "Thy sword is a beam of fire by thy side; thy spear is a pine that defies the storm. The varied face of the moon is not broader than thy shield. Ruddy is thy face of youth! soft the ringlets of thy hair! But this tree may fall, and his memory be forgot! The daughter of the stranger will be sad, looking to the rolling sea: the children will say, 'We see a ship; perhaps it is the king of Balclutha.' The tear starts from their mother's eye: her thoughts are of him who sleeps in Morven!"

Such were the words of the king when Ullin came to the mighty Carthon: he threw down the spear before him, he raised the song of peace. "Come to the feast of Fingal, Carthon, from the rolling sea! partake of the feast of the king, or lift the spear of war! The ghosts of our foes are many: but renowned are the friends of Morven! Behold that field, O Carthon! many a green hill rises there, with mossy stones and rustling grass; these are the tombs of Fingal's foes, the Sons of the rolling sea!"

"Dost thou speak to the weak in arms!" said Carthon, "bard of the woody Morven? Is my face pale for fear, son of the peaceful song? Why then dost thou think to darken my soul with the tales of those who fell? My arm has fought in battle, my renown is known afar. Go to the feeble in arms, bid them yield to Fingal. Have not I seen the fallen Balclutha? And shall I feast with Comhal's son? Comhal, who threw his fire in the midst of my father's hall? I was young, and knew not the cause why the virgins wept. The columns of smoke pleased mine eye, when they rose above my walls! I often looked back with gladness when my friends flew along the hill. But when the years of my youth came on, I beheld the moss of my fallen walls. My sigh arose with the morning, and my tears descended with night. Shall I not fight, I said to my soul, against the children of my foes? And I will fight, O bard! I feel the strength of my soul!"

His people gathered around the hero, and drew at once their shining swords. He stands in the midst, like a pillar of fire, the tear half–starting from his eye, for he thought of the fallen Balclutha. The crowded pride of his soul arose. Sidelong he looked up to the hill, where our heroes shone in arms: the spear trembled in his hand. Bending forward, he seemed to threaten the king.

Shall I, said Fingal to his soul, meet at once the youth? Shall I stop him in the midst of his course before his fame shall arise! But the bard hereafter may say, when he sees the tomb of Carthon, Fingal took his thousands to battle, before the noble Carthon fell. No: bard of the times to come! thou shalt not lessen Fingal's fame! my heroes will fight the youth, and Fingal behold the war. If he overcomes, I rush, in my strength, like the roaring stream of Cona. Who of my chiefs will meet the son of the rolling sea? Many are his warriors on the coast, and strong is his ashen spear!

Cathul rose in his strength, the son of the mighty Lormar: three hundred youths attend the chief, the race of his native streams. Feeble was his arm against Carthon: he fell, and his heroes fled. Connal resumed the battle, but he broke his heavy spear: he lay bound on the field: Carthon pursued his people.

Cless mmor, said the king of Morven, where is the spear of thy strength. Wilt thou behold Connal bound: thy friend at the stream of Lora? Rise, in the light of thy steel, companion of valiant Comhal! let the youth of Balclutha feel the strength of Morven's race. He rose

31

in the strength of his steel, shaking his grisly locks. He fitted the steel to his side; he rushed in the pride of valor.

Carthon stood on a rock: he saw the hero rushing on. He loved the dreadful joy of his face: his strength in the locks of age! "Shall I lift that spear," he said, "that never strikes but once a foe? Or shall I, with the words of peace, preserve the warrior's life? Stately are his steps of age! lovely the remnant of his years! Perhaps it is the husband of Moina, the father of car−borne Carthon. Often have I heard that he dwelt at the echoing stream of Lora."

Such were his words when Cless mmor came, and lifted high his spear. The youth received it on his shield, and spoke the words of peace. "Warrior of the aged locks! is there no youth to lift the spear? Hast thou no son to raise the shield before his father to meet the arm of youth? Is the spouse of thy love no more? or weeps she over the tombs of thy sons? Art thou of the kings of men? What will be the fame of my sword shouldst thou fall?"

It will be great, thou son of pride! begun the tall Cless mmor. I have been renowned in battle, but I − never told my name to a foe. Yield to me, son of the wave, then shalt thou know that the mark of my sword is in many a field. " I never yielded, king of spears!" replied the noble pride of Carthon: "I have also fought in war, I behold my future fame. Despise me not, thou chief of men! my arm, my spear is strong. Retire among thy friends; let younger heroes fight." Why dost thou wound my soul? replied Cless mmor, with a tear. Age does not tremble on my hand. I still can lift the sword. Shall I fly in Fingal's sight, in the sight of him I love? Son of the sea! I never fled: exalt thy pointed spear.

They fought like two contending winds, that strive to roil the wave. Calthon bade his spear to err: he still thought that the foe was the spouse of Moina. He broke Cless mmor's beamy spear in twain: he seized his shining sword. But as Carthon was binding the chief, the chief drew the dagger of his fathers. He saw the foe's uncovered side, and opened there a wound.

Fingal saw Cless mmor low: he moved in the sound of his steel. The host stood silent in his presence: they turned their eyes to the king. He came like the sullen noise of a storm before the winds arise: the hunter hears it in the vale, and retires to the cave of the rock. Carthon stood in his place, the blood is rushing down his side: he saw the coming down of the king, his hopes of fame arose, but pale was his cheek: his hair flew loose, his helmet shook on high: the force of Carthon failed, but his sword was strong.

Fingal beheld the hero's blood; he stopt the uplifted spear. "Yield, king of swords!" said Comhal's son, "I behold thy blood; thou hast been mighty in battle, and thy fame shall never fade." Art thou the king so far renowned? replied the car–borne Carthon: art thou that light of death, that frightens the kings of the world? But why should Carthon ask? for he is like the stream of his hills, strong as a river in his course, swift as the eagle of heaven. O that I had fought with the king, that my fame might be great in song! that the hunter, beholding my tomb, might say, he fought with the mighty Fingal. But Carthon dies unknown: he has poured out his force on the weak.

" But thou shalt not die unknown, replied the king of woody Morven: my bards are many, O Carthon! their songs descend to future times. The children of years to come shall hear the fame of Carthon, when they sit round the burning oak, and the night is spent in songs of old. The hunter, sitting in the heath, shall hear the rustling blast, and raising his eyes, behold the rock where Carthon fell. He shall turn to his son, and show the place where the mighty fought: There the king of Balclutha fought, like the strength of a thousand streams."

Joy rose in Carthon's face; he lifted his heavy eyes. He gave his sword to Fingal, to lie within his hall, that the memory of Balclutha's king might remain in Morven. The battle ceased along the field, the bard had sung the song of peace. The chiefs gathered round the falling Carthon; they heard his words with sighs. Silent they leaned on their spears, while Balclutha's hero spoke. His hair sighed in the wind, and his voice was sad and low.

"King of Morven," Carthon said, "I fall in the midst of my course. A foreign tomb receives, in youth, the last of Reuth mir's race. Darkness dwells in Balclutha; the shadows of grief in Crathmo. But raise my remembrance on the banks of Lora, where my fathers dwelt. Perhaps the husband of Moina will mourn over his fallen Carthon." His words reached the heart of Cless mmor: he fell in silence on his son. The host stood darkened around: no voice is on the plain. Night came: the moon, from the east, looked on the mournful field; but still they stood, like a silent grove that lifts its head on Gormal, when the loud winds are laid, and dark autumn is on the plain.

Three days they mourned above Carthon; on the fourth his father died. In the narrow plain of the rock they lie; a dim ghost defends their tomb. There lovely Moina is often seen, when the sunbeam darts on the rock, and all around is dark. There she is seen, Malvina; but not like the daughters of the hill. Her robes are from the stranger's land, and she is still alone!

Fingal was sad for Carthon; he commanded his bards to mark the day when shadowy autumn returned; and often did they mark the day, and sing the hero's praise. "Who comes so dark from ocean's roar, like autumn's shadowy cloud? Death is trembling in his hand! his eyes are flames of fire! Who roars along dark Lora's heath? Who but Carthon, king of swords! The people fall! see how he strides like the sullen ghost of Morven! But there he lies, a goodly oak which sudden blasts overturned! When shalt thou rise, Balclutha's joy? When, Carthon, shalt thou arise? Who comes so dark from ocean's roar, like autumn's shadowy cloud?" Such were the words of the bards in the day of their mourning; Ossian often joined their voice, and added to their song. My soul has been mournful for Carthon: he fell in the days of his youth; and thou, O Cless mmor! where is thy dwelling in the wind? Has the youth forgot his wound? Flies he on clouds with thee? I feel the sun, O Malvina! leave me to my rest. Perhaps they may come to my dreams: I think I hear a feeble voice! The beam of heaven delights to shine on the grave of Carthon: I feel it warm around.

O thou that rollest above, round as the shield of my fathers! Whence are thy beams, O sun! thy everlasting light! Thou comest forth in thy awful beauty; the stars hide themselves in the sky; the moon, cold and pale, sinks in the western wave; but thou thyself movest alone. Who can be a companion of thy course? The oaks of the mountains fall; the mountains themselves decay with years; the ocean shrinks and grows again; the moon herself is lost in heaven: but thou art forever the same, rejoicing in the brightness of thy course. When the world is dark with tempests, when thunder rolls and lightning flies, thou lookest in thy beauty from the clouds, and laughest at the storm. But to Ossian thou lookest in vain, for he beholds thy beams no more: whether thy yellow hair flows on the eastern clouds, or thou tremblest at the gates of the west. But thou art, perhaps, like me, for a season; thy years will have an end. Thou shalt sleep in thy clouds, careless of the voice of the morning. Exult then, O sun, in the strength of thy youth! age is dark and unlovely; it is like the glimmering light of the moon, when it shines through broken clouds, and the mist is on the hills: the blast of the north is on the plain, the traveller shrinks in the midst of his journey.

To tell one's name to an enemy, was reckoned, in those days of heroism, a manifest evasion of fighting him; for if it was once known that friendship subsisted of old, between the ancestors of the combatants. the battle immediately ceased, and the ancient amity of their forefathers was renewed. "A man who tells his name to his enemy," was of old an ignominious term for a coward.

OINA–MORUL.

ARGUMENT.

After an address to Malvina, the daughter of Toscar, Ossian proceeds to relate his own expedition to Furfed, an island of Scandinavia. Mal–orchol, king of Furfed, being hard pressed in war by Ton–thormod, chief of Sar–dronto (who had demanded in vain the daughter of Mal–orchol in marriage,) Fingal sent Ossian to his aid. Ossian, on the day after his arrival, came to battle with Ton–thormod, and took him prisoner. Mal–orchol offers his daughter, Oina–morul, to Ossian; but he, discovering her passion for Ton–thormod, generously surrenders her to her lover, and brings about a reconciliation between the two kings.

As flies the inconstant sun over Larmon's grassy hill so pass the tales of old along my soul by night! When bards are removed to their place, when harps are hung in Selma's hall, then comes a voice to Ossian, and awakes his soul! It is the voice of years that are gone! they roll before me with all their deeds! I seize the tales as they pass, and pour them forth in song. Nor a troubled stream is the song of the king, it is like the rising of music from Lutha of the strings. Lutha of many strings, not silent are thy streamy rocks, when the white hands of Malvina move upon the harp! Light of the shadowy thoughts that fly across my soul, daughter of Toscar of helmets, wilt thou not hear the song? We call back, maid of Lutha, the years that have rolled away! It was in the days of the king, while yet my locks were young, that I marked Con–cathlin on high, from ocean's nightly wave. My course was towards the isle of Furfed, woody dweller of seas! Fingal had sent me to the aid Mal–orchol, king of Furfed wild: for war was around him, and our fathers had met at the feast.

In Col–coiled I bound my sails. I sent my sword to Mal– orchol of shells. He knew the signal of Albion, and his joy arose. He came from his own high hall, and seized my hand in grief. "Why comes the race of heroes to a falling king? Ton–thormod of many spears is the chief of wavy Sar–dronlo. He saw and loved my daughter, white–bosomed Oina–morul. He sought. I denied the maid, for our fathers had been foes. He came with battle to Furfed; my people are rolled away. Why comes the race of heroes to a falling king?"

I come not, I said, to look, like a boy, on the strife. Fingal remembers Mal–orchol, and his hall for strangers. From his waves the warrior descended on thy woody isle: thou wert no cloud before him. Thy feast was spread with songs. For this my sword shall rise, and thy foes perhaps may fail. Our friends are not forgot in their danger, though distant is our land.

"Descendant of the daring Trenmor, thy words are like the voice of Cruth–Loda, when he speaks from his parting cloud, strong dweller of the sky! Many have rejoiced at my feast; but they all have forgot Mal–orchol. I have looked towards all the winds, but no white sails were seen! but steel resounds in my hall, and not the joyful shells. Come to my dwelling, race of heroes! dark–skirted night is near. Hear the voice of songs from the maid of Furfed wild."

We went. On the harp arose the white hands of Oina– morul. She waked her own sad tale from every trembling string. I stood in silence; for bright in her locks was the daughter of many isles! Her eyes were two stars, looking forward through a rushing shower. The mariner marks them on high, and blesses the lovely beams. With morning we rushed to battle, to Tormul's resounding stream: the foe moved to the sound of Ton–thormod's bossy shield. From wing to wing the strife was mixed. I met Ton– thormod in fight. Wide flew his broken steel. I seized the king in war. I gave his hand, fast bound with thongs, to Mal–orchol, the giver of shells. Joy rose at the feast of Furfed, for the foe had failed. Ton–thormod turned his face away from Oina–morul of isles.

Son of Fingal, began Mal–orchol, not forgot shalt thou pass from me. A light shall dwell in thy ship, Oina–morul of slow– rolling eyes. She shall kindle gladness along thy mighty soul. Nor unheeded shall the maid move in Selma through the dwelling of kings.

In the hall I lay in night. Mine eyes were half closed in sleep. Soft music came to mine ear. It was like the rising breeze, that whirls at first the thistle's beard, then flies dark–shadowy over the grass. It was the maid of Furfed wild! she raised the nightly song;

she knew that my soul was a stream that flowed at pleasant sounds. "Who looks," she said, "from his rock on ocean's closing mist? His long locks like the raven's wing, are wandering on the blast. — Stately are his steps in grief! The tears are in his eyes! His manly breast is heaving over his bursting soul! Retire, I am distant afar, a wanderer in lands unknown. Though the race of kings are around me, yet my soul is dark. Why have our fathers been foes, Ton–thormod, love of maids!"

"Soft voice of the streamy isle," I said, "why dost thou mourn by night? The race of daring Trenmor are not the dark in soul. Thou shalt not wander by streams unknown, blue–eyed Oina–morul! within this bosom is a voice: it comes not to other ears: it bids Ossian hear the hapless in their hour of woe. Retire, soft singer by night! Ton–thormod shall not mourn on his rock!"

With morning I loosed the king. I gave the long–haired maid. Mal–orchol heard my words in the midst of his echoing halls. "King of Furfed wild, why should Ton–thormod mourn? He is of the race of heroes, and a flame in war. Your fathers have been foes, but now their dim ghosts rejoice in death. They stretch their hands of mist to the same shell in Loda. Forget their rage, ye warriors! It was the cloud of other years."

Such were the deeds of Ossian, while yet his locks were young; though loveliness, with a robe of beams, clothed the daughter of many isles. We call back, of Lutha, the years that have rolled away!

Con–cathlin, "mild beam of the wave." What star was so called of old is not easily ascertained. Some now distinguish the pole–star by that name.

COLNA–DONA.

ARGUMENT.

Fingal despatches Ossian and Toscar, the son of Conloch, and father of Malvina, to raise a stone on the banks of the stream of Crona, to perpetuate the memory of a victory which he had obtained in that place. When they were employed in that work, Car–ul, a neighboring chief, invited them to a feast. They went, and Toscar fell desperately in love with Colna–dona, the daughter of Car–ul. Colna–dona became no less enamored of

THE POEMS OF OSSIAN

Toscar. An incident at a hunting party brings their loves to a happy issue.

COL–AMON of troubled streams, dark wanderer of distant vales, I behold thy course, between trees near Car–ul's echoing halls! There dwelt bright Colna–dona, the daughter of the king. Her eyes were rolling stars; her arms were white as the foam of streams. Her breast rose slowly to sight, like ocean's heaving wave. Her soul was a stream of light. Who, among the maids was like the love of heroes?

Beneath the voice of the king we moved to Crona of the streams, Toscar of grassy Lutha, and Ossian young in fields. Three bards attended with songs. Three bossy shields were borne before us; for we were to rear the stone in memory of the past. By Crona's mossy course Fingal had scattered his foes; he had rolled away the strangers like a troubled sea. We came to the place of renown; from the mountains descended night. I tore an oak from its hill, and raised a flame on high. I bade my fathers to look down from the clouds of their hall; for, at the fame of their race they brighten in the wind.

I took a stone from the stream, amidst the song of bards. The blood of Fingal's foes hung curdled in its ooze. Beneath I placed, at intervals, three bosses from the shield of foes, as rose or fell the sound of Ullin's nightly song. Toscar laid a dagger in earth, a mail of sounding steel. We raised the mould around the stone, and bade it speak to other years.

Oozy daughter of streams, that now art reared on high, speak to the feeble, O stone! after Selma's race have failed! Prone from the stormy night, the traveller shall lay him by thy side: thy whistling moss shall sound in his dreams; the years that were past shall return. Battles rise before him, blue–shielded kings descend to war: the darkened moon looks from heaven on the troubled field. He shall burst with morning from dreams, and see the tombs of warriors round. He shall ask about the stone, and the aged shall reply, "This gray stone was raised by Ossian, a chief of other years!"

From Col–amon came a bard, from Car–ul, the friend of strangers. He bade us to the feast of kings, to the dwelling of bright Colna–dona. We went to the hall of harps. There Car–ul brightened between his aged locks, when he beheld the sons of his friends, like two young branches before him.

"Sons of the mighty," he said, "ye bring back the days of old, when first I descended from waves, on Selma's streamy vale! I pursued Duthmocarglos, dweller of ocean's wind. Our fathers had been foes; we met by Clutha's winding waters. He fled along the sea, and my sails were spread behind him. Night deceived me on the deep. I came to the dwelling of kings, to Selma of high– bosomed maids. Fingal came forth with his bards, and Conloch, arm of heath. I feasted three days in the hall, and saw the blue eye. Erin, Roscrana, daughter of heroes, light of Cormac's race. Nor forgot did my steps depart: the kings gave their shields to Car–ul: they hang on high in Col–amon, in memory of the past. Sons of the daring kings, ye bring back the days of old!

Car–ul kindled the oak of feasts, he took two bosses from our shields. He laid them in earth beneath a stone, to speak to the hero's race. "When battle," said the king, "shall roar, and our sons are to meet in wrath, my race shall look perhaps on this stone, when they prepare the spear. Have not our fathers met in peace? they will say, and lay aside the shield."

Night came down. In her long locks moved the daughter of Car–ul. Mixed with the harp arose the voice of white–armed Colna–dona. Toscar darkened in his place before the love of heroes. She came on his troubled soul, like a beam to the dark– heaving ocean, when it bursts from a cloud, and brightens the foamy side of a wave.

* * * * * *

With morning we awaked the woods and hung forward on the path of the roes. They fell by their wonted streams. We returned through Crona's vale. From the wood a youth came forward, with a shield and pointless spear. — "Whence," said Toscar of Lutha, "is the flying beam? Dwells there peace at Col– amon, round bright Colna–dona of harps?"

"By Col–amon of streams," said the youth, "bright Colna– dona dwelt. She dwelt; but her course is now in deserts with the son of the king; he that seized with love her soul as it wandered through the hall." "Stranger of tales," said Toscar, "hast thou marked the warrior's course? He must fall; give thou that bossy shield." In wrath he took the shield. Fair behind it rose the breasts of a maid, white as the bosom of a swan, rising graceful on swift–rolling waves, It was Colna–dona of harps, the daughter of the king! Her blue eyes had rolled on Toscar, and her love arose!

Colna–dona signifies "the love of heroes." Col–amon, "narrow river." Car–ul, "dark–eyed."

39

Crona, "murmuring," was the name of a small stream which discharged itself in the river Carron.

Here an episode is entirely lost; or, at least, is handed down so imperfectly, that it does not deserve a place in the poem.

OITHONA.

ARGUMENT.

Gaul, the son of Morni, attended Lathmon into his own country, after his being defeated in Morven, as related in a preceding poem. He was kindly entertained by Nuth, the father of Lathmon, and fell in love with his daughter Oithona. The lady was no less enamored of Gaul, and a day was fixed for their marriage. In the mean time Fingal, preparing for an expedition into the country of the Britons, sent for Gaul. He obeyed, and went; but not without promising to Oithona to return, it he survived the war, by a certain day. Lathmon too was obliged to attend his father Nuth in his wars, and Oithona was left alone at Dunlathmon, the seat of the family. Dunrommath, Lord of Uthal, supposed to be one of the Orkneys, taking advantage of the absence of her friends, came and carried off, by force, Oithona, who had formerly rejected his love, into Trom thon, a desert island, where he concealed her in a cave.

Gaul returned on the day appointed; heard of the rape, and sailed to Trom thon, to revenge himself on Dunrommath. When he landed, he found Oithona disconsolate, and resolved not to survive the loss of her honor. She told him the story of her misfortunes, and she scarce ended when Dunrommath with his followers appeared at the farther end of the island. Gaul prepared to attack him, recommending to Uithona to retire till the battle was over. She seemingly obeyed; but she secretly armed herself rushed into the thickest of the battle, and was mortally wounded. Gaul, pursuing the flying enemy, found her just expiring on the field; he mourned over her, raised her tomb, and returned to Morven. Thus is the story handed down by tradition; nor is it given with any material difference in the poem, which opens with Gaul's return to Dunlathmon, after the rape of Oithona.

DARKNESS dwells around Dunlathmon, though the moon shows half her face on the hill. The daughter of night turns her eyes away; she beholds the approaching grief. The son of Morni is on the plain: there is no sound in the hall. No long streaming beam of light comes trembling through the gloom. The voice of Oithona is not heard amidst the noise of the streams of Dunranna. "Whither art thou gone in thy beauty, dark–haired daughter of Nuth? Lathmon is in the field of the valiant, but thou didst promise to remain in the hall till the son of Morni returned. Till he returned from Strumon, to the maid of his love! The tear was on thy cheek at his departure; the sigh rose in secret in thy breast. But thou dost not come forth with songs, with the lightly trembling sound of the harp!"

Such were the words of Gaul, when he came to Dunlathmon's towers. The gates were open and dark. The winds were blustering in the hall. The trees strewed the threshold with leaves; the murmur of night was abroad. Sad and silent, at a rock, the son of Morni sat: his soul trembled for the maid; but he knew not whither to turn his course! The son of Leth stood at a distance, and heard the winds in his bushy hair. But he did not raise his voice, for he saw the sorrow of Gaul!

Sleep descended on the chiefs. The visions of night arose. Oithona stood, in a dream, before the eyes of Morni's son. Her hair was loose and disordered; her lovely eye rolled deep in tears. Blood stained her snowy arm. The robe half hid the wound of her breast. She stood over the chief, and her voice was feebly heard. " Sleeps the son of Morni, he that was lovely in the eyes of Oithona? Sleeps Gaul at the distant rock, and the daughter of Nuth low? The sea rolls round the dark isle of Trom thon. I sit in my tears in the cave! Nor do I sit alone, O Gaul! the dark chief of Cuthal is there. He is there in the rage of his love. What can Oithona do?"

A rougher blast rushed through the oak. The dream of night departed. Gaul took his aspen spear. He stood in the rage of his soul. Often did hid turn to the east. He accused the lagging light. At length the morning came forth. The hero lifted up the sail. The winds came rustling from the hill; he bounded on the waves of the deep. On the third day arose Trom thon, like a blue shield in the midst of the sea. The white wave roared against its rocks; sad Oithona sat on the coast! She looked on the rolling waters, and her tears came down. But when she saw Gaul in his arms, she started, and turned her eyes away. Her lovely cheek is bent and red; her white arm trembles by her side. Thrice she strove to fly from his presence; thrice her steps failed as she went!

"Daughter of Nuth," said the hero, " why dost thou fly from Gaul? Do my eyes send forth the flame of death? Darkens hatred in my soul? Thou art to me the beam of the east, rising in a land unknown. But thou coverest thy face with sadness, daughter of car–borne Nuth! Is the foe of Oithona near! My soul burns to meet him in fight. The sword trembles by the side of Gaul, and longs to glitter in his hand. Speak, daughter of Nuth! Dost thou not behold my tears?"

" Young chief of Strumon," replied the maid, " why comest thou over the dark–blue wave, to Nuth's mournful daughter! Why did I not pass away in secret, like the flower of the rock, that lifts its fair head unseen, and strews its withered leaves on the blast! Why didst thou come, O Gaul! to hear my departing sigh! I vanish in my youth; my name shall not be heard. Or it will be heard with grief; the tears of Nuth must fall. Thou wilt be sad, son of Morni! for the departed fame of Oithona. But she shall sleep in the narrow tomb, far from the voice of the mourner. Why didst thou come, chief of Strumon! to the sea–beat rocks of Trom thon!"

"I came to meet thy foes, daughter of car–borne Nuth! The death of Cuthal's chief darkens before me; or Morni's son shall fall! Oithona! when Gaul is low, raise my tomb on that oozy rock. When the dark, bounding ship shall pass, call the sons of the sea; call them, and give this sword, to bear it hence to Morni's hall. The gray–haired chief will then cease to look towards the desert for the return of his son!"

"Shall the daughter of Nuth live?" she replied, with a bursting sig. "Shall I live in Trom thon, and the son of Morni low? My heart is not of that rock; nor my soul careless as that sea, which lifts its blue waves to every wind, and rolls beneath the storm! The blast which shall lay thee low, shall spread the branches of Oithona on earth. We shall wither together, son of car–borne Morni! The narrow house is pleasant to me, and the gray stone of the dead: for never more will I leave thy rocks, O sea–surrounded Trom thon! Night came on with her clouds after the departure of Lathmon, when he went to the wars of his fathers, to the moss–covered rock of Duth¢rmoth. Night came on. I sat in the hall, at the beam of the oak! The wind was abroad in the trees. I heard the sound of arms. Joy rose in my face. I thought of thy return. It was the chief of Cuthal, the red–haired strength of Dunrommath. His eyes rolled in fire: the blood of my people was on his sword. They who defended Oithona fell by the gloomy chief! What could I do? My arm was weak. I could not lift the spear. He took me in my grief; amidst my tears he raised the sail. He feared the returning Lathmon, the brother of unhappy Oithona! But behold, he comes with his people! the dark wave is divided before him! Whither wilt thou turn thy steps, son of Morni? Many are the warriors of thy foe!"

"My steps never turned from battle," Gaul said, and unsheathed his sword: " shall I then begin to fear, Oithona! when thy foes are near? Go to thy cave, my love, till our battle tease on the field. Son of Leth bring the bows of our fathers! the sounding quiver of Morni! Let our three warriors bend the yew. Ourselves will lift the spear. They are a host on the rock! our souls are strong in war!

Oithona went to the cave. A troubled joy rose on her mind, like the red path of lightning on a stormy cloud! Her soul was resolved: the tear was dried from her wildly-looking eye. Dunrommath slowly approached. He saw the son of Morni. Contempt contracted his face, a smile is on his dark-brown cheek; his red eye rolled half concealed, beneath his shaggy brows!

"Whence are the sons of the sea?" began the gloomy chief. Have the winds driven you on the rocks of Trom thon? or come you in search of the white-handed maid? the sons of the unhappy, ye feeble men, come to the hand of Dunrommath! His eye spares not the weak; he delights in the blood of strangers. Oithona is a beam of light, and the chief of Cuthal enjoys it in secret; wouldst thou come on its loveliness like a cloud, son of the feeble hand? Thou mayest come, but shalt thou return to the halls of thy fathers?"

" Dost thou not know me," said Gaul, "red-haired chief of Cuthal? Thy feet were swift on the heath, in the battle of car- borne Lathmon; when the sword of Morni's son pursued his host, in Morven's woody land. Dunrommath! thy words are mighty, for thy warriors gather behind thee. But do I fear them, son of pride? I am not of the race of the feeble!"

Gaul advanced in his arms; Dunrommath shrunk behind his people. But the spear of Gaul pierced the gloomy chief: his sword lopped off his head, as it bended in death. The son of Morni shook it thrice by the lock; the warriors of Dunrommath fled. The arrows of Morven pursued them: ten fell on the mossy rocks. The rest lift the sounding sail, and bound on the troubled deep. Gaul advanced towards the cave of Oithona. He beheld a youth leaning on a rock. An arrow had pierced his side; his eye rolled faintly beneath his helmet. The soul of Morni's son was sad; he came, and spoke the words of peace.

" Can the hand of Gaul heal thee, youth of the mournful brow? I have searched for the herbs of the mountains; I have gathered them on the secret banks of their streams. My hand has closed the wound of the brave, their eyes have blessed the son of Morni. Where dwelt thy fathers, warrior? Were they of the sons of the mighty! Sadness shall come, like night, on thy native streams. Thou art fallen in thy youth!"

" My fathers," replied the stranger, " were of the race of the mighty; but they shall not be sad; for my fame is departed like morning mist. High walls rise on the banks of Duvranna; and see their mossy towers in the stream; a rock ascends behind them with its bending pines. Thou mayest behold it far distant. There my brother dwells. He is renowned in battle: give him this glittering helmet."

The helmet fell from the hand of Gaul. It was the wounded Oithona! She had armed herself in the cave, and came in search of death. Her heavy eyes are half closed; the blood pours from her heaving side. "Son of Morni!" she said, "prepare the narrow tomb. Sleep grows, like darkness, on my soul. The eyes of Oithona are dim! O had I dwelt at Duvranna, in the bright beam of my fame! then had my years come on with joy; the virgins would then bless my steps. But I fall in youth, son of Morni! my father shall blush in his hall!"

She fell pale on the rock of Trom thon. The mournful warrior raised her tomb. He came to Morven; we saw the darkness of his soul. Ossian took the harp in the praise of Oithona. The brightness of the face of Gaul returned. But his sigh rose, at times, in the midst of his friends; like blasts that shake their unfrequent wings, after the stormy winds are laid!

CROMA.

ARGUMENT.

Malvina, the daughter of Toscar, is overheard by Ossian lamenting the death of Oscar her lover. Ossian, to divert her grief, relates his own actions in expedition which he undertook, at Fingal's command, to aid Crothar the petty king of Croma, a country in Ireland, against Rothmar, who invaded his dominions. The story is delivered down thus in tradition. Crothar, king of Croma, being blind with age, and his son too young for the field, Rothmar, the chief of Tromo resolved to avail himself of the opportunity offered of annexing the dominions of Crothar to his own. He accordingly marched into the country subject to Crothar, but which he held of Arth or Artho, who was, at the time, supreme king of Ireland.

Crothar being, on account of his age and blindness unfit for action, sent for aid to Fingal, king of Scotland; who ordered his son Ossian to the relief of Crothar. But before his arrival Fovargormo, the son of Crothar, attacking Rothmar, was slain himself, and his forces totally defeated. Ossian renewed the war; came to battle, killed Rothmar, and routed his army. Croma being thus delivered of its enemies, Ossian returned to Scotland.

"It was the voice of my love! seldom art thou in the dreams of Malvina! Open your airy halls, O father of Toscar of shields! Unfold the gates of your clouds: the steps of Malvina are near. I have heard a voice in my dream. I feel the fluttering of my soul. Why didst thou come, O blast! from the dark−rolling face of the lake? Thy rustling wing was in the tree; the dream of Malvina fled. But she beheld her love when his robe of mist flew on the wind. A sunbeam was on his skirts, they glittered like the gold of the stranger. It was the voice of my love! seldom comes he to my dreams!

"But thou dwellest in the soul of Malvina, son of mighty Ossian! My sighs arise with the beam of the east; my tears descend with the drops of night. I was a lovely tree, in thy presence, Oscar, with all my branches round me; but thy death came like a blast from the desert, and laid my green head low. The spring returned with its showers; no leaf of mine arose! The virgins saw me silent in the hall; they touched the harp of joy. The tear was on the cheek of Malvina: the virgins beheld me in my grief. Why art thou sad, they said, thou first of the maids of Lutha! Was he lovely as the beam of the morning, and stately in thy sight?"

Pleasant is thy song in Ossian's ear, daughter of streamy Lutha! Thou hast heard the music of departed bards in the dream of thy rest, when sleep fell on thine eyes, at the murmur of Moruth. When thou didst return from the chase in the day of the sun, thou hast heard the music of bards, and thy song is lovely! It is lovely, O Malvina! but it melts the soul. There is a joy in grief when peace dwells in the breast of the sad. But sorrow wastes the mournful, O daughter of Toscar! and their days are few! They fall away, like the flower on which the sun hath looked in his strength, after the mildew has passed over it, when its head is heavy with the drops of night. Attend to the tales of Ossian, O maid! He remembers the days of his youth!

The king commanded; I raised my sails, and rushed into the bay of Croma; into Croma's sounding bay in lovely Inisfail. High on the coast arose the towers of Crothar king of spears; Crothar renowned in the battles of his youth; but age dwelt then around the chief.

Rothmar had raised the sword against the hero; and the wrath of Fingal burned. He sent Ossian to meet Rothmar in war, for the chief of Croma was the friend of his youth. I sent the bard before me with songs. I came into the hall of Crothar. There sat the chief amidst the arms of his fathers, but his eyes had failed. His gray locks waved around a staff which the warrior leaned. He hummed the song of other times; when the sound of our arms reached his ears Crothar rose, stretched his aged hand, and blessed the son of Fingal.

"Ossian!" said the hero, "the strength of Crothar's arm has failed. O could I lift the sword, as on the day that Fingal fought at Strutha! He was the first of men; but Crothar had also his fame. The king of Morven praised me; he placed on my arm the bossy shield of Calthar, whom the king had slain in his wars. Dost thou not behold it on the wall? for Crothar's eyes have failed. Is thy strength like thy father's, Ossian! let the aged feel thine arm!"

I gave my arm to the king; he felt it with his aged hands. The sigh rose in his breast, and his tears came down. "Thou art strong, my son," he said, "but not like the king of Morven! But who is like the hero among the mighty in war? Let the feast of my hall be spread; and let my bards exalt the song. Great is he that is within my walls, ye sons of echoing Croma!" The feast is spread. The harp is heard; and joy is in the hall. But it was joy covering a sigh, that darkly dwelt in every breast. It was like the faint beam of the moon spread on a cloud in heaven. At length the music ceased, and the aged king of Croma spoke; he spoke without a tear, but sorrow swelled in the midst of his voice.

" Son of Fingal! beholdest thou not the darkness of Crothar's joy? My soul was not sad at the feast, when my people lived before me. I rejoiced in the presence of strangers, when my son shone in the hall. But, Ossian, he is a beam that is departed. He left no streak of light behind. He is fallen, son of Fingal! in the wars of his father. Rothmar the chief of grassy Tromlo heard that these eyes had failed; he heard that my arms were fixed in the hall, and the pride of his soul arose! He came towards Croma; my people fell before him. I took my arms in my wrath, but what could sightless Crothar do? My steps were unequal; my grief was great. I wished for the days that were past. Days! wherein I fought; and won in the field of blood. My son returned from the chase: the fair haired Fovargormo. He had not lifted his sword in battle, for his arm was young. But the soul of the youth was great; the fire of valor burned in his eyes. He saw the disordered steps of his father, and his sigh arose — "King of Croma," he said, "is it because thou hast no son; is it for the weakness of Fovargormo's arm that thy sighs arise? I begin, my father, to feel my strength; I have drawn the sword of my youth; and I have bent the bow. Let me meet this Rothmar, with the sons of Croma: let me meet him, O my father? I feel my burning soul!" — "And thou shalt meet him," I said, "son of the sightless Crothar! But let others advance before thee that I may hear the tread of thy feet at thy return; for my eyes behold thee not, fair haired Fovargormo!" He went; he met the foe; he fell. Rothmar advances to Croma. He who slew my son is near, with all his pointed spears."

This is no time to fill the shell, I replied, and took my spear! My people saw the fire of my eyes; they all arose around. Through night we strode along the heath. Gray morning rose in the east. A green narrow vale appeared before us; nor wanting are its winding streams. The dark host of Rothmar are on its banks with all their glittering arms. We fought along the vale. They fled. Rothmar sunk beneath my sword! Day had not descended in the west, when I brought his arms to Crothar. The aged hero felt them with his hands; and joy brightened over all his thoughts.

The people gather to the hall! The shells of the feast are heard. Ten harps are strung; five bards advance, and sing, by turns, the praise of Ossian; they poured forth their burning souls, and the string answered to their voice. The joy of Croma was great; for peace returned to the land. The night came on with silence; the morning returned with joy. No foe came in darkness with his glittering spear. The joy of Croma was great; for the gloomy Rothmar had fallen!

I raised my voice for Fovargormo, when they laid the chief in earth. The aged Crothar was there, but his sigh was not heard. He searched for the wound of his son, and found it in his breast. Joy rose in the face of the aged. He came and spoke to Ossian. "King of spears!" he said, "my son has not fallen without his fame. The young warrior did not fly; but met death as he went forward in his strength. Happy are they who die in youth, when their renown is heard! The feeble will not behold them in the hall; or smile at their trembling hands. Their memory shall be honored in song; the young tear of the virgin will fall. But the aged wither away by degrees; the fame of their youth, while yet they live, is all forgot. They fall in secret. The sigh of their son is not heard. Joy is around their tomb; the stone of their fame is placed without a tear. Happy are they who die in their youth, when their renown is around them!"

Inisfail: one of the ancient names of Ireland.

CALTHON AND COLMAL.

ARGUMENT.

This piece, as many more of Ossian's compositions, is addressed to one of the first Christian missionaries. The story of the poem is handed down by tradition thus:– In the country of the Britons, between the walls, two chiefs lived in the days of Fingal, Dunthalmo, Lord of Teutha, supposed to be the Tweed; and Rathmor, who dwelt at Clutha, well known to be the river Clyde. Rathmor was not more renowned for his generosity and hospitality, than Dunthalmo was infamous for his cruelty and ambition. Dunthalmo, through envy, or on account of some private feuds, which subsisted between the families, murdered Rathmor at a feast; but being afterward touched with remorse, he educated the two sons of Rathmor, Calthon and Colmar, in his own house. They growing up to man's estate, dropped some hints that they intended to revenge the death of their father, upon which Dunthalmo shut them up in two caves, on the banks of Teutha, intending to take them off privately. Colmal, the daughter of Dunthalmo, who was secretly in love with Calthon, helped him to make his escape from prison, and hied with him to Fingal, disguised in the habit of a young warrior, and implored his aid against Dunthalmo. Fingal sent Ossian with three hundred men to Colmar's relief. Dunthalmo, having previously murdered Colmar, came to a battle with Ossian, but he was killed by that hero, and his army totally defeated. Calthon married Colmal his deliverer; and Ossian returned to Morven.

Pleasant is the voice of thy song, thou lonely dweller of the rock! It comes on the sound of the stream, along the narrow vale. My soul awakes, O stranger, in the midst of my hall. I stretch my hand to the spear, as in the days of other years. I stretch my hand, but it is feeble: and the sigh of my bosom grows. Wilt thou not listen, son of the rock! to the song of Ossian? My soul is full of other times; the joy of my youth returns. Thus the sun appears in the west, after the steps of his brightness have moved behind a storm: the green hills lift their dewy heads: the blue streams rejoice in the vale. The aged hero comes forth on his stair; his gray hair glitters in the beam. Dost thou not behold, son of the rock! a shield in Ossian's hall? It is marked with the strokes of battle; and the brightness of its bosses has failed. That shield the great Dunthalmo bore, the chief of streamy Teutha. Dunthalmo bore it in battle before he fell by Ossian's spear. Listen, son of the rock! to the tale of other years.

Rathmor was a chief of Clutha. The feeble dwelt in his ball. The gates of Rathmor were never shut: his feast was always spread. The sons of the stranger came. They blessed the generous chief of Clutha. Bards raised the song, and touched the harp: joy brightened on the face of the sad! Dunthalmo came, in his pride, and rushed into the combat of Rathmor. The chief of Clutha overcame: the rage of Dunthalmo rose. He came, by night, with his warriors; the mighty Rathmor fell. He fell in his halls, where his feast was often spread for strangers.

Colmar and Calthon were young, the sons of car–borne Rathmor. They came, in the joy of youth, into their father's hall. They behold him in his blood; their bursting tears descend. The soul of Dunthalmo melted, when he saw the children of youth. He brought them to Alteutha's walls; they grew in the house of their foe. They bent the bow in his presence: and came forth to his wars. They saw the fallen walls of their fathers; they saw the green thorn in the hall. Their tears rushed forth in secret. At times their faces were sad. Dunthalmo beheld their grief; his darkening soul designed their death. He closed them in two caves, on the echoing banks of Teutha. The sun did not come there with his beams; nor the moon of heaven by night. The sons of Rathmor remained in darkness, and foresaw their death.

The daughter of Dunthalmo wept in silence, the fair–haired blue–eyed Colmal. Her eye had rolled in secret on Calthon; his loveliness swelled in her soul. She trembled for her warrior; but what could Colmal do? Her arm could not lift the spear; nor was the sword formed for her side. Her white breast never rose beneath a mail. Neither was her eye the terror of heroes. What canst thou do, O Colmal!! for the falling chief? Her steps are unequal; her hair is loose; her eye looks wildly through her tears. She came, by night, to the hall. She armed her lovely form in steel; the steel of a young warrior, who fell in the first of his battles. She came to the cave of Calthon, and loosed the thong from his hands.

"Arise, son of Rathmor," she said, "arise, the night is dark! Let us fly to the king of Selma, chief of fallen Clutha! I am the son of Lamgal, who dwelt in thy father's hall. I heard of thy dark dwelling in the cave, and my soul arose. Arise, son of Rathmor! arise, the night is dark!" — "Blest voice!" replied the chief, "comest thou from the clouds to Calthon? The ghosts of his fathers have often descended in his dreams, since the sun has retired from his eyes, and darkness has dwelt around him. Or art thou the son of Lamgal, the chief I often saw in Clutha? But shall I fly to Fingal, and Colmar my brother low? Will I fly to Morven, and the hero closed in night? No; give me that spear, son of

49

Lamgal; Calthon will defend his brother!"

"A thousand warriors," replied the maid, "stretch their spears round car–borne Colmar. What can Calthon do against a host so great? Let us fly to the king of Morven, he will come with war. His arm is stretched forth to the unhappy; the lightning of his sword is round the weak. Arise, thou son of Rathmor; the shadows will fly away. Arise, or thy steps may be seen, and thou must fall in youth."

The sighing hero rose; his tears descend for car–borne Colmar. He came with the maid to Selma's hall: but he knew not that it was Colmal. The helmet covered her lovely face. Her bosom heaved beneath the steel. Fingal returned from the chase, and found the lovely strangers. They were like two beams of light, in the midst of the hall of shells. The king heard the tale of grief, and turned his eyes around. A thousand heroes half rose before him; claiming the war of Teutha. I came with my spear from the hill; the joy of battle rose in my breast: for the king spoke to Ossian in the midst of a thousand chiefs.

" Son of my strength," began the king, "take thou the spear of Fingal. Go to Teutha's rushing stream, and save the car–borne Colmar. Let thy fame return before thee like a pleasant gale; that my soul may rejoice over my son, who renews the renown of fathers. Ossian! be thou a storm in war; but mild when the foe is low! it was thus my fame arose, O my son! be thou like Selma's chief. When the haughty come to my halls, my eyes behold them not. But my arm is stretched forth to the unhappy. My sword defends the weak."

I rejoiced in the words of the king. I took my rattling arms. Diaran rose at my side, and Dargo, king of spears. Three hundred youths followed our steps; the lovely strangers were at my side. Dunthalmo heard the sound of our approach. He gathered the strength of Teutha. He stood on a hill with his host. They were like rocks broken with thunder, when their bent trees are singed and bare, and the streams of their chinks have failed. The stream of Teutha rolled in its pride, before the gloomy foe. I sent a bard to Dunthalmo, to offer the combat on the plain; but he smiled in the darkness of his pride. His unsettled host moved on the hill; like the mountain cloud, when the blast has entered its womb, and scatters the curling gloom on every side.

They brought Colmar to Teutha's bank, bound with a thousand thongs. The chief is sad, but stately. His eye is on his friends; for we stood in our arms, whilst Teutha's waters

50

rolled between. Dunthalmo came with his spear, and pierced the hero's side: he rolled on the bank in his blood. We heard his broken sighs. Calthon rushed into the stream: I bounded forward on my spear. Teutha's race fell before us. Night came rolling down. Dunthalmo rested on a rock, amidst an aged wood. The rage of his bosom burned against the car–borne Calthon. But Calthon stood in grief; he mourned the fallen Colmar; Colmar slain in youth before his fame arose!

I bade the song of wo to rise, to soothe the mournful chief; but he stood beneath a tree, and often threw his spear on the earth. The humid eye of Colmar rolled near in a secret tear: she foresaw the fall of Dunthalmo, or of Clutha's warlike chief. Now half the night had passed away. Silence and darkness were on the field. Sleep rested on the eyes of the heroes: Calthon's settling soul was still. His eyes were half closed; but the murmur of Teutha had not yet failed in his ear. Pale, and showing his wounds, the ghost of Colmar came: he bent his head over the hero, and raised his feeble voice!

" Sleeps the son of Rathmor in his night, and his brother low? Did we not rise to the chase together? Pursued we not the dark–brown hinds? Colmar was not forgot till he fell, till death had blasted his youth I lie pale beneath the rock of Lona. O let Calthon rise! the morning comes with its beams; Dunthalmo will dishonor the fallen." He passed away in his blast The rising Calthon saw the steps of his departure. He rushed in the sound of his steel. Unhappy Colmal rose. She followed her hero through night, and dragged her spear behind. But when Calthon came to Lona's rock, he found his fallen brother. The rage of his bosom rose; he rushed among the foe. The groans of death ascend. They close around the chief. He is bound in the midst, and brought to gloomy Dunthalmo. The shout of joy arose; and the hills of night replied.

I started at the sound; and took my father's spear. Diaran rose at my side; and the youthful strength of Dargo. We missed the chief of Clutha, and our souls were sad. I dreaded the departure of my fame. The pride of my valor rose. "Sons of Morven," I said, "it is not thus our fathers fought. They rested not on the field of strangers, when the foe was not fallen before them. Their strength was like the eagles of heaven; their renown is in the song. But our people fall by degrees. Our fame begins to depart. What shall the king of Morven say, if Ossian conquers not at Teutha? Rise in your steel, ye warriors, follow the sound of Ossian's course. He will not return, but renowned, to the echoing walls of Selma."

Morning rose on the blue waters of Teutha. Colmal stood before me in tears. She told of the chief of Clutha: thrice the spear fell from her hand. My wrath turned against the stranger; for my soul trembled for Calthon. "'Son of the feeble hand!" I said, "do Teutha's warriors fight with tears? The battle is not won with grief; nor dwells the sigh in the soul of war. Go to the deer of Carmun, to the lowing herds of Teutha. But leave these arms, thou son of fear! A warrior may lift them in fight."

I tore the mail from her shoulders. Her snowy breast appeared. She bent her blushing face to the ground. I looked in silence to the chiefs. The spear fell from my hand; the sigh of my bosom rose! But when I heard the name of the maid, my crowding tears rushed down. I blessed the lovely beam of youth, and bade the battle move!

Why, son of the rock, should Ossian tell how warriors died? They are now forgot in their land; their tombs are not found on the heath. Years came on with their storms. The green mounds are mouldered away. Scarce is the grave of Dunthalmo seen, or the place where he fell by the spear of Ossian.

Some gray warrior, half blind with age, sitting by night at the flaming oak of the hall, tells now my deeds to his sons, and the fall of the dark Dunthalmo. The faces of youth bend sidelong towards his voice. Surprise and joy burn in their eyes! I found Calthon bound to an oak; my sword cut the thongs from his hands. I gave him the white–bosomed Colmal. They dwelt in the halls of Teutha.

THE WAR OF CAROS.

ARGUMENT.

Caros is probably the noted usurper Carausius, by birth a Menapran, who assumed the purple in the year 284; and, seizing on Britain, defeated the emperor Maximinian Herculius in several naval engagements, which gives propriety to his being called in this poem "the king of ships." He repaired Agricola's wall, in order to obstruct the incursions of the Caledonians, and when he was employed in that work, it appears he was attacked by a party under the command of Oscar the son of' Ossian. This battle is the foundation of the present poem, which is addressed to Malvina, the daughter of Toscar.

THE POEMS OF OSSIAN

Bring, daughter of Toscar, bring the harp! the light of the song rises in Ossian's soul! It is like the field, when darkness covers the hills around, and the shadow grows slowly on the plain of the sun. I behold my son, O Malvina! near the mossy rock of Crona. But it is the mist of the desert, tinged with the beam of the west! Lovely is the mist that assumes the form of Oscar! turn from it, ye winds, when ye roar on the side of Ardven!

Who comes towards my son, with the murmur of a song? His staff is in his hand, his gray hair loose on the wind. Surly joy lightens his face. He often looks back to Caros. It is Ryno of songs, he that went to view the foe. "What does Caros, king of ships?" said the son of the now mournful Ossian: "spreads he the wings of his pride, bard of the times of old?" "He spreads them, Oscar," replied the bard," but it is behind his gathered heap. He looks over his stones with fear. He beholds thee terrible, as the ghost of night, that rolls the waves to his ships!"

"Go, thou first of my bards!" says Oscar, "take the spear of Fingal. Fix a flame on its point. Shake it to the winds of heaven. Bid him in songs, to advance, and leave the rolling of his wave. Tell to Caros that I long for battle; that my bow is weary of the chase of Cona. Tell him the mighty are not here; and that my arm is young."

He went with the murmur of songs. Oscar reared his voice on high. It reached his heroes on Ardven, like the noise of a cave, when the sea of Togorma rolls before it, and its trees meet the roaring winds. They gather round my son like the streams of the hill; when, after rain, they roll in the pride of their course. Ryno came to the mighty Caros. He struck his flaming spear. Come to the battle of Oscar. O thou that sittest on the rolling waves! Fingal is distant far; he hears the songs of bards in Morven: the wind of his hall is in his hair. His terrible spear is at his side; his shield that is like the darkened moon Come to the battle of Oscar; the hero is alone.

He came not over the streamy Carun. The bard returned with his song. Gray night grows dim on Crona. The feast of shells is spread. A hundred oaks burn to the wind; faint light gleams over the heath. The ghosts of Ardven pass through the beam, and show their dim and distant forms. Comala is half unseen on her meteor; Hidallan is sullen and dim, like the darkened moon behind the mist of night.

" Why art thou sad?" said Ryno; for he alone beheld the chief. "Why art thou sad, Hidallan! hast thou not received thy fame? The songs of Ossian have been heard , thy ghost has brightened in wind, when thou didst bend from thy cloud to hear the song of Morven's bard!"—–" And do thine eyes," said Oscar, " behold the chief, like the dim meteor of night? Say, Ryno, say, how fell Hidallan, the renowned in the days of my fathers! His name remains on the rocks of Cona. I have often seen the streams of his hills!"

Fingal, replied the bard, drove Hidallan from his wars. The king's soul was sad for Comala, and his eyes could not behold the chief. Lonely, sad, along the heath he slowly moved, with silent steps. His arms hung disordered on his side. His hair flies loose from his brow. The tear is in his downcast eyes; a sigh half silent in his breast! Three days he strayed unseen, alone, before he came to Lamor's halls: the mossy halls of his fathers, at the stream of Balva. There Lamor sat alone beneath a tree; for he had sent his people with Hidallan to war. The stream ran at his feet; his gray head rested on his staff. Sightless are his aged eyes. He hums the song of other times. The noise of Hidallan's feet came to his ear: he knew the tread of his son.

"Is the son of Lamor returned; or is it the sound of his ghost? Hast thou fallen on the banks of Carun, son of the aged Lamor? Or, if I hear the sound of Hidallan's feet, where are the mighty in the war? where are my people, Hidallan! that were wont to return with their echoing shields? Have they fallen on the banks of Carun?"

"No," replied the sighing youth, "the people of Lamor live. They are renowned in war, my father! but Hidallan is renowned no more. I must sit alone on the banks of Balva, when the roar of the battle grows." " But thy fathers never sat alone," replied the rising pride of Lamor. "They never sat alone on the banks of Balva, when the roar of battle rose. Dost thou not behold that tomb? My eyes discern it not; there rests the noble Garm llon, who never fled from war! Come, thou renowned in battle, he says, come to thy father's tomb. How am I renowned, Garm llon? my son has fled from war!"

"King of the streamy Balva!" said Hidallan with a sigh, "why dost thou torment my soul? Lamor, I never fled. Fingal was sad for Comala; he denied his wars to Hidallan. Go to the gray streams of thy land, he said; moulder like a leafless oak, which the winds have bent over Balva, never more to grow."

"And must I hear," Lamor replied, "the lonely tread of Hidallan's feet? When thousands are renowned in battle, shall he bend over my gray streams? Spirit of the noble Garm

54

llon! carry Lamor to his place; his eyes are dark, his soul is sad, his son has lost his fame."

"Where," said the youth, " shall I search for fames to gladden the soul of Lamor? From whence shall return with renown, that the sound of my arms may be pleasant in his ear? If I go to the chase of hinds, my name will not be heard. Lamor will not feel my dogs with his hands, glad at my arrival from the hill. He will not inquire of his mountains, or of the dark–brown deer of his deserts!"

"I must fall," said Lamor, "like a leafless oak: it grew on a rock! it was overturned by the winds! My ghost will be seen on my hills, mournful for my young Hidallan. Will not ye, ye mists, as ye rise, hide him from my sight! My son, go to Lamor's ball: there the arms of our fathers hang. Bring the sword of Garm llon: he took it from a foe!"

He went and brought the sword with all its studded thongs. He gave it to his father. The gray–haired hero felt the point with his hand.

"My son, lead me to Garm llon's tomb: it rises beside that rustling tree. The long grass is withered; I hear the breezes whistling there. A little fountain murmurs near, and sends its waters to Balva. There let me rest; it is noon: the sun is on our fields!"

He led him to Garm llon's tomb. Lamor pierced the side of his son. They sleep together: their ancient halls moulder away. Ghosts are seen there at noon: the valley is silent, and the people shun the place of Lamor.

"Mournful is thy tale," said Oscar, "son of the times of old! My soul sighs for Hidallan; he fell in the days of his youth. He flies on the blast of the desert: his wandering is in a foreign land. Sons of the echoing Morven! draw near to the foes of Fingal. Send the night away in songs; watch the strength of Caros. Oscar goes to the people of other times; to the shades of silent Ardven, where his fathers sit dim in their clouds, and behold the future war. And art thou there, Hidallan, like a half–extinguished meteor? Come to my sight, in thy sorrow, chief of the winding Balva!"

The heroes move with their songs. Oscar slowly ascends the hill. The meteors of night set on the heath before him. A distant torrent faintly roars. Unfrequent blasts rush through aged oaks. The half enlightened moon sinks dim and red behind her hill. Feeble Voices are heard on the heath. Oscar drew his sword! " Come," said the hero, " O ye ghosts of my fathers! ye that fought against the kings of the world! Tell the deeds of future times; and your converse in our caves, when you talk together, and behold your sons in the fields of the brave!"

Trenmo came from his hill at the voice of his mighty son. A cloud, like the steed of the stranger, supported his airy limbs. His robe is of the mist of Lano, that brings death to the people. His sword is a green meteor, half−extinguished. His face is without form, and dark. He sighed thrice over the hero; thrice the winds of night roared around! Many were his words to Oscar; but they only came by halves to our ears; they were dark as the tales of other times, before the light of the song arose. He slowly vanished, like a mist that melts on the sunny hill. it was then, O daughter of Toscar! my son began first to be sad. He foresaw the fall of his race. At times he was thoughtful and dark, like the sun when he carries a cloud on his face, but again he looks forth from his darkness on the green hills of Cona.

Oscar passed the night among his fathers: gray morning met him on Carun's banks. A green vale surrounded a tomb which arose in the times of old. Little hills lift their heads at a distance, and stretch their old trees to the wind. The warriors of Caros sat there, for they had passed the stream by night. They appeared like the trunks of aged pines, to the pale light of the morning. Oscar stood at the tomb, and raised thrice his terrible voice. The rocking hills echoed around; the starting roes bounded away: and the trembling ghosts of the dead fled, shrieking on their clouds. So terrible was the voice of my son, when he called his friends!

A thousand spears arose around; the people of Caros rose. Why, daughter of Toscar, why that tear? My son, though alone, is brave. Oscar is like a beam of the sky; he turns around, and the people fall. his hand is the arm of a ghost, when he stretches it from a cloud; the rest of his thin form is unseen; but the people die in the vale! My son beheld the approach of the foe; he stood in the silent darkness of his strength. " Am I alone," said Oscar, " in the midst of a thousand foes? Many a spear is there! many a darkly−rolling eye. Shall I fly to Ardven? But did my fathers ever fly? The mark of their arm is in a thousand battles. Oscar too shall be renowned. Come, ye dim ghosts of my fathers, and behold my deeds in war! I may fall; but I will be renowned like the race of the echoing Morven." He stood, growing in his place, like a flood in a narrow vale! The battle came, but they fell: bloody was the sword of Oscar!

The noise reached his people at Crona; they came like a hundred streams. The warriors of Caros fled; Oscar remained like a rock left by the ebbing sea. Now dark and deep, with all his steeds, Caros rolled his might along: the little streams are lost in his course: the earth is rocking round. Battle spreads from wing to wing; ten thousand swords gleam at once in the sky. But why should Ossian sing of battles? For never more shall my steel shine in war. I remember the days of my youth with grief, when I feel the weakness of my arm. Happy are they who fell in their youth, in the midst of their renown! They have not beheld the tombs of their friends, or failed to bend the bow of their strength. Happy art thou, O Oscar, in the midst of thy rushing blast! Thou often goest to the fields of thy fame, where Caros fled from thy lifted sword!

Darkness comes on my soul, O fair daughter of Toscar! I behold not the form of my son at Carun, nor the figure of Oscar on Crona. The rustling winds have carried him far away, and the heart of his father is sad. But lead me, O Malvina! to the sound of my woods, to the roar of my mountain streams. Let the chase be heard on Cona: let me think on the days of other years. And bring me the harp, O maid! that I may touch it when the light of my soul shall arise. Be thou near to learn the song; future times shall hear of me! The sons of the feeble hereafter will lift the voice of Cona; and looking up to the rocks, say, "Here Ossian dwelt." They shall admire the chiefs of old, the race that are no more, while we ride on our clouds, Malvina! on the wings of the roaring winds. Our voices shall be heard at times in the desert; we shall sing on the breeze of the rock!

The wings of his pride: The Roman eagle.

His gathered heap: Agricola's wall, which Carausius repaired.

This is the scene of Comala's death, which is the subject of the dramatic poem.

CATHLIN OF CLUTHA.

ARGUMENT.

An address to Malvina, the daughter of Toscar. The poet relates the arrival of Cathlin in Selma, to solicit aid against Duth−carmor of Cluba, who had killed Cathmol for the sake of his daughter Lanul. Fingal declining to make a choice among his heroes, who were all claiming the command of the expedition, they retired "each to his hill of ghosts," to be determined by dreams. The spirit of Trenmor appears to Ossian and Oscar. They sail from the bay of Carmona, and on the fourth day, appear off the valley of Rath−col, in Inis−huna, where Duth−carmor had fixed his residence. Ossian despatches a bard to Duth−carmor to demand battle. Night comes on. The distress of Cathlin of Clutha. Ossian devolves the command on Oscar, who, according to the custom of the kings of Morven, before battle, retired to a neighboring hill. Upon the coming on of day, the battle joins. Oscar carries the mail and helmet of Duth−carmor to Cathlin, who had retired from the field. Cathlin is discovered to be the daughter of Cathmol in disguise, who had been carried off by force by, and had made her escape from, Duth−carmor.

COME, thou beam that art lonely, from watching in the night! The squalling winds are around thee, from all their echoing hills. Red, over my hundred streams, are the light−covered paths of the dead. They rejoice on the eddying winds, in the season of night. Dwells there no joy in song, white−hand of the harps of Lutha? Awake the voice of the string; roll my soul to me. It is a stream that has failed. Malvina, pour the song.

I hear thee from thy darkness in Selma, thou that watchest lonely by night! Why didst thou withhold the song from Ossian's falling soul? As the falling brook to the ear of the hunter, descending from his storm−covered hill, in a sunbeam rolls the echoing stream, he hears and shakes his dewy locks: such is the voice of Lutha to the friend of the spirits of heroes. My swelling bosom beats high. I look back on the days that are past. Come, thou beam that art lonely, from watching in the night!

In the echoing bay of Carmona we saw one day the bounding ship. On high hung a broken shield; it was marked with wandering blood. Forward came a youth in arms, and stretched his pointless spear. Long, over his tearful eyes, hung loose his disordered locks. Fingal gave the shell of kings. The words of the stranger arose. "In his hall lies Cathmol of Clutha, by the winding of his own dark streams. Duth−carmor saw white− bosomed Lanul, and pierced her father's side. In the rushy desert were my steps. He fled in the season of night. Give thine aid to Cathlin to revenge his father. I sought thee not as a beam in a land of clouds. Thou, like the sun, art known, king of echoing Selma!"

Selma's king looked around. In his presence we rose in arms. But who should lift the shield? for all had claimed the war. The night came down; we strode in silence, each to his hill of ghosts, that spirits might descend in our dreams to mark us for the field. We struck the shield of the dead: we raised the hum of songs. We thrice called the ghosts of our fathers. We laid us down in dreams. Trenmor came, before mine eyes, the tall form of other years! His blue hosts were behind him in half–distinguished rows. — Scarce seen is their strife in mist, or the stretching forward to deaths. I listened, but no sound was there. The forms were empty wind!

I started from the dream of ghosts. On a sudden blast flew my whistling hair. Low sounding. in the oak, is the departure of the dead. I took my shield from its bough. Onward came the rattling of steel. It was Oscar of Lego. He had seen his fathers. As rushes forth the blast on the bosom of whitening waves, so careless shall my course be, through ocean, to the dwelling of foes. I have seen the dead, my father! My beating soul is high! My fame is bright before me, like the streak of light on a cloud, when the broad sun comes forth, red traveller of the sky!"

" Grandson of Branno," I said, "not Oscar alone shall meet the foe. I rush forward, through ocean, to the woody dwelling of heroes. Let us contend, my son, like eagles from one rock, when they lift their broad wings against the stream of winds." We raised our sails in Carmona. From three ships they marked my shield on the wave, as I looked on nightly Ton–thena, red traveller between the clouds. Four days came the breeze abroad. Lumon came forward in mist. In winds were its hundred groves. Sunbeams marked at times its brown side. White leapt the foamy streams from all its echoing rocks.

A green field, in the bosom of hills, winds silent with its own blue stream. Here, "midst the waving of oaks, were the dwellings of kings of old." But silence, for many dark–brown years, had settled in grassy Rath–col; for the race of heroes had failed along the pleasant vale. Duth–carmor was here, with his people, dark rider of the wave! Ton–thena had hid her head in the sky. He bound his white–bosomed sails. His course is on the hills of Rath–col to the seats of roes. We came. I sent the bard, with songs, to call the foe to fight. Duth–carmor heard him with joy. The king's soul was like a beam of fire; a beam of fire, marked with smoke, rushing, varied through the bosom of night. The deeds of Duth–carmor were dark, though his arm was strong.

Night came with the gathering of clouds. By the beam of the oak we sat down. At a distance stood Cathlin of Clutha. I saw the changeful soul of the stranger. As shadows fly over the field of grass, so various is Cathlin's cheek. It was fair within locks, that rose on Rath–col's wind. I did not rush, amidst his soul, with my words. I bade the song to rise.

"Oscar of Lego," I said, "be thine the secret hill to–night. Strike the shield like Morven's kings. With day thou shalt lead in war. From my rock I shall see thee, Oscar, a dreadful form ascending in fight, like the appearance of ghosts amidst the storms they raise. Why should mine eyes return to the dim times of old, ere yet the song had bursted forth, like the sudden rising of winds? But the years that are past are marked with mighty deeds. As the nightly rider of waves looks up to Ton–thena of beams, so let us turn our eyes to Trenmor the father of kings."

"Wide, in Caracha's echoing field, Carmal had poured his tribes. They were a dark ridge of waves. The gray–haired bards were like moving foam on their face. They kindle the strife around with their red–rolling eyes. Nor alone were the dwellers of rocks; a son of Loda was there, a voice in his own dark land, to call the ghosts from high. On his hill he had dwelt in Lochlin, in the midst of a leafless grove. Five stones lifted near their heads. Loud roared his rushing stream. He often raised his voice to the winds, when meteors marked their nightly wings, when the dark–robed moon was rolled behind her hill. Nor unheard of ghosts was he! They came with the sound of eagle–wings. They turned battle, in fields, before the kings of men.

" But Trenmor they turned not from battle. He drew forward that troubled war: in its dark skirt was Trathal, like a rising light. It was dark, and Loda's son poured forth his signs on night. The feeble were not before thee, son of other lands! Then rose the strife of kings about the hill of night; but it was soft as two summer gales, shaking their light wings on a lake. Trenmor yielded to his son, for the fame of the king had been heard. Trathal came forth before his father, and the foes failed in echoing Caracha. The years that are past, my son, are marked with mighty deeds."

In clouds rose the eastern light. The foe came forth in arms. The strife is mixed on Rath–col, like the roar of streams. Behold the contending of kings! They meet beside the oak. In gleams of steel the dark forms are lost; such is the meeting of meteors in a vale by night: red light is scattered round, and men foresee the storm! — Duth–carmor is low in blood! The son of Ossian overcame! Not harmless, in battle, was he, Malvina, hand of harps!

Nor, in the field, were the steps of Cathlin. The strangers stood by secret stream, where the foam of Rath–col skirted the mossy stones. Above bends the branchy birch, and strews its leaves on wind. The inverted spear of Cathlin touched at times the stream.

Oscar brought Duth–carmor's mail: his helmet with its eagle–wing. He placed them before the stranger, and his words were heard. " The foes of thy father have fallen. They are laid in the field of ghosts. Renown returns to Morven like a rising wind. Why art thou dark, chief of Clutha? Is there cause for grief?"

" Son of Ossian of harps, my soul is darkly sad. I behold the arms of Cathmol, which lie raised in war. Take the mail of Cathlin, place it high in Selma's hall, that thou mayest remember the hapless in thy distant land." From white breasts descended the mail. It was the race of kings: the soft–handed daughter of Cathmol, at the streams of Clutha! Duth–carmor saw her bright in the hall; he had come by night to Clutha. Cathmol met him in battle, but the hero fell. Three days dwelt the foe with the maid. On the fourth she fled in arms. She remembered the race of kings, and felt her bursting soul!

Why, maid of Toscar of Lutha, should I tell how Cathlin failed? Her tomb is at rushy Lumon, in a distant land. Near it were the steps of Sul–malla, in the days of grief. She raised the song for the daughter of strangers, and touched the mournful harp.

Come from the watching of night, Malvina, lonely beam!

Ton–thena, " fire of the wave," was the remarkable star mentioned in the seventh book of Temora, which directed the course of Larthon to Ireland.

This passage alludes to the well–known custom among the ancient kings of Scotland, to retire from their army on the night preceding a battle. The story which Ossian introduces in the next paragraph, concerns the fall of the Druids.

SUL–MALLA OF LUMON.

ARGUMENT.

This poem, which, properly speaking, is a continuation of the last, opens with an address to Sul–malla, the daughter of the king of Inis–huna, whom Ossian met at the chase, as he returned from the battle of Rath–col. Sul–malla invites Ossian and Oscar to a feast, at the residence of her father, who was then absent on the wars. Upon hearing their names and family, she relates an expedition of Fingal into Inis–huna. She casually mentioning

THE POEMS OF OSSIAN

Cathmor, chief of Atha, (who then assisted her father against his enemies,) Ossian introduces the episode of Culgorm and Suran– dronlo, two Scandinavian kings, in whose wars Ossian himself and Cathmor were engaged on opposite sides. The story is imperfect, a part of the original being lost. Ossian, warned in a dream by the ghost of Trenmor, sets sail from Inis–huna.

WHO moves so stately on Lumon, at the roar of the foamy waters? Her hair falls upon her heaving breast. White is her arm behind, as slow she bends the bow. Why dost thou wander in deserts, like a light through a cloudy field? The young roes are panting by their secret rocks. Return, thou daughter of kings! the cloudy night is near! It was the young branch of green Inishuna, Sul–malla of blue eyes. She sent the bard from her rock to bid us to her feast. Amidst the song we sat down in Cluba's echoing hall. White moved the hands of Sul–malla on the trembling strings. Half–heard amidst the sound, was the name of Atha's king: he that was absent in battle for her own green land. Nor absent from her soul was he: he came 'midst her thoughts by night. Ton–thena looked in from the sky, and saw her tossing arms.

The sound of shells had ceased. Amidst long locks Sul– malla rose. She spoke with bended eyes, and asked of our course through seas; "for of the kings of men are ye, tall riders of the wave." "Not unknown," I said, "at his streams is he, the father of our race. Fingal has been heard of at Cluba, blue–eyed daughter of kings. Not only at Crona's stream is Ossian and Oscar known. Foes tremble at our voice and shrink in other lands."

"Not unmarked," said the maid, "by Sul–malla, is the shield of Morven's king. It hangs high in my father's hall, in memory of the past, when Fingal came to Cluba, in the days of other years. Loud roared the boar of Culdarnu, in the midst of his rocks and woods. Inis–huna sent her youths; but they failed, and virgins wept over tombs. Careless went Fingal to Culdarnu. On his spear rolled the strength of the woods. He was bright, they said, in his locks, the first of mortal men. Nor at the feast were heard his words. His deeds passed from his soul of fire, like the rolling of vapors from the face of the wandering sun. Not careless looked the blue eyes of Cluba on his stately steps. In white bosoms rose the king of Selma, in the midst of their thoughts by night. But the winds bore the stranger to the echoing vales of his roes. Nor lost to other lands was he, like a meteor, that sinks in a cloud. He came forth, at times in his brightness, to the distant dwelling of foes. His fame came, like the sound of winds, to Cluba's woody vale.

THE POEMS OF OSSIAN

"Darkness dwells in Cluba of harps! the race of kings is distant far: in battle is my father Conmor; and Lormar, my brother, king of streams. Nor darkening alone are they; a beam from other lands is nigh; the friend of strangers in Atha, the troubler of the field. High from their misty hills looks forth the blue eyes of Erin, for he is far away, young dweller of their souls! Nor harmless, white hands of Erin! is Cathmor in the skirts of war; he rolls ten thousand before him in his distant field."

"Not unseen by Ossian," I said, "rushed Cathmor from his streams, when he poured his strength on I–thorno, isle of many waves! In strife met two kings in I–thorno, Culgorm and Suran– dronlo: each from his echoing isle, stern hunters of the boar!

"They met a boar at a foamy stream; each pierced him with his spear. They strove for the fame of the deed, and gloomy battle rose. From isle to isle they sent a spear broken and stained with blood, to call the friends of their fathers in their sounding arms. Cathmor came from Erin to Colgorm, red–eyed king; I aided Suran–dronlo in his land of boars.

"We rushed on either side of a stream, which roared through a blasted heath. High broken rocks were round with all their bending trees. Near were two circles of Loda, with the stone of power, where spirits descended by night in dark–red streams of fire. There, mixed with the murmur of waters, rose the voice of aged men; they called the forms of night to aid them in their war.

"Heedless I stood with my people, where fell the foamy stream from rocks. The moon moved red from the mountain. My song at times arose. Dark, on the other side, young Cathmor heard my voice, for he lay beneath the oak in all his gleaming arms. Morning came: we rushed to the fight; from wing to wing is the rolling of strife. They fell like the thistle's head beneath autumnal winds.

"In armor came a stately form: I mixed my strokes with the chief. By turns our shields are pierced: loud rung our steely mail. His helmet fell to the ground. In brightness shone the foe. His eyes, two pleasant flames, rolled between his wandering locks. I knew Cathmor of Atha, and threw my spear on earth. Dark we turned, and silent passed to mix with other foes.

"Not so passed the striving kings. They mixed in echoing fray, like the meeting of ghosts in the dark wing of winds. Through either breast rushed the spears, nor yet lay the foes on earth! A rock received their fall; half—reclined they lay in death. Each held the lock of his foe: each grimly seemed to roll his eyes. The stream of the rock leapt on their shields, and mixed below with blood.

"The battle ceased in I—thorno. The strangers met in peace: Cathmor from Atha of streams, and Ossian king of harps. We placed the dead in earth. Our steps were by Runar's bay. With the bounding boat afar advanced a ridgy wave. Dark was the rider of seas, but a beam of light was there like the ray of the sun in Stromlo's rolling smoke. It was the daughter of Suran—dronlo, wild in brightened looks. Her eyes were wandering flames amidst disordered locks. Forward is her white arm with the spear; her high—heaving breast is seen, white as foamy waves that rise, by turns, amidst rocks. They are beautiful, but terrible, and mariners call the winds!

"Come, ye dwellers of Loda!" she said: "come, Carchar, pale in the midst of clouds! Sluthmor that stridest in airy halls! Corchtur, terrible in winds! Receive from his daughter's spear the foes of Suran—dronlo. No shadow at his roaring streams, no mildly looking form, was he! When he took up his spear, the hawks shook their sounding wings: for blood was poured a round the steps of dark—eyed Suran—dronlo. He lighted me no harmless beam to glitter on his streams. Like meteors I was bright, but I blasted the foes of Suran—dronlo."

* * * * * * * * * *

Nor unconcerned heard Sul—malla the praise of Cathmor of shields. He was within her soul, like a fire in secret heath, which awakes at the voice of the blast, and sends its beam abroad. Amidst the song removed the daughter of kings, like the voice of a summer breeze, when it lifts the heads of flowers, and curls the lakes and streams. The rustling Sound gently spreads o'er the vale, softly—pleasing as it saddens the soul.

By night came a dream to Ossian; formless stood the shadow of Trenmor. He seemed to strike the dim shield on Selma's streamy rock. I rose in my rattling steel: I knew that war was near; before the winds our sails were spread, when Lumon showed its streams to the morn.

Come from the watching night Malvina, lonely beam!

The friend of strangers: Cathmor, the son of Barbar–duthol.

THE WAR OF INIS–THONA

ARGUMENT.

Reflections on the poet's youth. An apostrophe to Selma. Oscar obtains leave to go to Inis–thona, an island of Scandinavia. The mournful story of Argon and Ruro, the two sons of the king of Inis–thona. Oscar revenges their death, and returns in triumph to Selma. A soliloquy by the poet himself.

Our youth is like the dream of the hunter on the hill of heath. He sleeps in the mild beams of the sun: he awakes amidst a storm; the red lightning flies around: trees shake their heads to the wind! He looks back with joy on the day of the sun, and the pleasant dreams of his rest! When shall Ossian's youth return? When his ear delight in the sound of arms? When shall I, like Oscar, travel in the light of my steel? Come with your streams, ye hills of Cona! listen to the voice of Ossian. The song rises, like the sun, in my soul. I feel the joys of other times.

I behold thy towers, O Selma! the oaks of thy shaded wall: thy streams sound in my ear; thy heroes gather round. Fingal sits in the midst. He leans on the shield of Trenmor; his spear stands against the wall; he listens to the songs of his bards. The deeds of his arm are heard; the actions of the king in his youth! Oscar had returned from the chase, and heard the hero's praise. He took the shield of Branno from the wall; his eyes were filed with tears. Red was the cheek of youth. His voice was trembling low. My spear shook its bright head in his hand: he spoke to Morven's king.

"Fingal! thou king of heroes! Ossian, next to him in war! ye have fought in your youth; your names are renowned in song. Oscar is like the mist of Cona; I appear and I vanish away. The bard will not know my name. The hunter will not search in the heath for my tomb. Let me fight, O heroes, in the battles of Inis– thona. Distant is the land of my war! ye shall not hear of Oscar's fall: some bard may find me there; some bard may give my name to song. The daughter of the stranger shall see my tomb, and weep over the youth, that came from afar. The bard shall say, at the feast, Hear the song of Oscar from the distant land!"

" Oscar," replied the king of Morven, " thou shalt fight, son of my fame! Prepare my dark–bosomed ship to carry my hero to Inis–thona. Son of my son, regard our fame; thou art of the race of renown: let not the children of strangers say, Feeble are the sons of Morven! Be thou, in battle, a roaring storm: mild as the evening sun in peace! Tell, Oscar, to Inis–thona's king, that Fingal remembers his youth; when we strove in the combat together, in the days of Agandecca." They lifted up the sounding sail: the wind whistled through the thongs of their masts. Waves lashed the oozy rocks: the strength of ocean roars. My son beheld, from the wave, the land of groves. He rushed into Runa's sounding bay, and sent his sword to Annir of spears. The gray–headed hero rose, when he saw the sword of Fingal. His eyes were full of tears; he remembered his battles in youth. Twice had they lifted the spear before the lovely Agandecca.: heroes stood far distant, as if two spirits were striving in winds.

" But now," began the king, " I am old; the Sword lies useless in my hall. Thou who art of Morven's race! Annir has seen the battle of spears; but now he is pale and withered, like the oak of Lano. I have no son to meet thee with joy, to bring thee to the halls of his fathers. Argon is pale in the tomb, and Ruro is no more. My daughter is in the hall of strangers: she longs to behold my tomb. Her spouse shakes ten thousand spears; he comes a cloud of death from Lano. Come, to share the feast of Annir, son of echoing Morven? Three days they feasted together. On the fourth, Annir heard the name of Oscar. They rejoiced in the shell. They pursued the boars of Runa. Beside the fount of mossy stones the weary heroes rest. The tear steals in secret from Annir: he broke the rising sigh. "Here darkly rest," the hero said, "the children of my youth. This stone is the tomb of Ruro; that tree sounds over the grave of Argon. Do ye hear my voice, O my sons, within your narrow house? Or do ye speak in these rustling leaves, when the wind of the desert rises?"

"King of Inis–thona," said Oscar, "how fell the children of youth? The wild boar rushes over their tombs, but he does not disturb their repose. They pursue deer formed of clouds, and bend their airy bow. They still love the sport of their youth; and mount the wind with joy." "Cormalo," replied the king, " is a chief of ten thousand spears. He dwells at the waters of Lano which sends forth the vapor of death. He came to Runa's echoing halls, and sought the honor of the spear. The youth was lovely as the first beam of the sun; few were they who could meet him in fight. My heroes yielded to Cormalo; my daughter was seized in his love. Argon and Ruro returned from the chase; the tears of their pride descend: they roll their silent eyes on Runa's heroes, who had yielded to stranger. Three days they feasted with Cormalo; on the fourth young Argon fought. But who could light with Argon? Cormalo is overcome. His heart swelled with the grief of pride; he resolved in secret to behold the death of my sons. They went to the hills of Runa; they pursued the dark–brown hinds. The arrow of Cormalo flew in secret; my children fell in blood. He came to the maid of his love; to Inis–thona's long–haired maid. They fled over the desert, Annir remained alone. Night came on, and day appeared; nor Argon's voice nor Ruro's came. At length their much–loved dog was seen; the fleet and bounding Runa. He came into the hall and howled; and seemed to look towards the place of their fall. We followed him; we found them here: we laid them by this mossy stream. This is the haunt of Annir, when the chase of the hinds is past. I bend like the trunk of an aged oak; my tears for ever flow!"

" O Ronnan!" said the rising Oscar, "Osgar, king of spears! call my heroes to my side, the sons of streamy Morven. To–day we go to Lano's water, that sends forth the vapor of death. Cormalo will not long rejoice: death is often at the point of our swords!"

They came over the desert like stormy clouds, when the winds roll them along the heath; their edges are tinged with lightning; the echoing groves foresee the storm! The horn of Oscar's battle is heard; Lano shook over all its waves. The children of the lake convened around the sounding shield of Cormalo. Oscar fought as he was wont in war. Cormalo fell beneath his sword: the sons of dismal Lano fled to their secret vales! Oscar brought the daughter of Inis–thona to Annir's echoing halls. The face of age is bright with joy; he blest the king of swords.

How great was the joy of Ossian, when he beheld the distant sail of his son! it was like a cloud of light that rises in the east, when the traveller is sad in a land unknown: and dismal night with her ghosts, is sitting around in shades! We brought him with songs to Selma's halls. Fingal spread the feast of shells. A thousand bards raised the name of Oscar: Morven answered to the sound. The daughter of Toscar was there; her voice was like the harp, when the distant sound comes in the evening, on the soft rustling breeze of the vale!

O lay me, ye that see the light, near some rock of my hills! let the thick hazels be around, let the rustling oak be near. Green be the place of my rest; let the sound of the distant torrent be heard. Daughter of Toscar, take the harp, and raise the lovely song of Selma; that sleep may overtake my soul in the midst of joy; that the dreams of my youth may return, and the days of the mighty Fingal. Selma! I behold thy towers, thy trees, thy shaded wall! I see the heroes of Morven; I hear the song of bards: Oscar lifts the sword of Cormalo; a thousand youths admire its studded thongs. They look with wonder on my son: they admire the strength of his arm. They mark the joy of his father's eyes; they long for an equal fame, and ye shall have your fame, O sons of streamy Morven! My soul is often brightened with song; I remember the friends of my youth. But sleep descends in the sound of the harp! pleasant dreams begin to rise! Ye Sons of the chase, stand far distant nor disturb my rest The bard of other times holds discourse with his fathers! the chiefs of the days of old! Sons of the chase, stand far distant! disturb not the dreams of Ossian!

Branno: The father of Everallin, and grandfather to Oscar

Leather thongs were used among the Celtic nations, instead of ropes

To "rejoice in the shell," is a phrase for feasting sumptuously and drinking freely.

Lano was a lake of Scandinavia, remarkable in the days of Ossian for emitting a pestilential vapor in autumn.

By " the honor of the spear," is meant the tournament practised among the ancient northern nations.

THE SONGS OF SELMA.

ARGUMENT.

Address to the evening star. Apostrophe to Fingal and his times. Minona sings before the king the song of the unfortunate Colma, and the bards exhibit other specimens of their poetical talents according to an annual custom established by the monarchs of the ancient Caledonians.

STAR of descending night! fair is thy light in the west! thou that liftest thy unshorn head from thy cloud: thy steps are stately on thy hill. What dost thou behold in the plain? The stormy winds are laid. The murmur of the torrent comes from afar. Roaring waves climb the distant rock. The flies of evening are on their feeble wings: the hum of their course is in the field. What dost thou behold, fair light? But thou dost smile and depart. The waves come with joy around thee: they bathe thy lovely hair. Farewell, thou silent beam! Let the light of Ossian's soul arise!

And it does arise in its strength! I behold my departed friends. Their gathering is on Lora, as in the days of other years. Fingal comes like a watery column of mist! his heroes are around: and see the bards of song, gray–haired Ullin! Stately Ryno! Alpin with the tuneful voice! the soft complaint of Minona! How are ye changed, my friends, since the days of Selma's feast! when we contended, like gales of spring, as they fly along the hill, and bend by turns the feebly whistling grass.

Minona came forth in her beauty: with downcast look and tearful eye. Her hair flew slowly on the blast, that rushed unfrequent from the hill. The souls of the heroes were sad when she raised the tuneful voice. Often had they seen the grave of Salgar, the dark dwelling of white–bosomed Colma. Colma left alone on the hill, with all her voice of song! Salgar promised to come: but the night descended around. Hear the voice of Colma, when she sat alone on the hill.

Colma. It is night, I am alone, forlorn on the hill of storms. The wind is heard on the mountain. The torrent pours down the rock. No hut receives me from the rain; forlorn on the hill of winds!

Rise, moon! from behind thy clouds. Stars of the night, arise! Lead me, some light, to the place where my love rests from the chase alone! his bow near him, unstrung: his dogs panting around him. But here I must sit alone, by the rock of the mossy stream. The stream and the wind roar aloud. I hear not the voice of my love! Why delays my Salgar, why the chief of the hill, his promise? here is the rock, and here the tree! here is the roaring stream! Thou didst promise with night to be here. Ah! whither is my Salgar gone? With thee, I would fly from my father; with thee, from my brother of pride. Our race have long been foes; we are not foes, O Salgar!

Cease a little while, O wind! stream, be thou silent awhile! let my voice be heard around. Let my wanderer hear me! Salgar! it is Colma who calls. Here is the tree, and the rock. Salgar, my love! I am here. Why delayest thou thy coming? Lo! the calm moon comes forth. The flood is bright in the vale. The rocks are gray on the steep, I see him not on the brow. His dogs come not before him, with tidings of his near approach. Here I must sit alone!

Who lie on the heath beside me? Are they my love and my brother? Speak to me, O my friends! To Colma they give no reply. Speak to me; I am alone! My soul is tormented with fears! Ah! they are dead! Their swords are red from the fight. O my brother! my brother! why hast thou slain my Salgar? why, O Salgar! hast thou slain my brother? Dear were ye both to me! what shalt I say in your praise? Thou wert fair on the hill among thousands! he was terrible in fight. Speak to me; hear my voice; hear me, song of my love! They are silent; silent for ever! Cold, cold, are their breasts of clay! Oh! from the rock on the hill, from the top of the windy steep, speak, ye ghosts of the dead! speak, I will not be afraid! Whither are ye gone to rest? In what cave of the hill shall I find the departed? No feeble voice is on the gale: no answer half– drowned in the storm!

I sit in my grief; I wait for morning in my tears! Rear the tomb, ye friends of the dead. Close it not till Colma come. My life flies away like a dream: why should I stay behind? Here shall I rest with my friends, by the stream of the sounding rock. When night comes on the hilt; when the loud winds arise; my ghost shall stand in the blast, and mourn the death of my friends. The hunter shall hear from his booth. he shall fear but love my voice! For sweet shall my voice be for my friends: pleasant were her friends to Colma!

Such was thy song, Minona, softly–blushing daughter of Torman. Our tears descended for Colma, and our souls were sad! Ullin came with his harp! he gave the song of Alpin. The voice of Alpin was pleasant: the soul of Ryno was a beam of fire! But they had rested in the narrow house: their voice had ceased in Selma. Ullin had returned, one day, from the chase, before the heroes fell. He heard their strife on the hilt; their song was soft but sad! They mourned the fall of Morar, first of mortal men! His soul was like the soul of Fingal: his sword like the sword of Oscar. But he fell, and his father mourned: his sister's eyes were full of tears. Minona's eyes were full of tears, the sister of car–borne Morar. She retired from the song of Ullin, like the moon in the west, when she foresees the shower, and hides her fair head in a cloud. I touched the harp with Ullin; the song of mourning rose!

Ryno. The wind and the rain are past; calm is the noon of day. The clouds are divided in heaven. Over the green hills flies the inconstant sun. Red through the stony vale comes down the stream of the hill. Sweet are thy murmurs, O stream! but more sweet is the

70

voice I hear. It is the voice of Alpin, the son of song, mourning for the dead! Bent is his head of age; red his tearful eye. Alpin, thou son of song, why alone on the silent hill? why complainest thou, as a blast in the wood; as a wave on the lonely shore?

Alpin. My tears, O Ryno! are for the dead; my voice for those that have passed away. Tall thou art on the hill; fair among the sons of the vale. But thou shalt fall like Morar; the mourner shall sit on thy tomb. The hills shall know thee no more; thy bow shall in thy hall unstrung.

Thou wert swift, O Morar! as a roe on the desert; terrible as a meteor of fire. Thy wrath was as the storm. Thy sword in battle, as lightning in the field. Thy voice was a stream after rain; like thunder on distant hills. Many fell by thy arm; they were consumed in the flames of thy wrath. But when thou didst return from war, how peaceful was thy brow! Thy face was like the sun after rain; like the moon in the silence of night; calm as the breast of the lake when the loud wind is laid.

Narrow is thy dwelling now! Dark the place of thine abode! With three steps I compass thy grave. O thou who wast so great before! Four stones, with their heads of moss, are the only memorial of thee. A tree with scarce a leaf, long grass, which whistles in the wind, mark to the hunter's eye the grave of the mighty Morar. Morar! thou art low indeed. Thou hast no mother to mourn thee; no maid with her tears of love. Dead is she that brought thee forth. Fallen is the daughter of Morglan.

Who on his staff is this? who is this whose head is white with age; whose eyes are red with tears? who quakes at every step? It is thy father, O Morar! the father of no son but thee. He heard of thy fame in war; he heard of foes dispersed. He heard of Morar's renown; why did he not hear of his wound? Weep, thou father of Morar! weep; but thy son heareth thee not. Deep is the sleep of the dead; low their pillow of dust. No more shall he hear thy voice; no more awake at thy call. When shall it be morn in the grave, to bid the slumberer awake Farewell, thou bravest of men! thou conqueror in the field! but the field shall see thee no more; nor the dark wood be lightened with the splendor of thy steel. Thou hast left no son. The song shall preserve thy name. Future times shall hear of thee; they shall hear of the fallen Morar.

The grief of all arose, but most the bursting sigh of Armin. He remembers the death of his son, who fell in the days of his youth. Carmor was near the hero, the chief of the echoing

Galmal. Why burst the sigh of Armin? he said. Is there a cause to mourn? The song comes, with its music, to melt and please the soul. It is like soft mist, that, rising from a lake, pours on the silent vale; the green flowers are filled with dew, but the sun returns in his strength, and the mist is gone. Why art thou sad, O Armin, chief of sea–surrounded Gorma?

Sad I am! nor small is my cause of wo. Carmor, thou hast lost no son; thou hast lost no daughter of beauty. Colgar the valiant lives; and Annira, fairest maid. The boughs of thy house ascend, O Carmor! but Armin is the last of his race. Dark is thy bed, O Daura! deep thy sleep in the tomb! When shalt thou awake with thy songs? with all thy voice of music?

Arise, winds of autumn, arise; blow along the heath! streams of the mountains, roar! roar, tempests, in the groves of my oaks! walk through broken clouds, O moon! show thy pale face, at intervals! bring to my mind the night, when all my children fell; when Arindal the mighty fell! when Daura the lovely failed! Daura, my daughter! thou wert fair; fair as the moon on Fura , white as the driven snow; sweet as the breathing gale. Arindal, thy bow was strong. Thy spear was swift on the field. Thy look was like mist on the wave: thy shield, a red cloud in a storm. Armar, renowned in war, came, and sought Daura's love. He was not long refused: fair was the hope of their friends!

Erath, son of Odgal, repined: his brother had been slain by Armar. He came disguised like a son of the sea: fair was his skiff on the wave; white his locks of age; calm his serious brow. Fairest of women, he said, lovely daughter of Armin! a rock not distant in the sea bears a tree on its side: red shines the fruit afar! There Armar waits for Daura. I come to carry his love! She went; she called on Armar. Nought answered, but the son of the rock. Armar, my love! my love! why tormentest thou me with fear! hear, son of Arnart, hear: it is Daura who calleth thee! Erath the traitor fled laughing to the land. She lifted up her voice; she called for her brother and for her father. Arindal! Armin! none to relieve your Daura!

Her voice came over the sea. Arindal my son descended from the hill; rough in the spoils of the chase. His arrows rattled by his side; his bow was in his hand; five dark–gray dogs attended his steps. He saw fierce Erath on the shore: he seized and bound him to an oak. Thick wind the thongs of the hide around his limbs: he loads the winds with his groans . Arindal ascends the deep in his boat, to bring Daura to land. Armar came in his wrath, and let fly the gray–feathered shaft. It sunk, it sunk in thy heart, O Arindal, my son! for Erath the traitor thou diest. The oar is stopped at once; he panted on the rock and expired. What is thy grief, O Daura, when round thy feet is poured thy brother's blood! The boat is broke in twain. Armar plunges into the sea, to rescue his Daura, or die. Sudden a blast from a hill came over the waves. He sunk, and he rose no more.

Alone on the sea–beat rock, my daughter was heard to complain. Frequent and loud were her cries. What could her father do? All night I stood on the shore. I saw her by the faint beam of the moon. All night I heard her cries. Loud was the wind; the rain beat hard on the hill. Before morning appeared her voice was weak. it died away, like the evening breeze among the grass of the rocks. Spent with grief, she expired; and left thee, Armin, alone. Gone is my strength in war! fallen my pride among women! When the storms aloft arise; when the north lifts the wave on high! I sit by the sounding shore, and look on the fatal rock. Often by the setting moon, I see the ghosts of my children. Half viewless, they walk in mournful conference together. Will none of you speak in pity. They do not regard their father. I am sad, O Carmor, nor small is my cause of wo.

Such were the words of the bards in the days of song: when the king heard the music of harps, the tales of other times! The chiefs gathered from all their hills, and heard the lovely sound. They praised the voice of Cona; the first among a thousand bards! But age is now on my tongue; my soul has failed: I hear, at times, the ghosts of bards, and learn their pleasant Song. But memory fails on my mind. I hear the call of years; they say, as they pass along, Why does Ossian sing? Soon shall he lie in the narrow house, and no bard shall raise his fame! Roll on, ye dark– brown years; ye bring no joy on your course! Let the tomb open to Ossian, for his strength has failed. The sons of song are gone to rest. My voice remains, like a blast, that roars, lonely, on a sea– surrounded rock, after the winds are laid. The dark moss whistles there; the distant mariner sees the waving trees!

By "the son of the rock," the poet means the echoing back of the human voice from a rock.

Ossian is sometimes poetically called "the voice of Cona".

FINGAL: AN ANCIENT EPIC POEM

FINGAL — BOOK I.

ARGUMENT.

Cuthullin (general of the Irish tribes, in the minority of Cormac, king of Ireland) sitting alone beneath a tree, at the gate of Tura, a castle of Ulster (the other chiefs having gone on a hunting party to Cromla, a neighboring hill,) is informed of the landing of Swaran, king of Lochlin, by Moran, the son of Fithil, one of his scouts. He convenes the chiefs; a council is held, and disputes run high about giving battle to the enemy. Connal, the petty king of Togorma, and an intimate friend of Cuthullin, was for retreating, till Fingal, king of those Caledonians who inhabited the north−west coast of Scotland, whose aid had been previously solicited, should arrive; but Calmar, the son of Matha, lord of Lara, a country in Connaught, was for engaging the enemy immediately. Cuthullin, of himself willing to fight, went into the opinion of Calmar. Marching towards the enemy, he missed three of his bravest heroes, Fergus, Duchomar, and C thba. Fergus arriving, tells Cuthullin of the death of the two other chiefs: which introduces the affecting episode of Morna, the daughter of Cormac. The army of Cuthullin is descried at a distance by Swaran, who sent the son of Arno to observe the motions of the enemy, while he himself ranged his forces in order of battle. The son of Arno returning to Swaran, describes to him Cuthullin's chariot, and the terrible appearance of that hero. The armies engage, but night coming on, leaves the victory undecided. Cuthullin, according to the hospitality of the times, sends to Swaran a formal invitation to a feast, by his bard Carril, the son of Kinfena. Swaran refuses to come. Carril relates to Cuthullin the story of Grudar and Brassolis. A party, by Connal's advice, is sent to observe the enemy; which closes the action of the first day.

CUTHULLIN sat by Tura's wall; by the tree of the rustling sound. His spear leaned against the rock. His shield lay on the grass by his side. Amid his thoughts of mighty Cairbar, a hero slain by the chief in war; the scout of ocean comes, Moran the son of Fithil!

"Arise," said the youth, "Cuthullin, arise. I see the ships of the north! Many, chief of men, are the foe. Many the heroes of the sea−borne Swaran!" — "Moran!" replied the blue−eyed chief "thou ever tremblest, son of Fithil! Thy fears have increased the foe. It is Fingal, king of deserts, with aid to green Erin of streams." — "I beheld their chief," says

74

Moran, "tall as a glittering rock. His spear is a blasted pine. His shield the rising moon! He sat on the shore! like a cloud of mist on the silent hill! Many, chief of heroes! I said, many are our hands of war. Well art thou named, the mighty man; but many mighty men are seen from Tura's windy walls.

"He spoke, like a wave on a rock, 'Who in this land appears like me? Heroes stand not in my presence: they fall to earth from my hand. Who can meet Swaran in fight? Who but Fingal, king of Selma of storms? Once we wrestled on Malmor; our heels overturned the woods. Rocks fell from their place; rivulets, changing their course, fled murmuring from our side. Three days we renewed the strife; heroes stood at a distance and trembled. On the fourth, Fingal says, that the king of the ocean fell! but Swaran says he stood! Let dark Cuthullin yield to him, that is strong as the storms of his land!'

"No!" replied the blue–eyed chief, "I never yield to mortal man! Dark Cuthullin shall be great or dead! Go, son of Fithil, take my spear. Strike the sounding shield of Semo. It hangs at Tura's rustling gale. The sound of peace is not its voice! My heroes shall hear and obey." He went. He struck the bossy shield. The hills, the rocks reply. The sound spreads along the wood: deer start by the lake of roes. Curach leaps from the sounding rock! and Connal of the bloody spear! Crugal's breast of snow beats high. The son of Favi leaves the dark–brown hind. It is the shield of war, said Ronnart; the spear of Cuthullin, said Lugar! Son of the sea, put on thy arms! Calmar, lift thy sounding steel! Puno! dreadful hero, arise! Cairbar, from thy red tree of Cromla! Bend thy knee, O Eth! descend from the streams of Lena Caolt, stretch thy side as thou movest along the whistling heath of Mora: thy side that is white as the foam of the troubled sea, when the dark winds pour it on rocky Cuthon.

Now I behold the chiefs, in the pride of their former deeds! Their souls are kindled at the battles of old; at the actions of other times. Their eyes are flames of fire. They roll in search of the foes of the land. Their mighty hands are on their swords. Lightning pours from their sides of steel. They come like streams from the mountains; each rushes roaring from the hill. Bright are the chiefs of battle, in the armor of their fathers. Gloomy and dark, their heroes follow like the gathering of the rainy clouds behind the red meteors of heaven. The sounds of crashing arms ascend. The gray dogs howl between. Unequal bursts the song of battle. Rocking Cromla echoes round. On Lena's dusky heath they stand, like mist that shades the hills of autumn; when broken and dark it settles high, and lifts its head to heaven.

"Hail," said Cuthullin, "Sons of the narrow vales! hail, hunters of the deer! Another sport is drawing near: it is like the dark rolling of that wave on the coast! Or shall we fight, ye sons of war! or yield green Erin to Lochlin? O Connal! speak, thou first of men! thou breaker of the shields! thou hast often fought with Lochlin: wilt thou lift thy father's spear?"

"Cuthullin!" calm the chief replied, "the spear of Connal is keen. it delights to shine in battle, to mix with the blood of thousands. But though my hand is bent on fight, my heart is for the peace of Erin. Behold, thou first in Cormac's war, the sable fleet of Swaran. His masts are many on our coasts, like reeds on the lake of Lego. His ships are forests clothed with mists, when the trees yield by turns to the squally wind. Many are his chiefs in battle. Connal is for peace! Fingal would shun his arm, the first of mortal men! Fingal who scatters the mighty, as stormy winds the echoing Cona; and night settles with all her clouds on the hill!"

"Fly, thou man of peace!" said Colmar, "fly," said the son of Matha; "go, Connal, to thy silent hills, where the spear never brightens in war! Pursue the dark−brown deer of Cromla: stop with thine arrows the bounding roes of Lena. But blue−eyed son of Semo, Cuthullin, ruler of the field, scatter thou the Sons of Lochlin! roar through the ranks of their pride. Let no vessel of the kingdom of snow bound on the dark−rolling waves of Inistore. Rise, ye dark winds of Erin, rise! roar, whirlwinds of Lara of hinds! Amid the tempest let me die, torn, in a cloud, by angry ghosts of men; amid the tempest let Calmar die, if ever chase was sport to him, so much as the battle of shields!

"Calmar!" Connal slow replied, "I never fled, young son of Matha! I was swift with my friends in fight; but small is the fame of Connal! The battle was won in my presence! the valiant overcame! But, son of Semo, hear my voice, regard the ancient throne of Cormac. Give wealth and half the land for peace, till Fingal shall arrive on our coast. Or, if war be thy choice, I lift the sword and spear. My joy shall be in midst of thousands; my soul shall alighten through the gloom of the fight!"

"To me," Cuthullin replies, "pleasant is the noise of arms! pleasant as the thunder of heaven, before the shower of spring! But gather all the shining tribes, that I may view the sons of war! Let then pass along the heath, bright as the sunshine before a storm; when the west wind collects the clouds, and Morven echoes over all her oaks! But where are my friends in battle? the supporters of my arm in danger? Where art thou, white–bosomed Cathba? Where is that cloud in war, Duchomar? Hast thou left me, O Fergus! in the day of the storm? Fergus, first in our joy at the feast! son of Rossa! arm of death! comest thou like a roe from Malmor? like a hart from thy echoing hills? Hall, thou son of Rossa! what shades the soul of war?"

"Four stones," replied the chief, "rise on the grave of Cathba. These hands have laid in earth Duchomar, that cloud in war! Cathba, son of Torman! thou wert a sunbeam in Erin. And thou, O valiant Duchomar! a mist of the marshy Lano; when it moves on the plains of autumn, bearing the death of thousands along. Morna! fairest of maids! calm is thy sleep in the cave of the rock! Thou hast fallen in darkness, like a star, that shoots across the desert; when the traveller is alone, and mourns the transient beam!"

"Say," said Semo's blue–eyed son, "say how fell the chiefs of Erin. Fell they by the sons of Lochlin, striving in the battle of heroes? Or what confines the strong in arms to the dark and narrow house?"

"Cathba," replied the hero, " fell by the sword of Duchomar at the oak of the noisy streams. Duchomar came to Tura's cave; he spoke to the lovely Morna. 'Morna, fairest among women, lovely daughter of strong–armed Cormac! Why in the circle of stones: in the cave of the rock alone? The stream murmurs along. The old tree groans in the wind. The lake is troubled before thee: dark are the clouds of the sky! But thou art snow on the heath; thy hair is the mist of Cromla; when it curls on the hill, when it shines to the beam of the west! Thy breasts are two smooth rocks seen from Branno of streams. Thy arms, like two white pillars in the halls of the great Fingal.'

"'From whence,' the fair–haired maid replied, 'from whence Duchomar, most gloomy of men? Dark are thy brows and terrible! Red are thy rolling eyes! Does Swaran appear on the sea? What of the foe, Duchomar?' 'From the hill I return, O Morna, from the hill of the dark–brown hinds. Three have I slain with my bended yew. Three with my long–bounding dogs of the chase. Lovely daughter of Cormac, I love thee as my soul: I have slain one stately deer for thee. High was his branchy head–and fleet his feet of wind.' 'Duchomar!' calm the maid replied, 'I love thee not, thou gloomy man! hard is thy heart of rock; dark is thy terrible brow. But Cathba, young son of Torman, thou art the love of Morna. Thou art a sunbeam, in the day of the gloomy storm. Sawest thou the son of Torman, lovely on the hill of his hinds? Here the daughter of Cormac waits the coming of Cathba!"

"'Long shall Morna wait,' Duchomar said, 'long shall Morna wait for Cathba! Behold this sword unsheathed! Here wanders the blood of Cathba. Long shall Morna wait. He fell by the stream of Branno. On Croma I will raise his tomb, daughter of blue– shielded Cormac! Turn on Duchomar thine eyes; his arm is strong as a storm.' 'Is the son of Torman fallen?' said the wildly– bursting voice of the maid; 'is he fallen on his echoing hills, the youth with the breast of snow? the first in the chase of hinds! the foe of the strangers of ocean! Thou art dark to me, Duchomar; cruel is thine arm to Morna! Give me that sword, my foe! I loved the wandering blood of Cathba!'

"He gave the sword to her tears. She pierced his manly breast! He fell, like the bank of a mountain stream, and stretching forth his hand, he spoke: 'Daughter of blue–shielded Cormac! Thou hast slain me in youth! the sword is cold in my breast! Morna; I feel it cold. Give me to Moina the maid. Duchomar was the dream of her night! She will raise my tomb; the hunter shall raise my fame. But draw the sword from my breast, Morna, the steel is cold!' She came, in all her tears she came; she drew the sword from his breast. He pierced her white side! He spread her fair locks on the ground! Her bursting blood sounds from her side: her white arm is stained with red. Rolling in death she lay. The cave re–echoed to her sighs."

"Peace," said Cuthullin, "to the souls of the heroes! their deeds were great in fight. Let them ride around me on clouds. Let them show their features of war. My soul shall then be firm in danger; mine arm like the thunder of heaven! But be thou on a moonbeam, O Morna! near the window of my rest; when my thoughts are of peace; when the din of arms is past. Gather the strength of the tribes! Move to the wars of Erin! Attend the car of my battles! Rejoice in the noise of my course! Place three spears by my side: follow the bounding of my steeds! that my soul may be strong in my friends, when battle darken around the beams of my steel!

As rushes a stream of foam from the dark shady deep of Cromla, when the thunder is traveling above, and dark–brown night sits on half the hill. Through the breaches of the tempest look forth the dim faces of ghosts. So fierce, so vast, so terrible rushed on the sons of Erin. The chief, like a whale of ocean, whom all his billows pursue, poured valor forth, as a stream, rolling his might along the shore. The sons of Lochlin heard the noise, as the sound of a winter storm. Swaran struck his bossy shield: he called the son of Arno. "What murmur rolls along the hill, like the gathered flies of the eve? The sons of Erin descend, or rustling winds roar in the distant wood! Such is the noise of Gormal, before the white tops of my waves arise. O son of Arno! ascend the hill; view the dark face of the heath!"

He went. He trembling swift returned. His eyes rolled wildly round. His heart beat high against his side. His words were faltering, broken, slow. "Arise, son of ocean, arise, chief of the dark-brown shields! I see the dark, the mountain-stream of battle! the deep. moving strength of the sons of Erin! the car of war comes on, like the flame of death! the rapid car of Cuthullin, the noble son of Semo! It bends behind like a wave near a rock; like a sun-streaked mist of the heath. Its sides are embossed with stones, and sparkle like the sea round the boat of night. Of polished yew is its beam; its seat of the smoothest bone. The sides are replenished with spears; the bottom is the foot-stool of heroes! Before the right side of the car is seen the snorting horse! the high-maned, broad-breasted, proud, wide-leaping strong steed of the hill. Loud and resounding is his hoof: the spreading of his mane above is like a stream of smoke on a ridge of rocks. Bright are the sides of his steed! his name Sulin-Sifadda!

"Before the left side of the car is seen the snorting horse! The thin-maned, high-headed, strong-hoofed fleet-bounding son of the hill: His name is Dusronnal, among the stormy sons of the sword! A thousand thongs bind the car on high. Hard polished bits shine in wreath of foam. Thin thongs, bright studded with gems, bend on the stately necks of the steeds. The steeds, that like wreaths of mist fly over the streamy vales! The wildness of deer is in their course, the strength of eagles descending on the prey. Their noise is like the blast of winter, on the sides of the snow-headed Gormal.

"Within the car is seen the chief; the strong-armed son of the sword. The hero's name is Cuthullin, son of Semo, king of shells. His red cheek is like my polished yew. The look of his blue-rolling eye is wide, beneath the dark arch of his brow. His hair flies from his head like a flame, as bending forward he wields the spear. Fly, king of ocean, fly! He comes, like a storm along the streamy vale!

"When did I fly?" replied the king; " when fled Swaran from the battle of spears? When did I shrink from danger, chief of the little soul? I met the storm of Gormal when the foam of my waves beat high. I met the storm of the clouds; shall Swaran fly from a hero? Were Fingal himself before me, my soul should not darken with fear. Arise to battle, my thousands! pour round me like the echoing main, gather round the bright steel of your king; strong as the rocks of my land; that meet the storm with joys and stretch their dark pines to the wind!"

Like autumn's dark storms pouring from two echoing hills, towards each other approached the heroes. Like two deep streams from high rocks meeting, mixing roaring on the plain; loud, rough, and dark in battle meet Lochlin and Ins–fail. Chief mixes his strokes with chief, and man with man: steel, clanging, sounds on steel. Helmets are cleft on high. Blood bursts and smokes around. Strings murmur on the polished yews. Darts rush along the sky. Spears fall like the circles of light, which gild the face of night: as the noise of the troubled ocean, when roll the waves on high. As the last peal of thunder in heaven, such is the din of war! Though Cormac's hundred bards were there to give the fight to song; feeble was the voice of a hundred bards to send the deaths to future times! For many were the deaths of heroes; wide poured the blood of the brave!

Mourn, ye sons of song, mourn the death of the noble Sith llin. Let the sons of Fiona rise, on the lone plains of her lovely Ardan. They fell, like two hinds of the desert, by the hands of the mighty Swaran; when, in the midst of thousands, he roared like the shrill spirit of a storm. He sits dim on the clouds of the north, and enjoys the death of the mariner. Nor slept thy hand by thy side, chief of the isle of mist! Many were the deaths of thine arm, Cuthullin, thou son of Semo! His sword was like the beam of heaven when it pierces the sons of the vale: when the people are blasted and fall, and all the hills are burning around. Dusronnal snorted over the bodies of heroes. Sifadda bathed his hoof in blood. The battle lay behind them, as groves overturned on the desert of Cromla; when the blast has passed the heath, laden with the spirits of night!

Weep on the rocks of roaring winds, O maid of Inistore! Bend thy fair head over the waves, thou lovelier than the ghost of the hills, when it moves on the sun–beam, at noon, over the silence of Morven. He is fallen: thy youth is low! pale beneath the sword of Cuthullin! No more shall valor raise thy love to match the blood of kings. Trenar, graceful Trenar died, O maid of Inistore! His gray dogs are howling at home: they see his passing ghost. His bow is in the hall unstrung. No sound is in the hall of his hinds!

As roll a thousand waves to the rocks, so Swaran's host came on. As meets a rock a thousand waves, so Erin met Swaran of spears. Death raises all his voices around, and mixes with the sounds of shields. Each hero is a pillar of darkness; the sword abeam of fire in his hand. The field echoes from wing to wing, as a hundred hammers, that rise, by turns, on the red son of the furnace. Who are these on Lena's heath, these so gloomy and dark? Who are these like two clouds, and their swords like lightning. above them? The little hills are troubled around; the rocks tremble with all their moss. Who is it but ocean's son and the car−borne chief of Erin? Many are the anxious eyes of their friends, as they see them dim on the heath. But night conceals the chiefs in clouds, and ends the dreadful fight!

It was on Cromla's shaggy side that Dorglas had placed the deer; the early fortune of the chase, before the heroes left the hill. A hundred youths collect the heath; ten warriors make the fire; three hundred choose the polished stones. The feast is smoking wide! Cuthullin, chief of Erin's war, resumed his mighty soul. He stood upon his beamy spear, and spoke to the son of songs; to Carril of other times, the gray−headed son of Kinfena. "Is this feast spread for me alone, and the king of Lochlin on Erin's shore, far from the deer of his hills, and sounding halls of his feasts? Rise, Carril of other times, carry my words to Swaran. Tell him from the roaring of waters, that Cuthullin gives his feast. Here let him listen to the sound of my groves, amidst the clouds of night, for cold and bleak the blustering winds rush over the foam of his seas. Here let him praise the trembling harp, and hear the songs of heroes!"

Old Carril went with softest voice. He called the king of dark−brown shields! Rise, from the skins of thy chase; rise, Swaran, king of groves! Cuthullin gives the joy of shells. Partake the feast of Erin's blue−eyed chief! He answered like the sullen sound of Cromla before a storm. Though all thy daughters, Inis− fail, should stretch their arms of snow, should raise the heavings of their breasts, softly roll their eyes of love, yet fixed as Lochlin's thousand rocks here Swaran should remain, till morn, with the young beams of the east, shall light me to the death of Cuthullin. Pleasant to my ear is Lochlin's wind! It rushes over my seas! It speaks aloft in all my shrouds, and brings my green forests to my mind: the green forests of Gormal, which often echoed to my winds when my spear was red in the chase of the boar. Let dark Cuthullin yield to me the ancient throne of Cormac, or Erin's torrents shall show from their hills the red foam of the blood of his pride!

"Sad is the sound of Swaran's voice," said Carril other times! "Sad to himself alone," said the blue−eyed son of Semo. "But, Carril, raise the voice on high; tell the deeds of other times. Send thou the night away in song, and give the joy of grief. For many heroes and maids of love have moved on Inis−fail, and lovely are the songs of wo that are heard on Albion's rocks, when the noise of the chase is past, and the streams of Cona answer to the voice of Ossian.

"In other days," Carril replies, "came the sons of ocean to Erin; a thousand vessels bounded on waves to Ullin's lovely plains. The sons of Inis–fail arose to meet the race of dark–brown shields. Cairbar, first of men, was there, and Grudar, stately youth! Long had they strove for the spotted bull that towed on Golbun's echoing heath. Each claimed him as his own. Death was often at the point of their steel. Side by side the heroes fought: the strangers of ocean fled. Whose name was fairer on the hill than the name of Cairbar and Grudar? But, ah! why ever lowed the bull on Golbun's echoing heath? they saw him leaping like snow. The wrath of the chiefs returned. "On Lubar's grassy banks they fought; Grudar fell in his blood. Fierce Cairbar came to the vale, where Brassolis, fairest of his sisters, all alone, raised the song of grief. She sung of the actions of Grudar, the youth of her secret soul. She mourned him in the field of blood, but still she hoped for his return. Her white bosom is seen from her robe, as the moon from the clouds of night, when its edge heaves white on the view from the darkness which covers its orb). Her voice was softer than the harp to raise the song of grief. Her soul was fixed on Grudar. The secret look of her eye was his. 'When shalt thou come in thine arms, thou mighty in the war?'

"'Take, Brassolis,' Cairbar came and said; 'take, Brassolis, this shield of blood. Fix it on high within my hall, the armor of my foe!' Her soft heart beat against her side. Distracted, pale, she flew. She found her youth in all his blood; she died on Cromla's heath. Here rests their dust, Cuthullin! these lonely yews sprung from their tombs, and shade them from the storm. Fair was Brassolis on the plain! Stately was Grudar on the hill! The bard shall preserve their names, and send them down to future times!"

"Pleasant is thy voice, O Carril," said the blue–eyed chief of Erin. Pleasant are the words of other times. They are like the calm shower of spring, when the sun looks on the field, and the light cloud flies over the hills. O strike the harp in praise of my love, the lonely sunbeam of Dunscaith! Strike the harp in the praise of Bragla, she that I left in the isle of mist, the spouse of Semo's son! Dost thou raise thy fair face from the rock to find the sails of Cuthullin? The sea is rolling distant far: its white foam deceives thee for my sails. Retire, for it is night, my love; the dark winds sigh in thy hair. Retire to the halls of my feasts, think of the times that are past. I will not return till the storm of war is ceased. O Connal! speak of war and arms, and send her from my mind. Lovely with her flowing hair is the white–bosomed daughter of Sorglan."

Connal, slow to speak, replied, "Guard against the race of ocean. Send thy troop of night abroad, and watch the strength of Swaran. Cuthullin, I am for peace till the race of Selma come, till Fingal come, the first of men, and beam, like the sun on our fields!" The hero struck the shield of alarms, the warriors of the night moved on. The rest lay in the heath of the deer, and slept beneath the dusky wind. The ghosts of the lately dead were near, and swam on the gloomy clouds; and far distant in the dark silence of Lena, the feeble voices of death were faintly heard.

Erin, a name of Ireland; for "ear," or "iar," west, and "in", an island.

Lochlin: The Gaelic name of a Scandinavian general.

Inistore: The Orkney islands.

This passage alludes to the manner of burial among the ancient Scots. They opened a grave six or eight feet deep; the bottom was lined with fine clay; and on this they laid the body of the deceased, and, if a warrior, his sword, and the heads of twelve arrows by his side. Above they laid another stratum of clay, in which they placed the horn of a deer, the symbol of hunting. The whole was covered with a fine mould, and four stones placed on end to mark the extent of the grave. These are the four stones alluded to here.

Thou art dark to me: She alludes to his name the " dark man."

The isle of mist: The isle of Sky; not improperly called the "isle of mist," as its high hills, which catch the clouds from the Western Ocean, occasion almost continual rains.

The Cona here mentioned is the small river that runs through Glenco in Argyleshire.

Lubar, a river in Ulster; "Labhar," loud, noisy.

It was long the opinion of the ancient Scots, that a ghost was heard shrieking near the place where a death was to happen soon after.

FINGAL — BOOK II.

ARGUMENT.

The ghost of Crugal, one of the Irish heroes who was killed in battle, appearing to Connal, foretells the defeat of Cuthullin in the next battle, and earnestly advises him to make peace with Swaran. Connal communicates the vision; but Cuthullin is inflexible; from a principle of honor he would not be the first to sue for peace, and he resolved to continue the war. Morning comes; Swaran proposes dishonorable terms to Cuthullin, which are rejected. The battle begins, and is obstinately fought for some time, until, upon the flight of Grumal, the whole Irish army gave way. Cuthullin and Connal cover their retreat. Carril leads them to a neighboring hill, whither they are soon followed by Cuthullin himself; who descries the fleet of Fingal making towards their coast; but night coming on, he lost sight of it again. Cuthullin, dejected after his defeat, attributes his ill success to the death of Ferda, his friend, whom he had killed some time before. Carril, to show that ill success did not always attend those who innocently killed their friends, introduces the episode of Connal and Galvina.

Connal lay by the sound of the mountain—stream, beneath the aged tree. A stone, with its moss, supported his head. Shrill, through the heath of Lena, he heard the voice of night. At distance from the heroes he lay; the son of the sword feared no foe! The hero beheld, in his rest, a dark—red stream of fire rushing down from the hill. Crugal sat upon the beam, a chief who fell in fight. He fell by the hand of Swaran, striving in the battle of heroes. His face is like the beam of the setting moon. His robes are of the clouds of the hill. His eyes are two decaying flames.

Dark is the wound of his breast! "Crugal," said the mighty Connal, "son of Dedgal famed on the hill of hinds! Why so pale and sad, thou breaker of shields? Thou hast never been pale for fear! What disturbs the departed Crugal?" Dim, and in tears he stood, and stretched his pale hand over the hero. Faintly he raised his feeble voice, like the gale of the reedy Lego.

"My spirit, Connal, is on my hills; my course on the sands of Erin. Thou shalt never talk with Crugal, nor find his lone steps in the heath. I am light as the blast of Cromla. I move like the shadow of mist! Connal, son of Colgar, I see a cloud of death: it hovers dark over the plains of Lena. The Sons of green Erin must fall. Remove from the field of ghosts." Like the darkened moon he retired, in the midst of the whistling blast. "Stay," said the mighty Connal " stay, my dark–red friend. Lay by that beam of heaven, son of windy Cromla! What cave is thy lonely house? What green– headed hill the place of thy repose? Shall we not hear thee in the storm? in the noise of the mountain–stream? when the feeble Sons of the wind come forth, and, scarcely seen, pass over the desert?"

The soft–voiced Connal rose, in the midst of his sounding arms. He struck his shield above Cuthullin. The son of battle waked. "Why," said the ruler of the car, "comes Connal through my night? My spear might turn against the sound, and Cuthullin mourn the death of his friend. Speak, Connal; son of Colgar, speak; thy counsel is the sun of heaven!" "Son of Semo!" replied the chief, "the ghost of Crugal came from his cave. The stars dim twinkled through his form His voice was like the sound of a distant stream He is a messenger of death! He speaks of the dark and narrow house! Sue for peace, O chief of Erin!, or fly over the heath of Lena!"

"He spoke to Connal," replied the hero, "though stars dim twinkled through his form. Son of Colgar, it was the wind that murmured across thy car. Or if it was the form of Crugal, why didst thou not force him to my sight? Hast thou inquired where is his cave? the house of that son of wind? My sword might find that voice, and force his knowledge from Crugal. But small is his knowledge, Connal; he was here to–day. He could not have gone beyond our hills! who could tell him there of our fall?" "Ghosts fly on clouds, and ride on winds," said Connal's voice of wisdom. "They rest together in their caves, and talk of mortal men."

"Then let them talk of mortal men; of every man but Erin's chief. Let me be forgot in their cave. I will not fly from Swaran! If fall I must, my tomb shall rise amidst the fame of future times. The hunter shall shed a tear on my stone: sorrow shall dwell around the high–bosomed Bragla. I fear not death; to fly I fear! Fingal has seen me victorious! Thou dim phantom of the hill, show thyself to me! come on thy beam of heaven, show me my death in thine hand! yet I will not fly, thou feeble son of the wind! Go, son of Colgar, strike the shield. It hangs between the spears. Let my warriors rise to the sound in the midst of the battles of Erin. Though Fingal delays his coming with the race of his stormy isles, we shall fight; O Colgar's son, and die in the battle of heroes!"

The sound spreads wide. The heroes rise, like the breaking of a blue-rolling wave. They stood on the heath, like oaks with all their branches round them, when they echo to the stream of frost, and their withered leaves are rustling to the wind! High Cromla's head of clouds is gray. Morning trembles on the half- enlightened ocean. The blue mist swims slowly by, and hides the Sons of Inis-fail!

"Rise ye," said the king of the dark-brown shields, "ye that came from Lochlin's waves. The sons of Erin have fled from our arms; pursue them over the plains of Lena! Morla, go to Cormac's hall. Bid them yield to Swaran, before his people sink to the tomb, and silence spread over his isle." They rose, rustling like a flock of sea-fowl, when the waves expel them from the shore. Their sound was like a thousand streams, that meet in Cona's vale, when after a stormy night, they turn their dark eddies beneath the pale light of the morn.

As the dark shades of autumn fly over the hills of grass, so gloomy, dark, successive came the chiefs of Lochlin's echoing woods. Tall as the stag of Morven, moved stately before them the king. His shining shield is on his side, like a flame on the heath at night, when the world is silent and dark, and the traveller sees some ghosts sporting in the beam! Dimly gleam the hills around, and show indistinctly their oaks! A blast from the troubled ocean removed the settled mist. The Sons of Erin appear, like a ridge of rocks on the coast; when mariners, on shores unknown, are trembling at veering winds!

"Go, Morla, go," said the king of Lochlin, "offer peace to these. Offer the terms we give to kings, when nations bow down to our swords. When the valiant are dead in war; when virgins weep on the field!" Tall Morla came, the son of Swaran, and stately strode the youth along! He spoke to Erin's blue-eyed chief, among the lesser heroes. "Take Swaran's peace," the warrior spoke, "the peace he gives to kings when nations bow to his sword. Leave Erin's streamy plains to us, and give thy spouse and dog. Thy spouse, high-bosomed heaving fair! Thy dog that overtakes the wind! Give these to prove the weakness of thine arm, live then beneath our power!"

"Tell Swaran, tell that heart of pride, Cuthullin never yields! I give him the dark-rolling sea; I give his people graves in Erin. But never shall a stranger have the pleasing sunbeam of my love. No deer shall fly on Lochlin's hills, before swift-footed Luth." "Vain ruler of the car," said Morla, " wilt thou then fight the king? the king whose ships of many groves could carry off thine isle! So little is thy green-hilled Erin to him who rules the stormy waves!" " In words I yield to many, Morla. My sword shall yield to none. Erin shall own the sway of Cormac while Connal and Cuthullin live! O Connal, first of mighty men, thou hearest the words of Morla. Shall thy thoughts then be of peace, thou breaker of the shields? Spirit of fallen Crugal, Why didst thou threaten us with death? The narrow house shall receive me in the midst of the light of renown. Exalt, ye sons of Erin, exalt the spear and bend the bow; rush on the foe in darkness, as the spirits of stormy nights!"

Then dismal, roaring fierce and deep, the gloom of battle poured along, as mist that is rolled on a valley when storms invade the silent sunshine of heaven. Cuthullin moves before me in arms, like an angry ghost before a cloud, when meteors enclose him with fire; when the dark winds are in his hand. Carril, far on the heath, bids the horn of battle sound. He raises the voice of song, and pours his soul into the minds of the brave.

"Where," said the mouth of the song, "where is the fallen Crugal? He lies forgot on earth; the hall of shells is silent. Sad is the spouse of Crugal. She is a stranger in the hall of her grief. But who is she that, like a sunbeam, flies before the ranks of the foe? It is Degrena, lovely fair, the spouse of fallen Crugal. Her hair is on the wind behind. Her eye is red; her voice is shrill. Pale, empty, is thy Crugal now! His form is in the cave of the hill. He comes to the ear of rest; he raises his feeble voice, like the humming of the mountain–bee, like the collected flies of the eve! But Degrena falls like a cloud of the morn; the sword of Lochlin is in her side. Cairbar, she is fallen, the rising thought of thy youth! She is fallen, O Cairbar! the thought of thy youthful hours!"

Fierce Cairbar heard the mournful sound. He rushed along like ocean's whale. He saw the death of his daughter: he roared in the midst of thousands. His spear met a son of Lochlin! battle spreads from wing to wing! As a hundred winds in Lochlin's groves, as fire in the pines of a hundred hills, so loud, so ruinous, so vast, the ranks of men are hewn down. Cuthullin cut off heroes like thistles; Swaran wasted Erin. Curach fell by his hand, Cairbar of the bossy shield! Morglan lies in lasting rest! Ca– olt trembles as he dies! His white breast is stained with blood! his yellow hair stretched in the dust of his native land! He often had spread the feast where he fell. He often there had raised the voice of the harp, when his dogs leapt round for joy, and the youths of the chase prepared the bow!

Still Swaran advanced, as a stream that bursts from the desert. The little hills are rolled in its course, the rocks are half– sunk by its side. But Cuthullin stood before him, like a hill, that catches the clouds of heaven. The winds contend on its head of pines, the hail rattles on its rocks. But, firm in its strength, it stands, and shades the silent vale of Cona. So Cuthullin shaded the sons of Erin, and stood in the midst of thousands. Blood rises like the fount of a rock from panting heroes around. But Erin falls on either wing, like snow in the day of the sun.

O sons of Erin," said Grumal, "Lochlin conquers in the field. Why strive we as reeds against the wind? Fly to the hill of dark—brown hinds." He fled like the stag of Morven; his spear is a trembling beam of light behind him. Few fled with Grumal, chief of the little soul: they fell in the battle of heroes on Lena's echoing heath. High on his car of many gems the chief of Erin stood. He slew a mighty son of Lochlin, and spoke in haste to Connal. "O Connal, first of mortal men, thou hast taught this arm of death! Though Erin's Sons have fled, shall we not fight the foe? Carril, son of other times, carry my friends to that bushy hill. Here, Connal, let us stand like rocks, and save our flying friends."

Connal mounts the car of gems. They stretch their shields, like the darkened moon, the daughter of the starry skies, when she moves a dun circle through heaven, and dreadful change is expected by men. Sith—fadda panted up the hill, and Stronnal, haughty steed. Like waves behind a whale, behind them rushed the foe. Now on the rising side of Cromla stood Erin's few sad sons: like a grove through which the flame had rushed, hurried on by the winds of the stormy night; distant, withered, dark, they stand, with not a leaf to shake in the vale.

Cuthullin stood beside an oak. He rolled his red eye in silence, and heard the wind in his bushy hair; the scout of ocean came, Moran the son of Fithil "The ships," he cried, "the ships of the lonely isles. Fingal comes, the first of men, the breaker of the shields! The waves foam before his black prows! His masts with sails are like groves in clouds!" — "Blow," said Cuthullin, "blow, ye winds that rush along my isle of mist. Come to the death of thousands, O king of resounding Selma! Thy sails, my friend, are to me the clouds of the morning; thy ships the light of heaven; and thou thyself a pillar of fire that beams on the world by night. O Connal, first of men, how pleasing in grief are our friends! But the night is gathering around. Where now are the ships of Fingal? Here let us pass the hours of darkness; here wish for the moon of heaven."

The winds came down on the woods. The torrents rush from the rocks. Rain gathers round the head of Cromla. The red stars tremble between the flying clouds. Sad, by the side of a stream, whose sound is echoed by a tree, sad by the side of a stream the chief of Erin sits. Connal, son of Colgar, is there, and Carril of other times. "Unhappy is the hand of Cuthullin," said the son of Semo, "unhappy is the hand of Cuthullin since he slew his friend! Ferda, son of Damman, I loved thee as myself!"

"How, Cuthullin, son of Semo, how fell the breaker of the shields? Well I remember," said Connal, "the son of the noble Damman. Tall and fair, he was like the rainbow of heaven. Ferda from Albion came, the chief of a hundred hills. In Muri's hall he learned the sword, and won the friendship of Cuthullin. We moved to the chase together: one was our bed in the heath."

Deugala was the spouse of Cairbar, chief of the plains of Ullin. She was covered with the light of beauty, but her heart was the house of pride. She loved that sunbeam of youth, the son of the noble Damman. "Cairbar," said the white-armed Deugala, "give me half of the herd. No more I will remain in your halls. Divide the herd, dark Cairbar!" "Let Cuthullin," said Cairbar, "divide my herd on the hill.

His breast is the seat of justice. Depart, thou light of beauty!" I went and divided the herd. One snow-white bull remained. I gave that bull to Cairbar. The wrath of Deugala rose!

"Son of Damman," began the fair, "Cuthullin hath pained my soul. I must hear of his death, or Lubar's stream shall roll over me. My pale ghost shall wander near thee, and mourn the wound of my pride. Pour out the blood of Cuthullin, or pierce this heaving breast." "Deugala," said the fair-haired youth, "how shall I slay the son of Semo? He is the friend of my secret thoughts. Shall I then lift the sword?" She wept three days before the chief; on the fourth he said he would fight. "I will fight my friend, Deugala, but may I fall by his sword! Could I wander on the hill alone? Could I behold the grave of Cuthullin?" We fought on the plain of Mori. Our swords avoid a wound. They slide on the helmets of steel, or sound on the slippery shields. Deugala was near with a smile, and said to the son of Damman: "Thine arm is feeble, sunbeam of youth! Thy years are not strong for steel. Yield to the son of Semo. He is a rock on Malmor."

The tear is in the eye of youth. He faltering said to me: "Cuthullin, raise thy bossy shield. Defend thee from the hand of thy friend. My soul is laden with grief, for I must slay the chief of men." I sighed as the wind in the cleft of a rock. I lifted high the edge of my steel. The sunbeam of battle fell: the first of Cuthullin's friends! Unhappy is the hand of Cuthullin since the hero fell!"

""Mournful is thy tale, son of the car," said Carril of other times. "It sends my soul back to the ages of old, to the days of other years. Often have I heard of Comal, who slew the friend he loved; yet victory attended his steel: the battle was consumed in his presence!"

Comal was the son of Albion, the chief of a hundred hills! His deer drunk of a thousand streams. A thousand rocks replied to the voice of his dogs. His face was the mildness of youth; his hand the death of heroes. One was his love, and fair was she, the daughter of the mighty Conloch. She appeared like a sunbeam among women. Her hair was the wing of the raven. Her dogs were taught to the chase. Her bowstring sounded on the winds. Her soul was fixed on Comal. Often met their eyes of love. Their course in the chase was one. Happy were their words in secret. But Grumal loved the maid, the dark chief of the gloomy Ardven. He watched her lone steps in the heath, the foe of unhappy Comal.

One day, tired of the chase, when the mist had concealed their friends, Comal and the daughter of Conloch met in the cave of Ronan. It was the wonted haunt of Comal. Its sides were hung with his arms. A hundred shields of thongs were there; a hundred helms of sounding steel. "Rest here," he said, "my love, Galbina: thou light of the cave of Ronan! A deer appears on Mora's brow. I go; but I will soon return." "I fear," she said, "dark Grumal, my foe: he haunts the cave of Ronan! I will rest among the arms; but soon return, my love!"

He went to the deer of Mora. The daughter of Conloch would try his love. She clothed her fair sides with his armor: she strode from the cave of Ronan! he thought it was his foe. His heart beat high. His color changed, and darkness dimmed his eyes. He drew the bow. The arrow flew. Galbina fell in blood! He run with wildness in his steps: he called the daughter of Conloch. No answer in the lonely rock. Where art thou, O my love? He saw at length her heaving heart, beating around the arrow he threw. "O Conloch's daughter! is it thou?" He sunk upon her breast! The hunters found the hapless pair! He afterward walked the hill. But many and silent were his steps round the dark dwelling of his love. The fleet of the ocean came. He fought; the strangers fled. He searched for death along the field. But who could slay the mighty Coma!? He threw away his dark–brown shield. An arrow found his manly breast. He sleeps with his loved Galbina at the noise of the sounding surge! Their green tombs are seen by the mariner, when he bounds on the waves of the north.

The ancient Scots, well as the present Highlanders, drunk in shells; hence it is, that we so often meet in the old poetry with "chief of shells," and "the hall of shells."

Muri: A place in Ulster.

FINGAL — BOOK III

ARGUMENT.

Cuthullin, pleased with the story of Carril, insists with that bard for more of his songs. He relates the actions of Fingal in Lochlin, and death of Agandecca, the beautiful sister of Swaran. He had scarce finished, when Calmar, the son of Matha, who had advised the first battle, came wounded from the field, and told them of Swaran's design to surprise the remains of the Irish army. He himself proposes to withstand singly the whole force of the enemy, in a narrow pass, till the Irish should make good their retreat. Cuthullin, touched with the gallant proposal of Calmar, resolves to accompany him and orders Carril to carry off the few that remained of the Irish. Morning comes, Calmar dies of his wounds; and the ships of the Caledonians appearing, Swaran gives over the pursuit of the Irish, and returns to oppose Fingal's landing. Cuthullin, ashamed, after his defeat, to appear before Fingal re tires to the cave of Tura. Fingal engages the enemy, puts them to flight: but the coming on of night makes the victory not decisive. The king, who had observed the gallant behavior of his grandson Oscar, gives him advice concerning his conduct in peace and war. He recommends to him to place the example of his fathers before his eyes, as the best model for his conduct; which introduces the episode concerning Fainasøllis, the daughter of the king of Craca, whom Fingal had taken under his protection in his youth. Fillan and Oscar are despatched to observe the motions of the enemy by night: Gaul, the son of Morni, desires the command of the army in the next battle, which Fingal promises to give him. Some general reflections of the poet close the third day.

"PLEASANT are the words of the song! "said Cuthullin, "lovely the tales of other times! They are like the calm dew of the morning on the hill of roes! when the sun is faint on its

91

side, and the lake is settled and blue on the vale. O Carril, raise again thy voice! let me hear the song of Selma: which was sung in my halls of joy, when Fingal, king of shields, was there, and glowed at the deeds of his fathers.

"Fingal! thou dweller of battle," said Carril, "early were thy deeds in arms. Lochlin was consumed in thy wrath, when thy youth strove in the beauty of maids. They smiled at the fair– blooming face of the hero; but death was in his hands. He was strong as the waters of Lora. His followers were the roar of a thousand streams. They took the king of Lochlin in war; they restored him to his ship. His big heart swelled with pride; the death of the youth was dark in his soul. For none ever but Fingal, had overcome the strength of the mighty Starno. He sat in the hall of his shells in Lochlin's woody land. He called the gray– haired Snivan, that often sung round the circle of Loda; when the stone of power heard his voice , and battle turned in the field of the valiant!

"'Go, gray–haired Snivan,' Starno said: 'go to Ardven's sea– surrounded rocks. Tell to the king of Selma; he the fairest among his thousands; tell him I give to him my daughter, the loveliest maid that ever heaved a breast of snow. Her arms are white as the foam of my waves. Her soul is generous and mild. Let him come with his bravest heroes to the daughter of the secret hall!' Snivan came to Selma's hall: fair–haired Fingal attended his steps. His kindled soul flew to the maid, as he bounded on the waves of the north. 'Welcome,' said the dark–brown Starno, 'welcome, king of rocky Morven! welcome his heroes of might, sons of the distant isle! Three days within thy halls shall we feast; three days pursue my boars; that your fame may reach the maid who dwells in the secret hall.'

"Starno designed their death. He gave the feast of shells. Fingal, who doubted the foe, kept on his arms of steel. The sons of death were afraid: they fled from the eyes of the king. The voice of sprightly mirth arose. The trembling harps of joy were strung. Bards sung the battles of heroes; they sung the heaving breast of love. Ullin, Fingal's bard, was there: the sweet voice of resounding Cona. He praised the daughter of Lochlin; and Morven's high–descended chief. The daughter of Lochlin overheard. She left the hall of her secret sigh! She came in all her beauty, like the moon from the cloud of the east. Loveliness was round her as light. Her steps were the music of songs. She saw the youth and loved him. He was the stolen sigh of her soul. Her blue eyes rolled on him in secret: she blessed the chief of resounding Morven.

THE POEMS OF OSSIAN

"The third day, with all its beams, shone bright on the wood of boars. Forth moved the dark–browed Starno; and Fingal, king of shields. Half the day they spent in the chase; the spear of Selma was red in blood. It was then the daughter of Starno, with blue eyes rolling in tears; it was then she came with her voice of love, and spoke to the king of Morven. 'Fingal, high–descended chief, trust not Starno's heart of pride. Within that wood he has placed his chiefs. Beware of the wood of death. But remember, son of the isle, remember Agandecca; save me from the wrath of my father, king of the windy Morven!'

"The youth with unconcern went on; his heroes by his side. The sons of death fell by his hand; and Germal echoed around! Before the halls of Starno the sons of the chase convened. The king's dark brows were like clouds; his eyes like meteors of night. 'Bring hither,' he said, 'Agandecca to her lovely king of Morven! His hand is stained with the blood of my people; her words have not been in vain!' She came with the red eye of tears. She came with loosely flowing locks. Her white breast heaved with broken sighs, like the foam of the streamy Lubar. Starno pierced her side with steel. She fell, like a wreath of snow, which slides from the rocks of Ronan, when the woods are still, and echo deepens in the vale! Then Fingal eyed his valiant chiefs: his valiant chiefs took arms! The gloom of battle roared: Lochlin fled or died. Pale in his bounding ship he closed the maid of the softest soul. Her tomb ascends on Ardven; the sea roars round her narrow dwelling."

"Blessed be her soul," said Cuthullin; "blessed be the mouth of the song! Strong was the youth of Fingal; strong is his arm of age. Lochlin shall fall again before the king of echoing Morven. Show thy face from a cloud, O moon! light his white sails on the wave: and if any strong spirit of heaven sits on that low– hung cloud; turn his dark ships from the rock, thou rider of the storm!"

Such were the words of Cuthullin at the sound of the mountain stream; when Calmar ascended the hill, the wounded son of Matha. From the field he came in his blood. He leaned on his bending spear. Feeble is the arm of battle! but strong the soul of the hero! "Welcome! O son of Matha," said Connal, "welcome art thou to thy friends! Why bursts that broken sigh from the breast of him who never feared before?" "And never, Connal, will he fear, chief of the pointed steel! My soul brightens in danger; in the noise of arms I am of the race of battle. My fathers never feared.

"Cormar was the first of my race. He sported through the storms of waves. His black skiff bounded on ocean; he travelled on the wings of the wind. A spirit once embroiled the night. Seas swell and rocks resound. Winds drive along the clouds. The lightning flies on wings of fire. He feared, and came to land, then blushed that he feared at all. He rushed again among the waves, to find the son of the wind. Three youths guide the bounding bark: he stood with sword unsheathed. When the low–hung vapor passed, he took it by the curling head. He searched its dark womb with his steel. The son of the wind forsook the air. The moon and the stars returned! Such was the boldness of my race. Calmar is like his fathers. Danger flies from the lifted sword. They best succeed who dare!

"But now, ye sons of green Erin, retire from Lena's bloody heath. Collect the sad remnant of our friends, and join the sword of Fingal. I heard the sound of Lochlin's advancing arms: Calmar will remain and fight. My voice shall be such, my friends, as if thousands were behind me. But, son of Semo, remember me. Remember Calmar's lifeless corse. When Fingal shall have wasted the field, place me by some stone of remembrance, that future times may hear my fame; that the mother of Calmar may rejoice in my renown."

"No: son of Matha," said Cuthullin, "I will never leave thee here. My joy is in an unequal fight: my soul increases in danger. Connal, and Carril of other times, carry off the sad sons of Erin. When the battle is over, search for us in this narrow way. For near this oak we shall fall, in the streams of the battle of thousands! O Fithal's son, with flying speed rush over the heath of Lena. Tell to Fingal that Erin is fallen. Bid the king of Morven come. O let him come like the sun in a storm, to lighten, to restore the isle!"

Morning is gray on Cromla. The sons of the sea ascend. Calmar stood forth to meet them in the pride of his kindling soul. But pale was the face of the chief. He leaned on his father's spear. That spear which he brought from Lara, when the soul of his mother was sad; the soul of the lonely Alcletha, waning in the sorrow of years. But slowly now the hero falls, like a tree on the plain. Dark Cuthullin stands alone like a rock in a sandy vale. The sea comes with its waves, and roars on its hardened sides. Its head is covered with foam; the hills are echoing round.

Now from the gray mist of the ocean the white–sailed ships of Fingal appear. High is the grove of their masts, as they nod, by turns, on the rolling wave. Swaran saw them from the hill. He returned from the sons of Erin. As ebbs the resounding sea, through the hundred isles of Inistore; so loud, so vast, so immense, returned the sons of Lochlin against the king. But bending, weeping, sad, and slow, and dragging his long spear behind, Cuthullin sunk in Cromla's wood, and mourned his fallen friends. He feared the face of Fingal, who was wont to greet him from the fields of renown!

"How many lie there of my heroes! the chiefs of Erin's race! they that were cheerful in the hall, when the sound of the shells arose! No more shall I find their steps in the heath! No more shall I hear their voice in the chase. Pale, silent, low on bloody beds, are they who were my friends! O spirits of the lately dead, meet Cuthullin on his heath! Speak to him on the winds, when the rustling tree of Tura's cave resounds. There, far remote, I shall lie unknown. No bard shall hear of me. No gray stone shall rise to my renown. Mourn me with the dead, O Bragla! departed is my fame." Such were the words of Cuthullin, when he sunk in the woods of Cromla!

Fingal, tall in his ship, stretched his bright lance before him. Terrible was the gleam of his steel: It was like the green meteor of death, setting in the heath of Malmor, when the traveller is alone, and the broad moon is darkened in heaven.

"The battle is past," said the king. "I behold the blood of my friends. Sad is the heath of Lena! mournful the oaks of Cromla! The hunters have fallen in their strength: the son of Semo is no more! Ryno and Fillan, my sons, sound the horn of Fingal! Ascend that hill on the shore; call the children of the foe. Call them from the grave of Lamderg, the chief of other times. Be your voice like that of your father, when he enters the battles of his strength! I wait for the mighty stranger. I wait on Lena's shore for Swaran. Let him come with all his race; strong in battle are the friends of the dead!"

Fair Ryno as lightning gleamed along: dark Fillan rushed like the shade of autumn. On Lena's heath their voice is heard. The sons of ocean heard the horn of Fingal. As the roaring eddy of ocean returning from the kingdom of snows: so strong, so dark, so sudden, came down the sons of Lochlin. The king in their front appears, in the dismal pride of his arms! Wrath burns on his dark–brown face; his eyes roll in the fire of his valor. Fingal beheld the son of Starno: he remembered Agandecca. For Swaran with tears of youth had mourned his white–bosomed sister. He sent Ullin of songs to bid him to the feast of shells: for pleasant on Fingal's soul returned the memory of the first of his loves!

Ullin came with aged steps, and spoke to Starno's son. "O thou that dwellest afar, surrounded, like a rock, with thy waves! come to the feast of the king, and pass the day in rest. To—morrow let us fight, O Swaran, and break the echoing shields." — "To— day," said Starno's wrathful son, "we break the echoing shields: to—morrow my feast shall be spread; but Fingal shall lie on earth." — "To—morrow let his feast be spread," said Fingal, with a smile. "To—day, O my sons! we shall break the echoing shields. Ossian, stand thou near my arm. Gaul, lift thy terrible sword. Fergus, bend thy crooked yew. Throw, Fillan, thy lance through heaven. Lift your shields, like the darkened moon. Be your spears the meteors of death. Follow me in the path of my fame. Equal my deeds in battle."

As a hundred winds on Morven; as the streams of a hundred hills; as clouds fly successive over heaven; as the dark ocean assails the shore of the desert: so roaring, so vast, so terrible, the armies mixed on Lena's echoing heath. The groans of the people spread over the hills: it was like the thunder of night, when the cloud bursts on Cona; and a thousand ghosts shriek at once on the hollow wind. Fingal rushed on in his strength, terrible as the spirit of Trenmor; when in a whirlwind he comes to Morven, to see the children of his pride. The oaks resound on their mountains, and the rocks fall down before him. Dimly seen as lightens the night, he strides largely from hill to hill. Bloody was the hand of my father, when he whirled the gleam of his sword. He remembers the battles of his youth. The field is wasted in its course!

Ryno went on like a pillar of fire. Dark is the brow of Gaul. Fergus rushed forward with feet of wind; Fillin like the mist of the hill. Ossian, like a rock, came down. I exulted in the strength of the king. Many were the deaths of my arm! dismal the gleam of my sword! My locks were not then so gray; nor trembled my hands with age. My eyes were not closed in darkness; my feet failed not in the race!

Who can relate the deaths of the people? who the deeds of mighty heroes? when Fingal, burning in his wrath, consumed the sons of Lochlin? Groans swelled on groans from hill to hill, till night had covered all. Pale, staring like a herd of deer, the sons of Lochlin convene on Lena. We sat and heard the sprightly harp, at Lubar's gentle stream. Fingal himself was next to the foe. He listened to the tales of his bards. His godlike race were in the song, the chiefs of other times. Attentive, leaning on his shield, the king of Morven sat. The wind whistled through his locks; his thoughts are of the days of other years. Near him, on his bending spear, my young, my valiant Oscar stood. He admired the king of Morven: his deeds were swelling in his soul.

"Son of my son," began the king, "O Oscar, pride of youth: I saw the shining of the sword. I gloried in my race. Pursue the fame of our fathers; be thou what they have been, when Trenmor lived, the first of men, and Trathal, the father of heroes! They fought the battle in their youth. They are the song of bards. O Oscar! bend the strong in arm; but spare the feeble hand. Be thou a stream of many tides against the foes of thy people; but like the gale, that moves the grass. to those who ask thine aid. So Trenmor lived; such Trathal was; and such has Fingal been. My arm was the support of the injured; the weak rested behind the lightning of my steel.

"Oscar! I was young, like thee, when lovely Fainas¢llis came: that sunbeam! that mild light of love! the daughter of Craca's king. I then returned from Cona's heath, and few were in my train. A white−sailed boat appeared far off; we saw it like a mist that rode on ocean's wind. It soon approached. We saw the fair. Her white breast heaved with sighs. The wind was in her loose dark hair; her rosy cheek had tears. 'Daughter of beauty,' calm I said, 'what sigh is in thy breast? Can I, young as I am, defend thee, daughter of the sea? My sword is not unmatched in war, but dauntless is my heart."

"'To thee I fly,' with sighs she said, 'O prince of mighty men! To thee I fly, chief of the generous shells, supporter of the feeble hand! The king of Craca's echoing isle owned me the sunbeam of his race. Cromla's hills have heard the sighs of love for unhappy Fainas¢llis! Sora's chief beheld me fair; he loved the daughter of Craca. His sword is a beam of light upon the warrior's side. But dark is his brow; and tempests are in his soul. I shun him on the roaring sea; but Sora's chief pursues.'

"'Rest thou,' I said, 'behind my shield! rest in peace, thou beam of light! The gloomy chief of Sora will fly, if Fingal's arm is like his soul. In some lone cave I might conceal thee, daughter of the sea. But Fingal never flies. Where the danger threatens, I rejoice in the storm of spears.' I saw the tears upon her cheek. I pitied Craca's fair. Now, like a dreadful wave afar, appeared the ship of stormy Borbar. His masts high−bended over the sea behind their sheets of snow. White roll the waters on either side. The strength of ocean sounds. 'Come thou,' I said, 'from the roar of ocean, thou rider of the storm. Partake the feast within my hall. It is the house of strangers.'

"The maid stood trembling by my side. He drew the bow. She fell. 'Unerring is thy hand,' I said, 'but feeble was the foe.' We fought, nor weak the strife of death. He sunk beneath my sword. We laid them in two tombs of stone; the hapless lovers of youth! Such have I been, in my youth, O Oscar! be thou like the age of Fingal. Never search thou for battle; nor shun it when it comes.

"Fillan and Oscar of the dark–brown hair! ye that are swift in the race fly over the heath in my presence. View the sons of Lochlin. Far off I hear the noise of their feet, like distant sounds in woods. Go: that they may not fly from my sword, along the waves of the north. For many chiefs of Erin's race lie here on the dark bed of death. The children of war are low; the sons of echoing Cromla."

The heroes flew like two dark clouds: two dark clouds that are the chariots of ghosts; when air's dark children come forth to frighten hapless men. It was then that Gaul, the son of Morni, stood like a rock in night. His spear is glittering to the stars; his voice like many streams.

"Son of battle," cried the chief, "O Fingal, king of shells! let the bards of many songs soothe Erin's friends to rest. Fingal, sheath thou thy sword of death; and let thy people fight. We wither away without our fame; our king is the only breaker of shields! When morning rises on our hills, behold at a distance our deeds. Let Lochlin feel the sword of Morni's son; that bards may sing of me. Such was the custom heretofore of Fingal's noble race. Such was thine own, thou king of swords, in battles of the spear."

O son of Morni," Fingal replied, "I glory in thy fame. Fight; but my spear shall be near, to aid thee in the midst of danger. Raise, raise the voice, ye sons of song, and lull me into rest. Here will Fingal lie, amidst the wind of night. And if thou, Agandecca, art near, among the children of thy land; if thou sittest on a blast of wind, among the high–shrouded masts of Lochlin; come to my dreams, my fair one! Show thy bright face to my soul ."

Many a voice and many a harp, in tuneful sounds arose. Of Fingal noble deeds they sung; of Fingal's noble race: and sometimes, on the lovely sound was heard the name of Ossian. I often fought, and often won in battles of the spear. But blind, and tearful, and forlorn, I walk with little men! O Fingal, with thy race of war I now behold thee not. The wild roes feed on the green tomb of the mighty king of Morven! Blest be thy soul, thou king of swords, thou most renowned on the hills of Cona!

The second night, since the opening of the poem, continues; and Cuthullin, Connal, and Carril, still sit in the place described in the preceding book.

This passage most certainly alludes to the religion of Lochlin, and "the stone of power," here mentioned, is the image of one of the deities of Scandinavia.

All the Northwest coast of Scotland probably went, of old under the name of Morven, which signifies a ridge of very high hills

What the Craca here mentioned was, it is not, at this distance of time, easy to determine. The most probable opinion is, that it was one of the Shetland Isles.

FINGAL — BOOK IV.

ARGUMENT. The action of the poem being suspended by night, Ossian takes the opportunity to relate his own actions at the lake of Lego, and his courtship of Everallin, who was the mother of Oscar, and had died some time before the expedition of Fingal into Ireland. Her ghost appears to him, and tells him that Oscar, who had been sent, the beginning of the night, to observe the enemy, was engaged with an advanced party, and almost overpowered. Ossian relieves his son; and an alarm is given to Fingal of the approach of Swaran. The king rises, calls his army together, and, as he had promised the preceding night, devolves the command on Gaul the son of Morni, while he himself, after charging his sons to behave gallantly and defend his people, retires to a hill, from whence he could have a view of the battle. The battle joins; the poet relates Oscar's great actions. But when Oscar, in conjunction with his father, conquered in one wing, Gaul, who was attacked by Swaran in person, was on the point of retreating in the other. Fingal sends Ullin his bard to encourage them with a war song, but notwithstanding Swaran prevails; and Gaul and his army are obliged to give way. Fingal descending from the hill, rallies them again; Swaran desists from the pursuit, possesses himself of a rising ground, restores the ranks, and waits the approach of Fingal. The king, having encouraged his men, gives the necessary orders, and renews the battle. Cuthullin, who, with his friend Connal, and Carril his bard, had retired to the cave of Tura, hearing the noise, came to the brow of the hill, which overlooked the field of battle, where he saw Fingal engaged with the enemy. He, being hindered by Connal from joining Fingal, who was himself upon the point of obtaining a complete victory, sends Carril to congratulate that hero on success.

THE POEMS OF OSSIAN

Who comes with her songs from the hill, like the bow of the showery Lena? It is the maid of the voice of love: the white–armed daughter of Toscar! Often hast thou heard my song; often given the tear of beauty. Hast thou come to the wars of thy people? to hear the actions of Oscar? When shall I cease to mourn, by the streams of resounding Cona? My years have passed away in battle. My age is darkened with grief!

"Daughter of the hand of snow, I was not so mournful and blind; I was not so dark and forlorn, when Everallin loved me! Everallin with the dark–brown hair, the white–bosomed daughter of Branno. A thousand heroes sought the maid, she refused her love to a thousand. The sons of the sword were despised: for graceful in her eyes was Ossian. I went, in suit of the maid, to Lego's sable surge. Twelve of my people were there, the sons of streamy Morven! We came to Branno, friend of strangers! Branno of the sounding mail! 'From whence,' he said, 'are the arms of steel? Not easy to win is the maid, who has denied the blue–eyed sons of Erin. But blest be thou, O son of Fingal! Happy is the maid that waits thee! Though twelve daughters of beauty were mine, thine were the choice, thou son of fame!'

"He opened the hall of the maid, the dark–haired Everallin. Joy kindled in our manly breasts. We blest the maid of Branno. Above us on the hill appeared the people of stately Cormac. Eight were the heroes of the chief. The heath flamed wide with their arms. There Colla; there Durra of wounds; there mighty Toscar, and Tago; there Fresta the victorious stood; Dairo of the happy deeds; Dala the battle's bulwark in the narrow way! The sword flamed in the hand of Cormac. Graceful was the look of the hero! Eight were the heroes of Ossian. Ullin, stormy son of war. Mullo of the generous deeds. The noble, the graceful Scelacha. Oglan, and Cerdan the wrathful. Dumariccan's brows of death. And why should Ogar be the last; so wide–renowned on the hills of Ardven?

"Ogar met Dala the strong face to face, on the field of heroes. The battle of the chiefs was like wind, on ocean's foamy waves. The dagger is remembered by Ogar; the weapon which he loved. Nine times he drowned it in Dala's side. The stormy battle turned. Three times I broke on Cormac's shield: three times he broke his spear. But, unhappy youth of love! I cut his head away. Five times I shook it by the lock. The friends of Cormac fled. Whoever would have told me, lovely maid, when then I strove in battle, that blind, forsaken, and forlorn, I now should pass the night; firm ought his mail to have been; unmatched his arm in war."

THE POEMS OF OSSIAN

On Lena's gloomy heath the voice of music died away. The inconstant blast blew hard. The high oak shook its leaves around. Of Everallin were my thoughts, when in all the light of beauty she came; her blue eyes rolling in tears. She stood on a cloud before my sight, and spoke with feeble voice! "Rise, Ossian, rise, and save my son; save Oscar, prince of men. Near the red oak of Luba's stream he fights with Lochlin's sons." She sunk into her cloud again. I covered me with steel. My spear supported my steps; my rattling armor rung. I hummed, as I was wont in danger, the songs of heroes of old. Like distant thunder Lochlin heard. They fled; my son pursued.

I called him like a distant stream. "Oscar, return over Lena. No further pursue the foe," I said, "though Ossian is behind thee." He came! and pleasant to my ear was Oscar's sounding steel. "Why didst thou stop my hand," he said, "till death had covered all? For dark and dreadful by the stream they met thy son and Fillin. They watched the terrors of the night. Our swords have conquered some. But as the winds of night pour the ocean over the white sands of Mora, so dark advance the sons of Lochlin, over Lena's rustling heat! The ghosts of night shriek afar: I have seen the meteors of death. Let me awake the king of Morven, he that smiles in danger! He that is like the sun of heaven, rising in a storm!"

Fingal had started from a dream, and leaned on Trenmor's shield! the dark–brown shield of his fathers, which they had lifted of old in war. The hero had seen, in his rest, the mournful form of Agandecca. She came from the way of the ocean. She slowly, lonely, moved over Lena. Her face was pale, like the mist of Cromla. Dark were the tears of her cheek. She often raised her dim hand from her robe, her robe which was of the clouds of the desert: she raised her dim hand over Fingal, and turned away silent eyes! "Why weeps the daughter of Starno?" said Fingal with a sigh; "why is thy face so pale, fair wanderer of the clouds?" She departed on the wind of Lena. She left him in the midst of the night. She mourned the sons of her people, that were to fall by the hand of Fingal.

The hero started from rest. Still he beheld her in his soul. The sound of Oscar's steps approached. The king saw the gray shield on his side: for the faint beam of the morning came over the waters of Ullin. "What do the foes in their fear?" said the rising king of Morven: "or fly they through ocean's foam, or wait they the battle of steel? But why should Fingal ask? I hear their voice on the early wind! Fly over Lena's heath: O Oscar, awake our friends!"

The king stood by the stone of Lubar. Thrice he reared his terrible voice. The deer started from the fountains of Cromla. The rocks shook, on all their hills. Like the noise of a hundred mountain–streams, that burst, and roar, and foam! like the clouds, that gather to a tempest on the blue face of the sky! so met the sons of the desert, round the terrible voice of Fingal. Pleasant was the voice of the king of Morven to the warriors of his land. Often had he led them to battle; often returned with the spoils of the foe.

"Come to battle," said the king, "ye children of echoing Selma! Come to the death of thousands! Comhal's son will see the fight. My sword shall wave on the hill, the defence of my people in war. But never may you need it, warriors; while the son of Morni fights, the chief of mighty men! He shall lead my battle, that his fame may rise in song! O ye ghosts of heroes dead! ye riders of the storm of Cromla! receive my falling people with joy, and bear them to your hills. And may the blast of Lena carry them over my seas, that they may come to my silent dreams, and delight my soul in rest. Fillan and Oscar of the dark–brown hair! fair Ryno, with the pointed steel! advance with valor to the fight. Behold the son of Morni! Let your swords be like his in strife: behold the deeds of his hands. Protect the friends of your father. Remember the chiefs of old. My children, I will see you yet, though here you should fall in Erin. Soon shall our cold pale ghosts meet in a cloud, on Cona's eddying winds."

Now like a dark and stormy cloud, edged round with the red lightning of heaven, flying westward from the morning's beam, the king of Selma removed. Terrible is the light of his armor; two spears are in his hand. His gray hair falls on the wind. He often looks back on the war. Three bards attend the son of fame, to bear his words to the chiefs high on Cromla's side he sat, waving the Lightning of his sword, and as he waved we moved.

Joy rises in Oscar's face. His cheek is red. His eye sheds tears. The sword is a beam of fire in his hand. He came, and smiling, spoke to Ossian. "O ruler of the fight of steel! my father, hear thy son! Retire with Morven's mighty chief. Give me the fame of Ossian. If here I fall, O chief, remember that breast of snow, the lonely sunbeam of my love, the white–handed daughter of Toscar! For, with red cheek from the rock, bending over the stream, her soft hair flies about her bosom, as she pours the sigh for Oscar. Tell her I am on my hills, a lightly–bounding son of the wind; tell her, that in a cloud I may meet the lovely maid of Toscar." "Raise, Oscar, rather raise my tomb. I will not yield the war to thee. The first and bloodiest in the strife, my arm shall teach thee how to fight. But remember, my son, to place this sword, this bow, the horn of my deer, within that dark and narrow house, whose mark is one gray stone! Oscar, I have no love to leave to the care of my son. Everallin is no more, the lovely daughter of Branno!"

Such were our words, when Gaul's loud voice came growing on the wind. He waved on high the sword of his father. We rushed to death and wounds. As waves, white bubbling over the deep, come swelling, roaring on; as rocks of ooze meet roaring waves; so foes attacked and fought. Man met with man, and steel with steel. Shields sound and warriors fall. As a hundred hammers on the red son of the furnace, so rose, so rung their swords!

Gaul rushed on, like a whirlwind in Ardven. The destruction of heroes is on his sword. Swaran was like the fire of the desert in the echoing heath of Gormal! How can I give to the song the death of many spears? My sword rose high, and flamed in the strife of blood. Oscar, terrible wert thou, my best, my greatest son! I rejoiced in my secret soul, when his sword flamed over the slain. They fled amain through Lena's heath. We pursued and slew. As stones that bound from rock to rock; as axes in echoing woods; as thunder rolls from hill to hill, in dismal broken peals; so blow succeeded to blow, and death to death, from the hand of Oscar and mine.

But Swaran closed round Morni's son, as the strength of the tide of Inistore. The king half rose from his hill at the sight. He half–assumed the spear. "Go, Ullin, go, my aged bard," began the king of Morven. "Remind the mighty Gaul of war. Remind him of his fathers. Support the yielding fight with song; for song enlivens war." Tall Ullin went, with step of age, and spoke to the king of swords. "Son of the chief of generous steeds! high–bounding king of spears! Strong arm in every perilous toil! Hard heart that never yields! Chief of the pointed arms of death! Cut down the foe; let no white sail bound round dark Inistore. Be thine arm like thunder, thine eyes like fire, thy heart of solid rock. Whirl round thy sword as a meteor at night: lift thy shield like the flame of death. Son of the chief of generous steeds, cut down the foe! Destroy!" The hero's heart beat high. But Swaran came with battle. He cleft the shield of Gaul in twain. The sons of Selma fled.

Fingal at once arose in arms. Thrice he reared his dreadful voice. Cromla answered around. The sons of the desert stood still. They bent their blushing faces to earth, ashamed at the presence of the king. He came like a cloud of rain in the day of the sun, when slow it rolls on the hill, and fields expect the shower. Silence attends its slow progress aloft; but the tempest is soon to rise. Swaran beheld the terrible king of Morven. He stopped in the midst of his course. Dark he leaned on his spear, rolling his red eyes around. Silent and tall he seemed as an oak on the banks of Lubar, which had its branches blasted of old by the lightning of heaven. It bends over the stream: the gray moss whistles in the wind: so stood the king. Then slowly he retired to the rising heath of Lena. His thousands pour round the hero. Darkness gathers on the hill!

Fingal, like a beam of heaven, shone in the midst of his people. His heroes gather around him. He sends forth the voice of his power. "Raise my standards on high; spread them on Lena's wind, like the flames of a hundred hills! Let them sound on the wind of Erin, and remind us of the fight. Ye sons of the roaring streams, that pour from a thousand hills be near the king of Morven! attend to the words of his power! Gaul, strongest arm of death! O Oscar, of the future fights! Connal, son of the blue shields of Sora! Dermid, of the dark–brown hair! Ossian, king of many songs, be near your father's arm!" We reared the sunbeam of battle; the standard of the king! Each hero exulted with joy, as, waving, it flew on the wind. It was studded with gold above, as the blue wide shell of the nightly sky. Each hero had his standard too, and each his gloomy men!

"Behold," said the king of generous shells, "how Lochlin divides on Lena! They stand like broken clouds on a hill, or a half–consumed grove of oaks, when we see the sky through its branches, and the meteor passing behind! Let every chief among the friends of Fingal take a dark troop of those that frown so high: nor let a son of the echoing groves bound on the waves of Inistore!"

"Mine," said Gaul, "be the seven chiefs that came from Lano's lake." "Let Inistore's dark king," said Oscar, "come to the sword of Ossian's son." "To mine the king of Iniscon," said Connal, heart of steel!" Or Mudan's chief or I," said brown–haired Dermid, "shall sleep on clay–cold earth." My choice, though now so weak and dark, was Terman's battling king; I promised with my hand to win the hero's dark–brown shield, "Blest and victorious be my chiefs," said Fingal of the mildest look. "Swaran, king of roaring waves, thou art the choice of Fingal!"

Now, like a hundred different winds that pour through many vales, divided, dark the sons of Selma advanced. Cromla echoed around! How can I relate the deaths, when we closed in the strife of arms? O, daughter of Toscar, bloody were our hands! The gloomy ranks of Lochlin fell like the banks of roaring Cona! Our arms were victorious on Lena: each chief fulfilled his promise. Beside the murmur of Branno thou didst often sit, O maid! thy white bosom rose frequent, like the down of the swan when slow she swims on the lake, and sidelong winds blow on her ruffled wing. Thou hast seen the sun retire, red and slow behind his cloud: night gathering round on the mountain, while the unfrequent blast roared in the narrow vales. At length the rain beats hard: thunder rolls in peals. Lightning glances on the rocks! Spirits ride on beams of fire! The strength of the mountain streams comes roaring down the hills. Such was the noise of battle, maid of the arms of snow! Why. daughter of Toscar, why that tear? The maids of Lochlin have cause to weep! The people of their country fell. Bloody were the blue swords of the race of my heroes! But I am sad, forlorn, and blind: no more the corn ion of heroes! Give, lovely maid to me thy tears. I have seen the tombs of all my friends!

It was then, by Fingal's hand, a hero fell, to his grief! Gray– haired he rolled in the dust. He lifted his faint eyes to the king. "And is it by me thou hast fallen," said the son of Comhal, "thou friend of Agandecca? I have seen thy tears for the maid of my love in the halls of the bloody Starno! Thou hast been the foe of the foes of my love, and hast thou fallen by my hand? Raise Ullin, raise the grave of Mathon, and give his name to Agandecca's song. Dear to my soul hast thou been, thou darkly–dwelling maid of Ardven!"

Cuthullin, from the cave of Cromla, heard the noise of the troubled war. He called to Connal, chief of swords: to Carril of other times. The gray–haired heroes heard his voice. They took their pointed spears. They came, and saw the tide of battle, like ocean's crowded waves, when the dark wind blows from the deep, and rolls the billows through the sandy vale! Cuthullin kindled at the sight. Darkness gathered on his brow. His hand is on the sword of his fathers: his red–rolling eyes on the foe. He thrice attempted to rush to battle. He thrice was stopped by Connal. "Chief of the isle of mist," he said, "Fingal subdues the foe. Seek not a part of the fame of the king; himself is like the storm!"

"Then, Carril, go," replied the chief, "go greet the king of Morven. When Lochlin falls away like a stream after rain; when the noise of the battle is past; then be thy voice sweet in his ear to praise the king of Selma! Give him the sword of Caithbat. Cuthullin is not worthy to lift the arms of his fathers! Come, o ye ghosts of the lonely Cromla! ye souls of chiefs that are no more! be near the steps of Cuthullin; talk to him in the cave of his grief. Never more shall I be renowned among the mighty in the land. I am a beam that has shone; a mist that has fled away when the blast of the morning came, and brightened the shaggy side of the hill. Connal, talk of arms no more! departed is my fame. My sighs shall be on Cromla's wind, till my footsteps cease to be seen. And thou, white–bosomed

Bragla! mourn over the fall of my fame: vanquished, I will never return to thee, thou sunbeam of my soul!"

Fingal's standard was distinguished by the name of "sunbeam", probably on account of its bright colour, and its being studded with gold. To begin a battle is expressed, in old composition, by "lifting of the sunbeam."

FINGAL — BOOK V.

ARGUMENT.

Cuthullin and Connal still remain on the hill. Fingal and Swaran meet: the combat is described. Swaran is overcome, bound, and delivered over as a prisoner to the care of Ossian, and Gaul, the son of Morni; Fingal, his younger sons and Oscar still pursue the enemy. The episode of Orla, a chief of Lochlin, who was mortally wounded in the battle, is introduced. Fingal, touched with the death of Orla, orders the pursuit to be discontinued; and calling his sons together, he is informed that Ryno, the youngest of them, was slain. He laments his death, hears the story of Lamderg and Gelchossa, and returns towards the place where he had left Swaran. Carril, who had been sent by Cuthullin to congratulate Fingal on his victory, comes in the mean time to Ossian. The conversation of the two poets closes the action of the fourth day.

On Cromla's resounding side Connal spoke to the chief of the noble car. Why that gloom, son of Semo? Our friends are the mighty in fight. Renowned art thou, O warrior! many were the deaths of thy steel. Often has Bragla met, with blue−rolling eyes of joy: often has she met her hero returning in the midst of the valiant, when his sword was red with slaughter, when his foes were silent in the fields of the tomb. Pleasant to her ears were thy bards, when thy deeds, arose in song.

But behold the king of Morven! He moves, below, like a pillar of fire. His strength is like the stream of Lubar, or the wind of the echoing Cromla, when the branchy forests of night are torn from all their rocks. Happy are thy people, O Fingal! thine arm shall finish their wars. Thou art the first in their dangers: the wisest in the days of their peace. Thou speakest, and thy thousands obey: armies tremble at the sound of thy steel. Happy are thy people, O Fingal! king of resounding Selma. Who is that so dark and terrible coming in the thunder of his course? who but Starno's son, to meet the king of Morven? Behold the battle of the chiefs! it is the storm of the ocean, when two spirits meet far distant, and contend for the rolling of waves. The hunter hears the noise on his bill. He sees the high billows advancing to Ardven's shore.

Such were the words of Connal when the heroes met in fight. There was the clang of arms! there every blow, like the hundred hammers of the furnace! Terrible is the battle of the kings; dreadful the look of their eyes. Their dark–brown shields are cleft in twain. Their steel flies, broken, from their helms. They fling their weapons down. Each rushes to his hero's grasp; their sinewy arms bend round each other: they turn from side to side, and strain and stretch their large–spreading limbs below. But when the pride of their strength arose they shook the hill with their heels. Rocks tumble from their places on high; the green– headed bushes are overturned. At length the strength of Swaran fell; the king of the groves is bound. Thus have I seen on Cona; but Cona I behold no more! thus have I seen two dark hills removed from their place by the strength of their bursting stream. They turn from side to side in their fall; their tall oaks meet one another on high. Then they tumble together with all their rocks and trees. The streams are turned by their side. The red ruin is seen afar. "Sons of distant Morven, "said Fingal, "guard the king of Lochlin. He is strong as his thousand waves. His hand is taught to war. His race is of the times of old. Gaul, thou first of my heroes; Ossian, king of songs attend. He is the friend of Agandecca; raise to joy his grief. But Oscar, Fillan, and Ryno, ye children of the race, pursue Lochlin over Lena, that no vessel may hereafter bound on the dark–rolling waves of Inistore."

They flew sudden across the heath. He slowly moved, like a cloud of thunder, when the sultry plain of summer is silent and dark. His sword is before him as a sunbeam; terrible as the streaming meteor of night. He came towards a chief of Lochlin. He spoke to the son of the wave. — "Who is that so dark and sad, at the rock of the roaring stream? He cannot bound over its course. How stately is the chief! His bossy shield is on his side; his spear like the tree f the desert. Youth of the dark–red hair, art thou of the foes of Fingal?"

"I am a son of Lochlin," he cries; "strong is my arm in war. My spouse is weeping at home. Orla shall never return!" "Or fights or yields the hero?" said Fingal of the noble deeds; "foes do not conquer in my presence: my friends are renowned in the hall. Son of the wave, follow me: partake the feast of my shells: pursue the deer of my desert: be thou the friend of Fingal." "No," said the hero: "I assist the feeble. My strength is with the

107

weak in arms. My sword has been always unmatched, O warrior! let the king of Morven yield!" "I never yielded, Orla. Fingal never yielded to man. Draw thy sword, and choose thy foe. Many are my heroes!"

"Does then the king refuse the fight?" said Orla of the dark– brown shield. "Fingal is a match for Orla; and he alone of all his race! But, king of Morven, if I shall fall, as one time the warrior must die; raise my tomb in the midst: let it be the greatest on Lena. Send over the dark–blue wave, the sword of Orla to the spouse of his love, that she may show it to her son, with tears to kindle his soul to war." "Son of the mournful tale," said Fingal, "why dost thou awaken my tears! One day the warriors must die, and the children see their useless arms in the hall. But, Orla, thy tomb shall rise. Thy white–bosomed spouse shall weep over thy sword."

They fought on the heath of Lena. Feeble was the arm of Orla. The sword of Fingal descended, and cleft his shield in twain. It fell and glittered on the ground, as the moon on the ruffled stream. "King of Morven," said the hero, "lift thy sword and pierce my breast. Wounded and faint from battle, my friends have left me here. The mournful tale shall come to my love on the banks of the streamy Lota, when she is alone in the wood, and the rustling blast in the leaves!"

"No," said the king of Morven: "I will never wound thee, Orla. On the banks of Lota let her see thee, escaped from the hands of war. Let thy gray–haired father, who, perhaps, is blind with age, let him hear the sound of thy voice, and brighten within his hall. With joy let the hero rise, and search for the son with his hands!" "But never will he find him, Fingal," said the youth of the streamy Lota: "on Lena's heath I must die: foreign bards shall talk of me. My broad belt covers my wound of death. I give it to the wind!"

The dark blood poured from his side; he fell pale on the heath of Lena. Fingal bent over him as he died, and. called his younger chiefs. "Oscar and Fillan, my sons, raise high the memory of Orla. Here let the dark–haired hero rest, far from the spouse of his love. Here let him rest in his narrow house, far from the sound of Lota. The feeble will find his bow at home, but will not be able to bend it. His faithful dogs howl on his hills; his boars which he used to pursue, rejoice. Fallen is the arm of battle! the mighty among the valiant is low! Exalt the voice, and blow the horn, ye sons of the king of Morven! Let us go back to Swaran, to send the night away in song. Fillan, Oscar, and Ryno, fly over the heath of Lena. Where, Ryno, art thou, young son of fame? thou art not wont to be the last to answer thy father's voice!"

"Ryno," said Ullin, first of bards, "is with the awful forms of his fathers. With Trathal, king of shields; with Trenmor of mighty deeds. The youth is low, the youth is pale, he lies on Lena's heath!" "Fell the swiftest of the race," said the king, "the first to bend the bow? Thou scarce hast been known to me! Why did young Ryno fall? But sleep thou softly on Lena; Fingal shall soon behold thee. Soon shall my voice be heard no more, and my footsteps cease to be seen. The bards will tell of Fingal's name. The stones will talk of me. But, Ryno, thou art low, indeed: thou hast not received thy fame. Ullin, strike the harp for Ryno; tell what the chief would have been. Farewell, thou first in every field. No more shall I direct thy dart. Thou that hast been so fair! I behold thee not. Farewell." The tear is on the cheek of the king, for terrible was his son in war. His son that was like a beam of fire by night on a hill, when the forests sink down in its course, and the traveller trembles at the sound. But the winds drive it beyond the steep. It sinks from sight, and darkness prevails.

"Whose fame is in that dark–green tomb?" began the king of generous shells: "four stones with their heads of moss stand there. They mark the narrow house of death. Near it let Ryno rest. A neighbor to the brave let him lie. Some chief of fame is here, to fly with my son on clouds. O Ullin! raise the songs of old. Awake their memory in their tomb. If in the field they never fled, my son shall rest by their side. He shall rest, far distant from Morven, on Lena's resounding plains."

"Here," said the bard of song, "here rest the first of heroes. Silent is Lamderg in this place, dumb is Ullin, king of swords. And who, soft smiling from her cloud, shows me her face of love? Why, daughter, why so pale art thou, first of the maids of Cromla? Dost thou sleep with the foes in battle, white–bosomed daughter of Tuathal? Thou hast been the love of thousands, but Lamderg was thy love. He came to Tura's mossy towers, and striking his dark buckler, spoke: 'Where is Gelchossa, my love, the daughter of the noble Tuathal? I left her in the hall of Tura, when I fought with the great Ulfada. Return soon, O Lamderg! she said, for here I sit in grief. Her white breast rose with sighs. Her cheek was wet with tears. But I see her not coming to meet me to soothe my soul after war. Silent is the hull of my joy. I near not the voice of the bard. Bran does not shake his chains at the gate, glad at the coming of Lamderg. Where is Gelchossa, my love, the mild daughter of generous Tuathal?'

109

"'Lamderg,' says Ferchios, son of Aidon, 'Gelchossa moves stately on Cromla. She and the maids of the bow pursue the flying deer!' 'Ferchios!' replied the chief of Cromla, 'no noise meets the ear of Lamderg! No sound is in the woods of Lena. No deer fly in my sight. No panting dog pursues. I see not Gelchossa, my love, fair as the full moon setting on the hills.. Go, Ferchios, go to Allad, the gray–haired son of the rock. His dwelling is in the circle of stones He may know of the bright Gelchossa!'

"The son of Aidon went. He spoke to the ear of age. 'Allad, dweller of rocks, thou that tremblest alone, what saw thine eyes of age?' 'I saw,' answered Allad the old, 'Ullin the son of Cairbar. He came, in darkness, from Cromla. He hummed a surly song, like a blast in a leafless wood. He entered the hall of Tura. "Lamderg," he said, "most dreadful of men, fight or yield to Ullin." "Lamderg," replied Gelchossa, "the son of battle is not here. He fights Ulfada, mighty chief. He is not here, thou first of men! But Lamderg never yields. He will fight the son of Cairbar!" "Lovely thou," said terrible Ullin, "daughter of the generous Tuathal. I carry thee to Cairbar's halls. The valiant shall have Gelchossa. Three days I remain on Cromla, to wait that son of battle, Lamderg. On the fourth Gelchossa is mine, if the mighty Lamderg flies."'

"'Allad,' said the chief of Cromla, 'peace to thy dreams in the cave! Ferchios, sound the horn of Lamderg, that Ullin may hear in his halls.' Lamderg, like a roaring storm ascended the hill from Tura. He hummed a surly song as he went, like the noise of a falling stream. He darkly stood upon the hill, like a cloud varying its form to the wind. He rolled a stone, the sign of war. Ullin heard in Cairbar's hall. The hero heard, with joy, his foe. He took his father's spear. A smile brightens his dark–brown cheek, as he places his sword by his side. The dagger glittered in his hand, he whistled as he went.

"Gelchossa saw the silent chief, as a wreath of mist ascending the hill. She struck her white and heaving breast; and silent, tearful, feared for Lamderg. 'Cairbar, hoary chief of shells,' said the maid of the tender hand, 'I must bend the bow on Cromla. I see the dark–brown hinds.' She hasted up the hill. In vain the gloomy heroes fought. Why should I tell to Selma's king how wrathful heroes fight? Fierce Ullin fell. Young Lamderg came, all pale, to the daughter of generous Tuathal! 'What blood, my love;' she trembling said, 'what blood runs down my warrior's side?' ' It is Ullin's blood,' the chief replied, 'thou fairer than the snow! Gelchossa, let me rest here a little while.' The mighty Lamderg died! 'And sleepest thou so soon on earth, O chief of shady Tura?' Three days she mourned beside her love. The hunters found her cold. They raised this tomb above the three. Thy son, O king of Morven, may rest here with heroes!"

"And here my son shall rest," said Fingal. "The voice of their fame is in mine ears. Fillan and Fergus, bring hither Orla, the pale youth of the stream of Lota! not unequalled shall Ryno lie in earth, when Orla is by his side. Weep, ye daughters of Morven! ye maids of the streamy Lota, weep! Like a tree they grew on the hills. They have fallen like the oak of the desert, when it lies across a stream, and withers in the wind. Oscar, chief of every youth, thou seest how they have fallen. Be thou like them on earth renowned. Like them the song of bards. Terrible were their forms in battle; but calm was Ryno in the days of peace. He was like the bow of the shower seen far distant on the stream, when the sun is setting on Mora, when silence dwells on the hill of deer. Rest, youngest of my sons! rest, O Ryno! on Lena. We too shall be no more. Warriors one day must fall!"

Such was thy grief, thou king of swords, when Ryno lay on earth. What must the grief of Ossian be, for thou thyself art gone! I hear not thy distant voice on Cona. My eyes perceive thee not. Often forlorn and dark I sit at thy tomb, and feel it with my hands. When I think I hear thy voice, it is but the passing blast. Fingal has long since fallen asleep, the ruler of the war!

Then Gaul and Ossian sat with Swaran, on the soft green banks of Lubar. I touched the harp to please the king; but gloomy was his brow. He rolled his red eyes towards Lena. The hero mourned his host. I raised mine eyes to Cromla's brow. I saw the son of generous Semo. Sad and slow he retired from his hilt, towards the lonely cave of Tura. He saw Fingal victorious, and mixed his joy with grief. The sun is bright on his armor. Connal slowly strode behind. They sunk behind the hill, like two pillars of the fire of night, when winds pursue them over the mountain, and the flaming death resounds! Beside a stream of roaring foam his cave is in a rock. One tree bends above it. The rushing winds echo against its sides. Here rests the chief of Erin, the son of generous Semo. His thoughts are on the battles he lost. The tear is on his cheek. He mourned the departure of his fame, that fled like the mist of Cona. O Bragla! thou art too far remote to cheer the soul of the hero. But let him see thy bright form in his mind, that his thoughts may return to the lonely sunbeam of his love!

Who comes with the locks of age? It is the son of songs. "Hail, Carril of other times! Thy voice is like the harp in the halls of Tura. Thy words are pleasant as the shower which falls on the sunny field. Carril of the times of old, why comest thou from the son of the generous Semo?"

"Ossian, king of swords," replied the bard, "thou best canst raise the song. Long hast thou been known to Carril, thou ruler of war! Often have I touched the harp to lovely Everallin. Thou too hast often joined my voice in Branno's hall of generous shells. And often, amidst our voices, was heard the mildest Everallin. One day she sung of Cormac's fall, the youth who died for her love. I saw the tears on her cheek, and on thine, thou chief of men. Her soul was touched for the unhappy, though she loved him not. How fair among a thousand maids was the daughter of generous Branno!"

Bring not, Carril," I replied, "bring not her memory to my mind. My soul must melt at the remembrance. My eyes must have their tears. Pale in the earth is she, the softly–blushing fair of my love! But sit thou on the heath, O bard! and let us hear thy voice. It is pleasant as the gale of spring, that sighs on the hunter's ear, when he awakens from dreams of joy, and has heard the music of the spirits of the hill!"

FINGAL — BOOK VI.

ARGUMENT.

Night comes on. Fingal gives a feast to his army, at which Swaran is present. The king commands Ullin his bard to give "the song of peace;" a custom always observed at the end of a war. Ullin relates the actions of Trenmor, great–grandfather to Fingal, in Scandinavia, and his marriage with Inibaca, the daughter of a king of Lochlin, who was ancestor to Swaran; which consideration, together with his being brother to Agandecca, with whom Fingal was in love in his youth, induced the king to release him, and permit him to return with the remains of his army into Lochlin, upon his promise of never returning to Ireland in a hostile manner. The night is spent in settling Swaran's departure, in songs of bards, and in a conversation in which the story of Grumal is introduced by Fingal. Morning comes. Swaran departs. Fingal goes on a hunting party, and finding Cuthullin in the cave of Tura, comforts him, and sets sail the next day for Scotland, which concludes the poem.

THE clouds of night came rolling down. Darkness rests on the steeps of Cromla. The stars of the north arise over the rolling of Erin's waves; they show their heads of fire through the flying mist of heaven. A distant wind roars in the wood. Silent and dark is the plain of death! Still on the dusky Lena arose in my ears the voice of Carril. He sung of the friends of our youth; the days of former years; when we met on the banks of Lego; when we sent round the joy of the shell. Cromla answered to his voice. The ghosts of those he sung came in their rustling winds. They were seen to bend with joy, towards the sound of their praise!

Be thy soul blest, O Carril! in the midst of thy eddying winds. O that thou wouldst come to my hall, when I am alone by night! And thou dost come, my friend. I hear often thy light hand on my harp, when it hangs on the distant wall, and the feeble sound touches my ear. Why dost thou not speak to me in my grief: and tell when I shall behold my friends? But thou passest away in thy murmuring blast; the wind whistles through the gray hair of Ossian!

Now, on the side of Mora, the heroes gathered to the feast. A thousand aged oaks are burning to the wind. The strength of the shell goes round. The souls of warriors brighten with joy. But the king of Lochlin is silent. Sorrow reddens in the eyes of his pride. He often turned towards Lena. He remembered that he fell. Fingal leaned on the shield of his fathers. His gray locks slowly waved on the wind, and glittered to the beam of night. He saw the grief of Swaran, and spoke to the first of bards.

"Raise, Ullin, raise the song of peace. O soothe my soul from war! Let mine ear forget, in the sound, the dismal noise of arms. Let a hundred harps be near to gladden the king of Lochlin. He must depart from us with joy. None ever went sad from Fingal. Oscar! the lightning of my sword is against the strong in fight. Peaceful it lies by my side when warriors yield in war."

"Trenmor," said the mouth of songs, "lived in the days of other years. He bounded over the waves of the north; companion of the storm! The high reeks of the land of Lochlin, its groves of murmuring sounds, appeared to the hero through mist; he bound his white. bosomed sails. Trenmor pursued the boar that roared through the woods of Gormal. Many had fled from its presence; but it rolled in death on the spear of Trenmor. Three chiefs, who beheld the deed, told of the mighty stranger. They told that he stood, like a pillar of fire, in the bright arms of his valor. The king of Lochlin prepared the feast. He called the blooming Trenmor. Three days he feasted at Gormal's windy towers, and received his choice in the combat. The land of Lochlin had no hero that yielded not to

113

Trenmor. The shell of joy went round with songs in praise of the king of Morven. He that came over the waves, the first of mighty men.

"Now when the fourth gray morn arose, the hero launched his ship. He walked along the silent shore, and called for the rushing wind; for loud and distant he heard the blast murmuring behind the groves. Covered over with arms of steel, a son of the woody Gormal appeared. Red was his cheek, and fair his hair. His skin was like the snow of Morven. Mild rolled his blue and smiling eye, when he spoke to the king of swords.

"'Stay, Trenmor, stay, thou first of men; thou hast not conquered Lonval's son. My sword has often met the brave. The wise shun the strength of my bow.' 'Thou fair–haired youth,' Trenmor replied, 'I will not fight with Lonval's son. Thine arm is feeble, sunbeam of youth! Retire to Gormal's dark–brown hinds.' 'But I will retire,' replied the youth, 'with the sword of Trenmor; and exult in the sound of my fame. The virgins shall gather with smiles around him who conquered mighty Trenmor. They shall sigh with the sighs of love, and admire the length of thy spear: when I shall carry it among thousands; when I lift the glittering point to the sun.'

"'Thou shalt never carry my spear,' said the angry king of Morven. 'Thy mother shall find thee pale on the shore; and looking over the dark–blue deep, see the sails of him that slew her son!' 'I will not lift the spear,' replied the youth, 'my arm is not strong with years. But with the feathered dart I have learned to pierce a distant foe. Throw down that heavy mail of steel. Trenmor is covered from death. I first will lay my mail on earth. Throw now thy dart, thou king of Morven!' He saw the heaving of her breast. It was the sister of the king. She had seen him in the hall: and loved his face of youth. The spear dropt from the hand of Trenmor: he bent his red cheek to the ground. She was to him a beam of light that meets the sons of the cave; when they revisit the fields of the sun, and bend their aching eyes!

"'Chief of the windy Morven,' began the maid of the arms of snow, 'let me rest in thy bounding ship, far from the love of Corlo. For he, like the thunder of the desert, is terrible to Inibaca. He loves me in the gloom of pride. He shakes ten thousand spears!' – – ' Rest thou in peace,' said the mighty Trenmor, 'rest behind the shield of my fathers. I will not fly from the chief, though he shakes ten thousand spears.' Three days he waited on the shore. He sent his horn abroad. He called Corlo to battle, from all his echoing hills. But Corlo came not to battle. The king of Lochlin descends from his hall. He feasted on the roaring shore. He gave the maid to Trenmor!"

"King of Lochlin," said Fingal, "thy blood flows in the veins of thy foe. Our fathers met in battle, because they loved the strife of spears. But often did they feast in the hall, and send round the joy of the shell. Let thy thee brighten with gladness, and thine ear delight in the harp. Dreadful as the storm of thine ocean, thou hast poured thy valor forth; thy voice has been like the voice of thousands when they engage in war. Raise, to—morrow, raise thy white sails to the wind, thou brother of Agandecca! Bright as the beam of noon, she comes on my mournful soul. I have seen thy tears for the fair one. I spared thee in the halls of Starno; when my sword was red with slaughter: when my eye was full of tears for the maid. Or dost thou choose the fight? The combat which thy fathers gave to Trenmor is thine! that thou mayest depart renowned, like the sun setting in the west!"

"King of the race of Morven!" said the chief of resounding Lochlin, "never will Swaran fight with thee, first of a thousand heroes! I have seen thee in the halls of Starno; few were thy years beyond my own. When shall I, I said to my soul, lift the spear like the noble Fingal? We have fought heretofore, O warrior, on the side of the shaggy Malmor; after my waves had carried me to thy halls, and the feast of a thousand shells was spread. Let the bards send his name who overcame to future years, for noble was the strife of Malmor! But many of the ships of Lochlin have lost their youths on Lena. Take these, thou king of Morven, and be the friend of Swaran! When thy sons shall come to Gormal, the feast of shells shall be spread, and the combat offered on the vale." "Nor ship," replied the king, "shall Fingal take, nor land of many hills. The desert is enough to me, with all its deer and woods. Rise on thy waves again, thou noble friend of Agandecca! Spread thy white sails to the beam of the morning; return to the echoing hills of Gormal." — "Blest be thy soul, thou king of shells," said Swaran of the dark—brown shield." In peace thou art the gale of spring; in war the mountain storm. Take now my hand in friendship, king of echoing Selma! Let thy bards mourn those who fell. Let Erin give the sons of Lochlin to earth. Raise high the mossy stones of their fame: that the children of the north hereafter may behold the place where their fathers fought. The hunter may say, when he leans on a mossy tomb, Here Fingal and Swaran fought, the heroes of other years. Thus hereafter shall he say, and our fame shall last for ever."

"Swaran," said the king of hills, "to—day our fame is greatest. We shall pass away like a dream. No sound will remain in our fields of war. Our tombs will be lost in the heath. The hunter shall not know the place of our rest. Our names may be heard in song. What avails it, when our strength hath ceased? O Ossian, Carril, and Ullin! you know of heroes that are no more. Give us the song of other years. Let the night pass away on the sound, and morning return with joy."

We gave the song to the kings. A hundred harps mixed their sound with our voice. The face of Swaran brightened, like the full moon of heaven; when the clouds vanish away, and leave her calm and broad in the midst of the sky.

"Where, Carril," said the great Fingal, "Carril of other times! where is the son of Semo, the king of the isle of mist? Has he retired like the meteor of death, to the dreary cave of Tura?" — "Cuthullin," said Carril of other times, "lies in the dreary cave of Tura. His hand is on the sword of his strength. His thoughts on the battles he lost. Mournful is the king of spears: till now unconquered in war. He sends his sword, to rest on the side of Fingal: for, like the storm of the desert, thou hast scattered all his foes. Take, O Fingal! the sword of the hero. His fame is departed like mist, when it flies, before the rustling wind, along the brightening vale."

"No," replied the king, "Fingal shall never take his sword. His arm is mighty in war: his fame shall never fail. Many have been overcome in battle; whose renown arose from their fall. O Swaran, king of resounding woods, give all thy grief away. The vanquished, if brave, are renowned. They are like the sun in a cloud, when he hides his face in the south, but looks again on the hills of grass."

"Grumal was a chief of Cona. He sought the battle on every coast. His soul rejoiced in blood; his ear in the din of arms. He poured his warriors on Craca; Craca's king met him from his grove; for then, within the circle of Brumo, he spoke to the stone of power. Fierce was the battle of the heroes, for the maid of the breast of snow. The fame of the daughter of Craca had reached Grumal at the streams of Cona; he vowed to have the white– bosomed maid, or die on echoing Craca. Three days they strove together, and Grumal on the fourth was bound. Far from his friends they placed him in the horrid circle of Brumo; where often, they said, the ghosts of the dead howled round the stone of their fear. But he afterward shone, like a pillar of the light of heaven. They fell by his mighty hand. Grumal had all his fame!

"Raise, ye bards of other times," continued the great Fingal, "raise high the praise of heroes: that my soul may settle on their fame; that the mind of Swaran may cease to be sad." They lay in the heath of Mora. The dark winds rustled over the chiefs. A hundred voices, at once, arose; a hundred harps were strung. They sung of other times; the mighty chiefs of former years! When now shall I hear the bard? When rejoice at the fame of my fathers? The harp is not strung on Morven. The voice of music ascends not on Cona. Dead, with the mighty, is the bard. Fame is in the desert no more."

Morning trembles with the beam of the east; it glimmers on Cromla's side. Over Lena is heard the horn of Swaran. The sons of the ocean gather around. Silent and sad they rise on the wave. The blast of Erin is behind their sails. White, as the mist of Morven, they float along the sea. "Call," said Fingal, "call my dogs, the long–bounding sons of the chase. Call white–breasted Bran, and the surly strength of Luath! Fillan, and Ryno; — but he is not here! My son rests on the bed of death. Fillan and Fergus! blow the horn, that the joy of the chase may arise; that the deer of Cromla may hear, and start at the lake of roes."

The shrill sound spreads along the wood. The sons of heathy Cromla arise. A thousand dogs fly off at once, gray– bounding through the heath. A deer fell by every dog; three by the white–breasted Bran. He brought them, in their flight, to Fingal, that the joy of the king might be great! One deer fell at the tomb of Ryno. The grief of Fingal returned. He saw how peaceful lay the stone of him, who was the first at the chase! "No more shalt thou rise, O my son! to partake of the feast of Cromla. Soon will thy tomb be hid, and the grass grow rank on thy grave. The sons of the feeble shall pass along. They shall not know where the mighty lie.

"Ossian and Fillan, sons of my strength! Gaul, chief of the blue steel of war! Let us ascend the hill to the cave of Tura. Let us find the chief of the battles of Erin. Are these the walls of Tura? gray and lonely they rise on the heath. The chief of shells is sad, and the halls are silent and lonely. Come, let us find Cuthullin, and give him all our joy. But is that Cuthullin, O Fillan, or a pillar of smoke on the heath? The wind of Cromla is on my eyes. I distinguish not my friend."

"Fingal!" replied the youth, "it is the son of Semo! Gloomy and sad is the hero! his hand is on his sword. Hail to the son of battle, breaker of the shields!" "Hail to thee," replied Cuthullin, "hail to all the sons of Morven! Delightful is thy presence, O Fingal! it is the sun on Cromla: when the hunter mourns his absence for a season, and sees him between the clouds. Thy sons are like stars that attend thy course. They give light in the night! It is not thus thou hast seen me, O Fingal! returning from the wars of thy land: when the kings of the world had fled, and joy returned to the hills of hinds!"

"Many are thy words, Cuthullin," said Connan of small renown. "Thy words are many, son of Semo, but where are thy deeds in arms? Why did we come, over ocean, to aid thy feeble sword? Thou fliest to thy cave of grief, and Connan fights thy battles. Resign to me these arms of light. Yield them, thou chief of Erin." — "No hero," replied the chief," ever sought the arms of Cuthullin! and had a thousand heroes sought them, it were in vain, thou gloomy youth! I fled not to the cave of grief, till Erin failed at her streams."

"Youth of the feeble arm," said Fingal, "Connan, cease thy words! Cuthullin is renowned in battle: terrible over the world. Often have I heard thy fame, thou stormy chief of Inis–fail. Spread now thy white sails for the isle of mist. See Bragla leaning on her rock. Her tender eye is in tears, the winds lift her long hair from her heaving breast. She listens to the breeze of night, to hear the voice of thy rowers; to hear the song of the sea; the sound of thy distant harps."

"Long shall she listen in vain. Cuthullin shall never return. How can I behold Bragla, to raise the sigh of her breast? Fingal, I was always victorious, in battles of other spears." — "And hereafter thou shalt be victorious," said Fingal of generous shells. "The fame of Cuthullin shall grow, like the branchy tree of Cromla. Many battles await thee, O chief! Many shall be the wounds of thy hand! Bring hither, Oscar, the deer! Prepare the feast of shells; Let our souls rejoice after danger, and our friends delight in our presence."

We sat. We feasted. We sung. The soul of Cuthullin rose. The strength of his arm returned. Gladness brightened along his face. Ullin gave the song; Carril raised the voice. I joined the bards, and sung of battles of the spear. Battles! where I often fought. Now I fight no more! The fame of my former deeds is ceased. I sit forlorn at the tombs of my friends!

Thus the night passed away in song. We brought back the morning with joy. Fingal arose on the heath, and shook his glittering spear. He moved first to wards the plains of Lena. We followed in all our arms. "Spread the sail," said the king, "seize the winds as they pour from Lena." We rose on the wave with songs. We rushed, with joy, through the foam of the deep.

LATHMON.

ARGUMENT.

Lathmon, a British prince, taking advantage of Fingal's absence on an expedition to Ireland, made a descent on Morven, and advanced within sight of Selma, the royal residence. Fingal arrived in the mean time, and Lathmon retreated to a hill, where his army was surprised by night, and himself taken prisoner by Ossian and Gaul the son of Morni. The poem opens with the first appearance of Fingal on the coast of Morven, and ends, it may be supposed, about noon the next day.

SELMA, thy halls are silent. There is no sound in the woods of Morven. The wave tumbles along on the coast. The silent beam of the sun is on the field. The daughters of Morven come forth, like the bow of the shower; they look towards green Erin for the white sails of the king. He had promised to return, but the winds of the north arose!

Who pours from the eastern hill, like a stream of darkness? It is the host of Lathmon. He has heard of the absence of Fingal. He trusts in the winds of the north. His soul brightens with joy. Why dost thou come, O Lathmon? The mighty are not in Selma. Why comest thou with thy forward spear? Will the daughters of Morven fight? But stop, O mighty stream, in thy course! Does not Lathmon behold these sails? Why dost thou vanish, Lathmon, like the mist of the lake? But the squally storm is behind thee; Fingal pursues thy steps!

The king of Morven had started from sleep, as we rolled on the dark−blue wave. He stretched his hand to his spear, his heroes rose around. We knew that he had seen his fathers, for they often descended to his dreams, when the sword of the foe rose over the land and the battle darkened before us. "Whither hast thou fled, O wind?" said the king of Morven. "Dost thou rustle in the chambers of the south? pursuest thou the shower in other lands? Why dost thou not come to my sails? to the blue face of my seas? The foe is in the land of Morven, and the king is absent far. But let each bind on his mail, and each assume his shield. Stretch every spear over the wave; let every sword be unsheathed. Lathmon is before us with his host; he that fled from Fingal on the plains of Lona. But he returns like a collected stream, and his roar is between our hills."

Such were the words of Fingal. We rushed into Carmon's bay. Ossian ascended the hill! he thrice struck his bossy shield. The rock of Morven replied: the bounding roes came forth. The foe was troubled in my presence: he collected his darkened host. I stood like a cloud on the hill, rejoicing in the arms of my youth.

Morni sat beneath a tree on the roaring waters of Strumon: his locks of age are gray: he leans forward on his staff; young Gaul is near the hero, hearing the battles of his father. Often did he rise in the fire of his soul, at the mighty deeds of Morni. The aged heard the sound of Ossian's shield; he knew the sign of war. He started at once from his place. His gray hair parted on his back. lie remembered the deeds of other years.

"My son," he said, to fair-haired Gaul, "I hear the sound of war. The king of Morven is returned; his signals are spread on the wind. Go to the halls of Strumon; bring his arms to Morni. Bring the shield of my father's latter years, for my arm begins to fail. Take thou thy armor, O Gaul! and rush to the first of thy battles. Let thine arm reach to the renown of thy fathers. Be thy course in the field like the eagle's wing. Why shouldst thou fear death, my son? the valiant fall with fame; their shields turn the dark stream of danger away; renown dwells on their aged hairs. Dost thou not see, O Gaul! low the steps of my age are honored? Morni moves forth. and the young men meet him, with silent joy, on his course. But I never fled from danger, my son! my sword lightened through the darkness of war. The stranger melted before me; the mighty were blasted in my presence."

Gaul brought the arms to Morni: the aged warrior is covered with steel. He took the spear in his hand, which was stained with the blood of the valiant. He came towards Fingal; his son attended his steps. The son of Comhal arose before him with joy, when he came in his locks of age.

"Chief of the roaring Strumon!" said the rising soul of Fingal; "do I behold thee in arms, after thy strength has failed? Often has Morni shone in fight, like the beam of the ascending sun; when he disperses the storms of the hill, and brings peace to the glittering fields. But why didst thou not rest in thine age? Thy renown is in the song. The people behold thee, and bless the departure of mighty Morni. Why didst thou not rest in thine age? The foe will vanish before Fingal!" "Son of Comhal," replied the chief, "the strength of Morni's arm has failed. I attempt to draw the sword of my youth, but it remains in its place. I throw the spear, but it falls short of the mark. I feel the weight of my shield. We decay like the grass of the hill; our strength returns no more. I have a son, O Fingal! his soul has delighted in Morni's deeds; but his sword has not been lifted against a foe, neither has his fame begun. I come with him to the war; to direct his arm in fight. His renown will be a light to my soul in the dark hour of my departure. O that the name of Morni were forgot among the people! that the heroes would only say, 'Behold the father of Gaul!'"

"King of Strumon," Fingal replied, "Gaul shall lift the sword in fight. But he shall lift it before Fingal; my arm shall defend his youth. But rest thou in the halls of Selma, and hear of our renown. Bid the harp to be strung, and the voice of the bard to arise, that those who fall may rejoice in their fame, and the soul of Morni brighten with joy. Ossian, thou hast fought in battles: the blood of strangers is on thy spear: thy course be with Gaul in the strife; but depart not from the side of Fingal, lest the foe should find you alone, and your fame fail in my presence."

[Ossian speaks] "I saw Gaul in his arms; my soul was mixed with his. The fire of the battle was in his eyes! he looked to the foe with joy. We spoke the words of friendship in secret; the lightning of our swords poured together; for we drew them behind the wood, and tried the strength of our arms on the empty air!"

Night came down on Morven. Fingal sat at the beam of the oak. Morni sat by his side with all his gray–waving locks. Their words were of other times, of the mighty deeds of their fathers. Three bards, at times, touched the harp: Ullin was near with his song. He sung of the mighty Comhal; but darkness gathered on Morni's brow. He rolled his red eye on Ullin: at once ceased the song of the bard. Fingal observed the aged hero, and he mildly spoke: "Chief of Strumon, why that darkness? Let the days of other years be forgot. Our fathers contended in war; but we meet together at the feast. Our swords are turned on the foe of our land: he melts before us on the field. Let the days of our fathers be forgot, hero of mossy Strumon!"

King of Morven," replied the chief, "I remember thy father with joy. He was terrible in battle, the rage of the chief was deadly. My eyes were full of tears when the king of heroes fell. The valiant fall, O Fingal! the feeble remain on the hills! How many heroes have passed away in the days of Morni! Yet I did not shun the battle; neither did I fly from the strife of the valiant. Now let the friends of Fingal rest, for the night is around, that they may rise with strength to battle against car–borne Lathmon. I hear the sound of his host, like thunder moving on the hills. Ossian! and fair–haired Gaul! ye are young and swift in the race. Observe the foes of Fingal from that woody hill. But approach them not: your fathers are near to shield you. Let not your fame fall at once. The valor of youth may fail!"

We heard the words of the chief with joy. We moved in the clang of our arms. Our steps are on the woody hill. Heaven burns with all its stars. The meteors of death fly over the field. The distant noise of the foe reached our ears. It was than Gaul spoke, in his valor: his hand half unsheathed his sword.

"Son of Fingal!" he said, "why burns the soul of Gaul? my heart beats high. My steps are disordered; my hand trembles on my sword. When I look towards the foe, my soul lightens before me. I see their sleeping host. Tremble thus the souls of the valiant in battles of the spear? How would the soul of Morni rise if we should rush on the foe? Our renown should grow in song: our steps would be stately in the eyes of the brave."

"Son of Morni," I replied, "my soul delights in war. I delight to shine in battle alone, to give my name to the bards. But what if the foe should prevail? can I behold the eyes of the king? They are terrible in his displeasure, and like the flames of death. But I will not behold them in his wrath! Ossian shall prevail or fall. But shall the fame of the vanquished rise? They pass like a shade away. But the fame of Ossian shall rise! His deeds shall be like his father's. Let us rush in our arms; son of Morni, let us rush to fight. Gaul, if thou shouldst return, go to Selma's lofty hall. Tell to Everallin that I fell with fame; carry this sword to Branno's daughter. Let her give it to Oscar, when the years of his youth shall arise."

"Son of Fingal," Gaul replied with a sigh, "shall I return after Ossian is low? What would my father say? what Fingal, the king of men? The feeble would turn their eyes and say, 'Behold Gaul, who left his friend in his blood!' Ye shall not behold me, ye feeble, but in the midst of my renown! Ossian, I have heard from my father the mighty deeds of heroes; their mighty deeds when alone! for the soul increases in danger!"

"Son of Morni," I replied, and strode before him on the heath, "our fathers shall praise our valor when they mourn our fall. A beam of gladness shall rise on their souls, when their eyes are full of tears. They will, say, 'Our sons have not fallen unknown: they spread death around them.' But why should we think of the narrow house? The sword defends the brave. But death pursues the flight of the feeble; their renown is never heard."

We rushed forward through night; we came to the roar of a stream, which bent its blue course round the foe, through trees that echoed to its sound. We came to the bank of the stream, and saw the sleeping host. Their fires were decayed on the plain: the lonely steps of their scouts were distant far. I stretched my spear before me, to support my steps over the stream. But Gaul took my hand, and spoke the words of the brave. "Shall the son of Fingal rush on the sleeping foe? Shall he come like a blast by night, when it overturns the young trees in secret? Fingal did no receive his fame, nor dwells renown on the gray hairs of Morni, for actions like these. Strike, Ossian, strike the shield, and let their thousands rise! Let them meet Gaul in his first battle, that he may try the strength of his arm."

My soul rejoiced over the warrior; my bursting tears came down. "And the foe shall meet thee, Gaul," I said: "the fame of Morni's son shall arise. But rush not too far, my hero: let the gleam of thy steel be near to Ossian. Let our hands join in slaughter. Gaul! dost thou not behold that rock? Its gray side dimly gleams to the stars. Should the foe prevail, let our back be towards the rock. Then shall they fear to approach our spears; for death is in our hands!"

I struck thrice my echoing shield. The startling foe arose. We rushed on in the sound of our arms. Their crowded steps fly over the heath. They thought that the mighty Fingal was come. The strength of their arms withered away. The sound of their flight was like that of flame, when it rushes through the blasted groves. It was then the spear of Gaul flew in its strength; it was then his sword arose. Cramo fell; and mighty Leth! Dunthormo struggled in his blood. The steel rushed through Crotho's side, as bent he rose on his spear; the black stream poured from the wound, and hissed on the half–extinguished oak. Cathmin saw the steps of the hero behind him: he ascended a blasted tree; but the spear pierced him from behind. Shrieking, panting, he fell. Moss and withered branches pursue his fall, and strew the blue arms of Gaul.

Such were thy deeds, son of Morni, in the first of thy battles. Nor slept the sword by thy side, thou last of Fingal's race! Ossian rushed forward in his strength; the people fell before him; as the grass by the stall of the boy, when he whistles along the field, and the gray beard of the thistle falls. But careless the youth moves on; his steps are towards the desert. Gray morning rose around us; the winding streams are bright along the heath. The foe gathered on a bill; and the rage of Lathmon rose. He bent the red eye of his wrath: he is silent in his rising grief. He often struck his bossy shield: and his steps are unequal on the heath. I saw the distant darkness of the hero, and I spoke to Morni's son.

"Car–borne chief of Strumon, dost thou behold the foe? 'They gather on the hill in their wrath. Let our steps be toward the king. He shall rise in his strength, and the host of Lathmon vanish. Our fame is around us, warrior; the eyes of the aged will rejoice. But let us fly, son of Morni, Lathmon descends the hill." "Then let our steps be slow," replied the fair– haired Gaul;" lest the foe say with a smile, 'Behold the warriors of night! They are, like ghosts, terrible in darkness; they melt away before the beam of the east.' Ossian, take the shield of Gormar, who fell beneath thy spear. The aged heroes will rejoice, beholding the deeds of their sons."

Such were our words on the plain, when Sulmath came to car–borne Lathmon: Sulmath chief of Datha, at the dark–rolling stream of Duvranna." Why dost thou not rush, son of Nuth, with a thousand of thy heroes? Why dost thou not descend with thy host before the warriors fly? Their blue arms are beaming to the rising light, and their steps are before us on the heath!" "Son of the feeble hand," said Lathmon," shall my host descend? They are but two, son of Dutha! shall a thousand lift the steel? Nuth would mourn in his hall, for the departure of his fame. His eyes would turn from Lathmon, when the tread of his feet approached. Go thou to the heroes, chief of Dutha! I behold the stately steps of Ossian. His fame is worthy of my steel! let us contend in fight."

The noble Sulmath came. I rejoiced in the words of the king. I raised the shield on my arm: Gaul placed in my hand the sword of Morni. We returned to the murmuring stream; Lathmon came down in his strength. His dark host rolled, like clouds, behind him; but the son of Nuth was bright in his steel.

"Son of Fingal," said the hero, "thy fame has grown on our fall. How many lie there of my people by thy hand, thou king of men! Lift now thy spear against Lathmon; lay the son of Nuth low! Lay him low among his warriors, or thou thyself must fall! It shall never be told in my halls, that my people fell in my presence: that they fell in the presence of Lathmon when his sword rested by his side: the blue eyes of Couth would roll in tears; her steps be lonely in the vales of Dunlathmon!"

"Neither shall it be told," I replied, "that the son of Fingal fled. Were his steps covered with darkness, yet would not Ossian fly! His soul would meet him and say, 'Does the bard of Selma fear the foe?" No: he does not fear the foe. His joy is in the midst of battle."

Lathmon came on with his spear. He pierced the shield of Ossian. I felt the cold steel by my side. I drew the sword of Morni. I cut the spear in twain. The bright point fell glittering on earth. The son of Nuth burnt in his wrath. He lifted high his sounding shield. His dark eyes rolled above it, as bending forward, it shone like a gate of brass. But Ossian's spear pierced the brightness of its bosses, and sunk in a tree that rose behind. The shield hung on the quivering lance! But Lathmon still advanced! Gaul foresaw the fall of the chief. He stretched his buckler before my sword, when it descended, in a stream of light, over the king of Dunlathmon!

Lathmon beheld the son of Morni. The tear started from his eye. He threw the sword of his fathers on the earth, and, spoke the words of the brave.

"Why should Lathmon fight against the first of men? Your souls are beams from heaven; your swords the flames of death! Who can equal the renown of the heroes, whose deeds are so great in youth? O that ye were in the halls of Nuth, in the green dwelling of Lathmon! Then would my father say that his son did not yield to the weak. But who comes, a mighty stream, along the echoing heath? The little hills are troubled before him. A thousand ghosts are on the beams of his steel; the ghosts of those who are to fall by the king of resounding Morven. Happy art thou, O Fingal! thy son shall fight thy wars. They go forth before thee: they return with the steps of their renown!"

Fingal came in his mildness, rejoicing in secret over the deeds of his son. Morni's face brightened with gladness. His aged eyes look faintly through tears of joy. We came to the halls of Selma. We sat around the feasts of shells. The maids of song came in to our presence, and the mildly–blushing Everallin! Her hair spreads on her neck of snow, her eye rolls in secret on Ossian. She touched the harp of music! we blessed the daughter of Branno!

Fingal rose in his place, and spoke to Lathmon, king of spears. The sword of Trenmor shook by his side, as high he raised his mighty arm Son of Nuth," he said, "why dost thou search for fame in Morven? We are not of the race of the feeble; our swords gleam not over the weak. When did we rouse thee, O Lathmon, with the sound of war? Fingal does not delight in battle, though his arm is strong! My renown grows on the fall of the haughty. The light of my steel pours on the proud in arms. The battle comes! and the tombs of the valiant rise; the tombs of my people rise, O my fathers! I at last must remain alone! But I will remain renowned: the departure of my soul shall be a stream of light.

Lathmon! retire to thy place! Turn thy battles to other lands! The race of Morven are renowned; their foes are the sons of the unhappy."

DAR–THULA

ARGUMENT.

It may not be improper here to give the story which is the foundation of this poem, as it is handed down by tradition. Usnoth, lord of Etha, which is probably that part of Argyleshire which is near Loch Eta, an arm of the sea in Lorn, had three sons, Nathos, Althos, and Ardan, by Sliss ma, the daughter of Semo, and sister to the celebrated Cuthullin. The three brothers, when very young, were sent over to Ireland by their father, to learn the use of arms under their uncle Cuthullin, who made a great figure in that kingdom. They were just landed in Ulster, when the news of Cuthullin's death arrived. Nathos, though very young, took the command of Cuthullin's army, made head against Cairbar the usurper, and defeated him in several battles. Cairbar at last, having found means to murder Cormac, the lawful king, the army of Nathos shifted sides, and he himself was obliged to return into Ulster, in order to pass over into Scotland.

Dar–thula, the daughter of Colla, with whom Cairbar was in love, resided at that time in Sel ma, a castle in Ulster. She saw, fell in love, and fled with Nathos; but a storm rising at sea, they were unfortunately driven back on that part of the coast of Ulster, where Cairbar was encamped with his army. The three brothers, after having defended themselves for some time with great bravery, were overpowered and slain, and the unfortunate Dar–thula killed herself upon the body of her beloved Nathos. The poem opens, on the night preceding the death of the sons of Usnoth, and brings in, by way of episode, what passed before. it relates the death of Dar–thula differently from the common tradition. This account, is the most probable, as suicide seems to have been unknown in those early times, for no traces of it are found in the old poetry.

DAUGHTER of heaven, fair art thou! the silence of thy face is pleasant! Thou comest forth in loveliness. The stars attend thy blue course in the east. The clouds rejoice in thy presence, O moon! They brighten their dark–brown sides. Who is like thee in heaven, light of the silent night? The stars are shamed in thy presence. They turn away their sparkling eyes. Whither dost thou retire from thy course when the darkness of thy countenance grows? Hast thou thy hall, like Ossian? Dwellest thou in the shadow of grief? Have thy sisters fallen from heaven? Are they who rejoiced with thee, at night, no more? Yes, they have fallen, fair light! and thou dost often retire to mourn. But thou thyself shalt fail one night and leave thy blue path in heaven. The stars will then lift their heads: they who were ashamed in thy presence, will rejoice. Thou art now clothed with thy brightness. Look from thy gates in the sky. Burst the cloud, O wind! that the daughters of night may look forth; that the shaggy mountains may brighten, and the ocean roll its white waves in light!

Nathos is on the deep, and Althos, that beam of youth! Ardan is near his brothers. They move in the gloom of their course. The sons of Usnoth move in darkness, from the wrath of Cairbar of Erin. Who is that, dim by their side? The night has covered her beauty! Her hair sighs on ocean's wind. Her robe streams in dusky wreaths. She is like the fair spirit of heaven in the midst of the shadowy mist. Who is it but Dar–thula, the first of Erin's maids? She has fled from the love of Cairbar, with blue– shielded Nathos. But the winds deceive thee, O Dar–thula! They deny the woody Etha to thy sails. These are not the mountains of Nathos; nor is that the roar of his climbing waves. The halls of Cairbar are near: the towers of the foe lift their heads! Erin stretches its green head into the sea. Tura's bay receives the ship. Where have ye been, ye southern Winds, when the sons of my love were deceived? But ye have been sporting on the plains, pursuing the thistle's beard. O that ye had been rustling in the sails of Nathos, till the hills of Etha arose! till they arose in their clouds, and saw their returning chief! Long hast thou been absent, Nathos! the day of thy return is past!

But the land of strangers saw thee lovely! thou wast lovely in the eyes of Dar–thula. Thy face was like the light of the morning. Thy hair like the raven's wing. Thy soul was generous and mild, like tho hour of the setting sun. Thy words were the gale of the reeds; the gliding stream of Lora! But when the rage of battle rose, thou wast a sea in a storm. The clang of thy arms was terrible: the host vanished at the sound of thy course. It was then Dar–thula beheld thee, from the top of her mossy tower; from the tower of Sel ma, where her fathers dwelt.

"Lovely art thou, O stranger!" she said, for her trembling soul arose. "Fair art thou in thy battles, friend of the fallen Cormac! Why dost thou rush on in thy valor, youth of the ruddy look? Few are thy hands in fight against the dark–brown Cairbar! O that I might be freed from his love, that I might rejoice in the presence of Nathos! Blest are the rocks of

Etha! they will behold his steps at the chase; they will see his white bosom, when the winds lift his flowing hair!" Such were thy words, Dar–thula, in Sel ma's mossy towers. But now the night is around thee. The winds have deceived thy sails– — the winds have deceived thy sails, Dar–thula! Their blustering sound is high. Cease a little while, O north wind! Let me hear the voice of the lovely. Thy voice is lovely, Dar–thula, between the rustling blasts!

"Are these the rocks of Nathos?" she said, "this the roaring of his mountain streams? Comes that beam of light from Usnoth's nightly hall? The mist spreads around; the beam is feeble and distant far. But the light of Dar–thula's soul dwells in the chief of Etha! Son of the generous Usnoth, why that broken sigh? Are we in the land of strangers, chief of echoing Etha?"

"These are not the rocks of Nathos," he replied, "nor this the roar of his stream. No light comes from Etha's hall, for they are distant far. We are in the land of strangers, in the land of cruel Cairbar. The winds have deceived us, Dar–thula. Erin lifts here her hills. Go towards the north, Althos: be thy steps, Ardan, along the coast; that the foe may not come in darkness, and our hopes of Etha fail. I will go towards that mossy tower, to see who dwells about the beam. Rest, Dar–thula, on the shore! rest in peace, thou lovely light! the sword of Nathos is around thee, like the lightning of heaven!"

He went. She sat alone: she heard the roiling of the wave. The big tear is in her eye. She looks for returning Nathos. Her soul trembles at the bast. She turns her ear towards the tread of his feet. The tread of his feet is not heard. "Where art thou, son of my love! The roar of the blast is around me. Dark is the cloudy night. But Nathos does not return. What detains thee, chief of Etha? Have the foes met the hero in the strife of the night?"

He returned; but his face was dark. He had seen his departed friend! it was the wall of Tura. The ghost of Cuthullin stalked there alone; the sighing of his breast was frequent. The decayed flame of his eyes was terrible! His spear was a column of mist. The stars looked dim through his form. His voice was like hollow wind in a cave: his eye a light seen afar. He told the tale of grief. The soul of Nathos was sad, like the sun in the day of mist, when his face watery and dim.

"Why art thou sad, O Nathos!" said the lovely daughter of Colla. "Thou art a pillow of light to Dar–thula. The joy of her eyes is in Etha's chief. Where is my friend, but Nathos?

THE POEMS OF OSSIAN

My father, my brother is fallen! Silence dwells on Sel ma. Sadness spreads on the blue streams of my land. My friends have fallen with Cormac. The mighty were slain in the battles of Erin. Hear, son of Usnoth! hear, O Nathos! my tale of grief.

"Evening darkened on the plain. The blue streams failed before mine eyes. The unfrequent blast came rustling in the tops of Sel ma's groves. My seat was beneath a tree, on the walls of my fathers. Truthil past before my soul; the brother of my love: he that was absent in battle against the haughty Cairbar! Bending on his spear, the gray-haired Colla came. His downcast face is dark, and sorrow dwells in his soul. His sword is on the side of the hero; the helmet of his fathers on his head. The battle grows in his breast. He strives to hide the tear.

"'Dar-thula, my daughter,' he said, 'thou art the last of Colla's race! Truthil is fallen in battle. The chief of Sel ma is no more! Cairbar comes, with his thousands, towards Sel ma's walls. Colla will meet his pride, and revenge his son. But where shall I find thy safety, Dar-thula with the dark-brown hair! thou art lovely as the sunbeam of heaven, and thy friends are low!' 'Is the son of battle fallen?' I said, with a bursting sigh. 'Ceased the generous soul of Truthil to lighten through the field? My safety, Colla, is in that bow. I have learned to pierce the deer. Is not Cairbar like the hart of the desert, father of fallen Truthil?'

"The face of age brightened with joy. The crowded tears of his eyes poured down. The lips of Colla trembled. His gray beard whistled in the blast. 'Thou art the sister of Truthil,' he said; 'thou burnest in the fire of his soul. Take, Dar-thula, take that spear, that brazen shield, that burnished helm; they are the spoils of a warrior, a son of early youth! When the light rises on Sel ma, we go to meet the car-borne Cairbar. But keep thou near the arm of Colla, beneath the shadow of my shield. Thy father, Dar-thula, could once defend thee; but age is trembling On his hand. The strength of his arm has failed. His soul is darkened with grief.'

"We passed the night in sorrow. The light of morning rose. I shone in the arms of battle. The gray haired hero moved before. The sons of Sel ma convened around the sounding shield of Colla. But few were they in the plain, and their locks were gray. The youths had fallen with Truthil, in the battle of car-borne Cormac. 'Friends of my youth,' said Colla, 'it was not thus you have seen me in arms. It was not thus I strode to battle when the great Confaden fell. But ye are laden with grief. The darkness of age comes like the mist of the

129

desert. My shield is worn with years! my sword is fixed in its place! I said to my soul, Thy evening shall be calm; thy departure like a fading light. But the storm has returned. I bend like an aged oak. My boughs are fallen on Sel ma. I tremble in my place. Where art thou, with thy fallen heroes, O my beloved Truthil! Thou answerest not from thy rushing blast. The soul of thy father is sad. But I will be sad no more! Cairbar or Colla must fall! I feel the returning strength of my arm. My heart leaps at the sound of war.'

"The hero drew his sword. The gleaming blades of his people rose. They moved along the plain. Their gray hair streamed in the wind. Cairbar sat at the feast, in the silent plain of Lena. He saw the coming of the heroes. He called his chiefs to war. Why should I tell to Nathos how the strife of battle grew? I have seen thee in the midst of thousands, like the beam of heaven's fire: it is beautiful, but terrible; the people fall in its dreadful course. The spear of Colla flew. He remembered the battles of his youth. An arrow came with its sound. It pierced the hero's side. He fell on his echoing shield. My soul started with fear. I stretched my buckler over him: but my heaving breast was seen! Cairbar came with his spear. He beheld Sel ma's maid. Joy rose on his dark–brown Taco. He stayed his lifted steel. He raised the tomb of Colla. He brought me weeping to Sel ma. He spoke the words of love, but my soul was sad. I saw the shields of my fathers; the sword of car–borne Truthil. I saw the arms of the dead; the tear was on my cheek! Then thou didst come, O Nathos! and gloomy Cairbar fled. He fled like the ghost of the desert before the morning's beam. His host was not near; and feeble was his arm against thy steel! Why art thou sad, O Nathos?" said the lovely daughter of Colla.

"I have met," replied the hero, "the battle in my youth. My arm could not lift the spear when danger first arose. My soul brightened in the presence of war, as the green narrow vale, when the sun pours his streamy beams, before he hides his head in a storm. The lonely traveller feels a mournful joy. He sees the darkness that slowly comes. My soul brightened in danger before I saw Sel ma's fair; before I saw thee, like a star that shines on the hill at night; the cloud advances, and threatens the lovely light! We are in the land of foes. The winds have deceived us, Dar–thula! The strength of our friends is not near, nor the mountains of Etha. Where shall I find thy peace, daughter of mighty Colla! The brothers of Nathos are brave, and his own sword has shone in fight. But what are the sons of Usnoth to the host of dark–brown Cairbar! O that the winds had brought thy sails, Oscar king of men! Thou didst promise to come to the battles of fallen Cormac! Then would my hand be strong as the flaming arm of death. Cairbar would tremble in his halls, and peace dwell round the lovely Dar–thula. But why dost thou fall, my soul? The sons of Usnoth may prevail!"

"And they will prevail, O Nathos!" said the rising soul of the maid. "Never shall Dar–thula behold the halls of gloomy Cairbar. Give me those arms of brass, that glitter to the passing meteor. I see them dimly in the dark–bosomed ship. Dar–thula will enter the battles of steel. Ghost of the noble Colla! do I behold thee on that cloud! Who is that dim beside thee? Is it the car–borne Truthil? Shall I behold the halls of him that slew Sel ma's chief? No: I will not behold them, spirits of my love!"

Joy rose in the face of Nathos when he heard the white– bosomed maid. "Daughter of Sel ma! thou shinest along my soul. Come, with thy thousands, Cairbar! the strength of Nathos is returned! Thou O aged Usnoth! shalt not hear that thy son has fled. I remembered thy words on Etha, when my sails began to rise: when I spread them towards Erin, towards the mossy walls of Tura! 'Thou goest,' he said, 'O Nathos, to the king of shields! Thou goest to Cuthullin, chief of men, who never fled from danger. Let not thine arm be feeble: neither be thy thoughts of flight; lest the son of Semo should say that Etha's race are weak. His words may come to Usnoth, and sadden his soul in the hall.' The tear was on my father's cheek. He gave this shining sword!

"I came to Tura's bay; but the halls of Tara were silent. I looked around, and there was none to tell of the son of generous Semo. I went to the hall of shells, where the arms of his fathers hung. But the arms were gone, and aged Lamhor sat in tears. 'Whence are the arms of steel?' said the rising Lamhor. 'The light of the spear has long been absent from Tura's dusky walls. Come ye from the rolling sea? or from Temora's mournful halls?'

"'We come from the sea,' I said, 'from Usnoth's rising towers. We are the sons of Sliss ma, the daughter of car–borne Semo. Where is Tura's chief, son of the silent hall? But why should Nathos ask? for I behold thy tears. How did the mighty fall, son of the lonely Tura?' 'He fell not,' Lamhor replied, 'like the silent star of night, when it flies through darkness and is no more. But he was like a meteor that shoots into a distant land. Death attends its dreary course. Itself is the sign of wars. Mournful are the banks of Lego; and the roar of streamy Lara! There the hero fell, son of the noble Usnoth!' 'The hero fell in the midst of slaughter,' I said with a bursting sigh. 'His hand was strong in war. Death dimly sat behind his sword.'

"We came to Lego's sounding banks. We found his rising tomb. His friends in battle are there: his bards of many songs. Three days we mourned over the hero: on the fourth I struck the shield of Caithbat. The heroes gathered around with joy, and shook their beamy spears. Corlath was near with his host, the friend of car–borne Cairbar. We came like a stream by night. His heroes fell before us. When the people of the valley rose, they saw their blood with morning's light. But we rolled away, like wreaths of mist, to Cormac's echoing hall. Our swords rose to defend the king. But Temora's halls were empty. Cormac had fallen in his youth. The king of Erin was no more!

"Sadness seized the sons of Erin. They slowly gloomily retired: like clouds that long having threatened rain, vanish behind the hills. The sons of Usnoth moved, in their grief, towards Tura's sounding bay. We passed by Sel ma. Cairbar retired like Lena's mist, when driven before the winds. It was then I beheld thee, O Dar–thula! like the light of Etha's sun. 'Lovely is that beam!' I said. The crowded sigh of my bosom rose. Thou camest in thy beauty, Dar–thula, to Etha's mournful chief. But the winds have deceived us, daughter of Colla, and the foe is near!"

"Yes, the foe is near," said the rushing strength of Althos." I heard their clanging arms on the coast. I saw the dark wreaths of Erin's standard. Distinct is the voice of Cairbar; loud as Cromla's falling stream. He had seen the dark ship on the sea, before the dusky night came down. His people watch on Lena's plain. They lift ten thousand swords." "And let them lift ten thousand swords," said Nathos with a smile." The sons of car–borne Usnoth will never tremble in danger! Why dost thou roll with all thy foam, thou roaring sea of Erin? Why do ye rustle on your dark wings, ye whistling storms of the sky? Do ye think, ye storms, that ye keep Nathos on the coast? No: his soul detains him, children of the night! Althos, bring my father's arms: thou seest them beaming to the stars. Bring the spear of Semo. It stands in the dark– bosomed ship!"

He brought the arms. Nathos covered his limbs in all their shining steel. The stride of the chief is lovely. The joy of his eyes was terrible. He looks towards the coming of Cairbar. The wind is rustling in his hair. Dar–thula is silent at his side. Her look is fixed on the chief. She strives to hide the rising sigh. Two tears swell in her radiant eyes! "Althos!" said the child of Etha, "I see a cave in that rock. Place Dar–thula there. Let thy arm, my brother, be strong. Ardan! we meet the foe; call to battle gloomy Cairbar. O that he came in his sounding steel, to meet the son of Usnoth! Dar–thula, if thou shalt escape, look not on the fallen Nathos! Lift thy sails, O Althos! towards the echoing groves of my land.

132

"Tell the chief that his son fell with fame; that my sword did not shun the fight. Tell him I fell in the midst of thousands. Let the joy of his grief be great. Daughter of Colla! call the maids to Etha's echoing hall! Let their songs arise for Nathos, when shadowy autumn returns. O that the voice of Cona, that Ossian might be heard in my praise! then would my spirit rejoice in the midst of the rushing winds." "And my voice shall praise thee, Nathos, chief of the woody Etha! The voice of Ossian shall rise in thy praise, son of the generous Usnoth! Why was I not on Lena when the battle rose? Then would the sword of Ossian defend thee, or himself fall low!"

We sat that night in Selma, round the strength of the shell. The wind was abroad in the oaks. The spirit of the mountain roared. The blast came rustling through the hall, and gently touched my harp. The sound was mournful and low, like the song of the tomb. Fingal heard it the first. The crowded sighs of his bosom rose. "Some of my heroes are low," said the gray– haired king of Morven. "I hear the sound of death on the harp. Ossian, touch the trembling string. Bid the sorrow rise, that their spirits may fly with joy to Morven's woody hills!" I touched the harp before the king; the sound was mournful and low. "Bend forward from your clouds," I said, "ghosts of my fathers! bend. Lay by the red terror of your course. Receive the fallen chief; whether he comes from a distant land, or rises from the rolling sea. Let his robe of mist be near; his spear that is formed of a cloud. Place an half–extinguished meteor by his side, in the form of the hero's sword. And, oh! let his countenance be lovely, that his friends may delight in his presence. Bend from your clouds," I said, "ghosts of my fathers! bend!"

Such was my song in Selma, to the lightly–trembling harp. But Nathos was on Erin's shore, surrounded by the night. He heard the voice of the foe, amidst the roar of tumbling waves. Silent he heard their voice, and rested on his spear! Morning rose, with its beams. The sons of Erin appear: like gray rocks, with all their trees, they spread along the coast. Cairbar stood in the midst. He grimly smiled when he saw the foe. Nathos rushed forward in his strength: nor could Dar–thula stay behind. She came with the hero, lifting her shining spear. "And who are these, in their armor, in the pride of youth? Who but the sons of Usnoth, Althos and dark–haired Ardan?"

"Come," said Nathos, "come, chief of high Temora! Let our battle be on the coast, for the white bosomed maid. His people are not with Nathos: they are behind these rolling seas. Why dost thou bring thy thousands against the chief of Etha? Thou didst fly from him in battle, when his friends were around his spear." "Youth of the heart of pride, shall Erin's king fight with thee? Thy fathers were not among the renowned, nor of the kings of men. Are the arms of foes in their halls? or the shields of other times? Cairbar is renowned in Temora, nor does he fight with feeble men

The tear started from car-borne Nathos. He turned his eyes to his brothers. Their spears flew at once. Three heroes lay on earth. Then the light of their swords gleamed on high. The ranks of Erin yield, as a ridge of dark clouds before a blast of wind! Then Cairbar ordered his people, and they drew a thousand bows. A thousand arrows flew. The sons of Usnoth fell in blood. They fell like three young oaks, which stood alone on the hill: the traveller saw the lovely trees, and wondered how they grew so lonely: the blast of the desert came by night, and laid their green heads low. Next day he returned, but they were withered, and the heath was bare!

Dar-thula stood in silent grief, and beheld their fall! No tear is in her eye. But her look is wildly sad. Pale was her cheek. Her trembling lips broke short an half-formed word. Her dark hair flew on wind. The gloomy Cairbar came. "Where is thy lover now? the car-borne chief of Etha? Hast thou beheld the halls of Usnoth? or the dark-brown hills of Fingal? My battle would have roared on Morven, had not the winds met Dar-thula. Fingal himself would have been low, and sorrow dwelling in Selma!" Her shield fell from Dar-thula's arm. Her breast of snow appeared. It appeared; but it was stained with blood. An arrow was fixed in her side. She fell on the fallen Nathos, like a wreath of snow! Her hair spreads wide on his face. Their blood is mixing round!

"Daughter of Colla! thou art low!" said Cairbar's hundred bards. "Silence is at the blue streams of Sel ma. Truthil's race have failed. When wilt thou rise in thy beauty, first of Erin's maids? Thy sleep is long in the tomb. The morning distant far. The sun shall not come to thy bed and say, Awake, Dar-thula! awake, thou first of women! the wind of spring is abroad. The flowers shake their heads on the green hills. The woods wave their growing leaves. Retire, O sun! the daughter of Colla is asleep. She will not come forth in her beauty. She will not move in the steps of her loveliness."

Such was the song of the bards, when they raised the tomb. I sung over the grave, when the king of Morven came: when he came to green Erin to fight with car-borne Cairbar!

It was the custom of ancient times, that every warrior, at a certain age, or when he became unfit for the field, fixed his arms in the great ball, where the tribes feasted upon joyful occasions. He was afterward never to appear in battle; and this stage of life was called "the time of fixing the arms."

By the spirit of the mountain, is meant that deep and melancholy sound which precedes a storm, well known to those who live in a high country.

THE DEATH OF CUTHULLIN.

ARGUMENT.

Cuthullin, after the arms of Fingal had expelled Swaran from Ireland, continued to manage the affairs of that kingdom as the guardian of Cormac the young king. In the third year of Cuthullin's administration, Torlath, the son of Cantela, rebelled in Connaught: and advanced to Temora to dethrone Cormac. Cuthullin marched against him, came up with him at the lake of Lego, and totally defeated his forces. Torlath fell in battle by Cuthullin's hand; but as he too eagerly pressed on the enemy, he was mortally wounded. The affairs of Cormac, though for some time supported by Nathos, as mentioned in the preceding poem, fell into confusion at the death of Cuthullin. Cormac himself was slain by the rebel Cairbar; and the re—establishment of the royal family of Ireland, by Fingal, furnishes the subject of the epic poem of Temora.

Is the wind on the shield of Fingal? Or is the voice of past times in my hall? Sing on, sweet voice! for thou art pleasant. Thou carriest away my night with joy. Sing on, O Bragla, daughter of car—borne Sorglan!

"It is the white wave of the rock, and not Cuthullin's sails. Often do the mists deceive me for the ship of my love! when they rise round some ghost, and spread their gray skirts on the wind. Why dost thou delay thy coming, son of the generous Semo? Four times has autumn returned with its winds, and raised the seas of Togorma, since thou hast been in the roar of battles, and Bragla distant far! Hills of the isle of mist! when will ye answer to his hounds? But ye are dark in your clouds. Sad Bragla calls in vain! Night comes rolling down. The face of ocean falls. The heath—cock's head is beneath his wing. The hind sleeps with the hart of the desert. They shall rise with morning's light, and feed by the mossy stream. But my tears return with the sun. My sighs come on with the night. When wilt thou come in thine arms, O chief of Erin's wars?"

THE POEMS OF OSSIAN

Pleasant is thy voice in Ossian's ear, daughter of car–borne Sorglan! But retire to the hall of shells, to the beam of the burning oak. Attend to the murmur of the sea: it rolls at Dunsci's walls: let sleep descend on thy blue eyes. Let the hero arise in thy dreams!

Cuthullin sits at Lego's lake, at the dark rolling of waters. Night is around the hero. His thousands spread on the heath. A hundred oaks burn in the midst. The feast of shells is smoking wide. Carril strikes the harp beneath a tree. His gray locks glitter in the beam. The rustling blast of night is near, and lifts his aged hair. His song is of the blue Togorma, and of its chief, Cuthullin's friend! "Why art thou absent, Connal, in the days of the gloomy storm? The chiefs of the south have convened against the car– borne Cormac. The winds detain thy sails. Thy blue waters roll around thee. But Cormac is not alone. The son of Semo fights his wars! Semo's son his battles fights! the terror of the stranger! He that is like the vapor of death, slowly borne by sultry winds. The sun reddens in its presence; the people fall around."

Such was the song of Carril, when a son of the foe appeared. He threw down his pointless spear. He spoke the words of Torlath; Torlath chief of heroes, from Lego's sable surge! He that led his thousands to battle, against car–borne Cormac. Cormac, who was distant far, in Temora's echoing halls: he learned to bend the bow of his fathers; and to lift the spear. Nor long didst thou lift the spear, mildly–shining beam of youth! death stands dim behind thee, like the darkened half of the moon behind its growing light. Cuthullin rose before the bard, that came from generous Torlath. He offered him the shell of joy. He honored the son of songs. "Sweet voice of Lego!" he said, "what are the words of Torlath? Comes he to our feast or battle, the car– borne son of Cantela?"

"He comes to thy battle," replied the bard, "to the sounding strife of spears. When morning is gray on Lego, Torlath will fight on the plain. Wilt thou meet him, in thine arms, king of the isle of mist? Terrible is the spear of Torlath! it is a meteor of night. He lifts it, and the people fall! death sits in the lightning of his sword!" — "Do I fear," replied Cuthullin, "the spear of car–borne Torlath? He is brave as a thousand heroes: but my soul delights in war! The sword rests not by the side of Cuthullin, bard of the times of old! Morning shall meet me on the plain, and gleam on the blue arms of Semo's son. But sit thou on the heath, O bard, and let us hear thy voice. Partake of the joyful shell: and hear the songs of Temora!"

"This is no time," replied the bard, "to hear the song of joy: when the mighty are to meet in battle, like the strength of the waves of Lego. Why art thou so dark, Slimora! with all thy silent woods? No star trembles on thy top. No moonbeam on thy side. But the meteors of death are there: the gray watery forms of ghosts. Why art thou dark, Slimora! why thy silent woods?" He retired, in the sound of his song. Carril joined his voice. The music was like the memory of joys that are past, pleasant and mournful to the soul. The ghosts of departed bards heard on Slimora's side. Soft sounds spread along the wood. The silent valleys of night rejoice. So when he sits in the silence of the day, in the valley of his breeze, the humming of the mountain bee comes to Ossian's ear: the gale drowns it in its course: but the pleasant sound returns again! Slant looks the sun on the field! gradual grows the shade of the hill!

"Raise," said Cuthullin to his hundred bards, "the song of the noble Fingal: that song which he hears at night, when the dreams of his rest descend; when the bards strike the distant harp, and the faint light gleams on Selma's walls. Or let the grief of Lara rise: the sighs of the mother of Calmar, when he was sought, in vain, on his hills; when she beheld his bow in the hall. Carril, place the shield of Caithbat on that branch. Let the spear of Cuthullin be near; that the sound of my battle may rise, with the gray beam of the east."

The hero leaned on his father's shield: the song of Lara rose! The hundred bards were distant far: Carril alone is near the chief. The words of the song were his: the sound of his harp was mournful.

"Alcletha with the aged locks! mother of car–borne Calmar! why dost thou look towards the desert, to behold the return of thy son? These are not his heroes, dark on the heath: nor is that the voice of Calmar. It is but the distant grove, Alcletha! but the roar of the mountain–wind — [Alcletha speaks] 'Who bounds over Lara's stream, sister of the noble Calmar? Does not Alcletha behold his spear? But her eyes are dim! Is it not the son of Matha, daughter of my love?'

"'It is but an aged oak, Alcletha!' replied the lovely weeping Alona. 'It is but an oak, Alcletha, bent over Lara's stream. But who comes along the plain? sorrow is in his speed. He lifts high the spear of Calmar. Alcletha, it is covered with blood!' —

"[Alcletha speaks] 'But it is covered with the blood of foes, sister of car–borne Calmar! His spear never returned unstained with blood: nor his bow from the strife of the mighty.

THE POEMS OF OSSIAN

The battle is consumed in his presence: he is a flame of death, Alona! — Youth of the mournful speed! where is the son of Alcletha! Does he return with his fame, in the midst of his echoing shields? Thou art dark and silent! Calmar is then no more! Tell me not, warrior, how he fell. I must not hear of his wound!' Why dost thou look towards the desert, mother of low–laid Calmar?"

Such was the song of Carril, when Cuthullin lay on his shield. The bards rested on their harps. Sleep fell softly around. The son of Semo was awake alone. His soul fixed on war. The burning oaks began to decay. Faint red light is spread around. A feeble voice is heard! The ghost of Calmar came! He stalked dimly along the beam. Dark is the wound in his side. His hair is disordered and loose. Joy sits pale on his face. He seems to invite Cuthullin to his cave.

"Son of the cloudy night!" said the rising chief of Erin; "why dost thou bend thy dark eyes on me, ghost of the noble Calmar? wouldst thou frighten me, O Matha's son! from the battles of Cormac? Thy hand was not feeble in war: neither was thy voice for peace. How art thou changed, chief of Lara! if thou now dost advise to fly! But, Calmar, I never fled. I never feared the ghosts of night. Small is their knowledge, weak their hands; their dwelling is in the wind. But my soul grows in danger, and rejoices in the noise of steel. Retire thou to thy cave. Thou art not Calmar's ghost. He delighted in battle. His arm was like the thunder of heaven! He retired in his blast with joy, for he had heard the voice of his praise."

The faint beam of the morning rose. The sound of Caithbat's buckler spread. Green Erin's warriors convened, like the roar of many streams. The horn of war is heard over Lego. The mighty Torlath came! "Why dost thou come with thy thousands, Cuthullin," said the chief of Lego." I know the strength of thy arm. Thy soul is an unextinguished fire. Why fight we not on the plain, and let our hosts behold our deeds? Let them behold us like roaring waves, that tumble round a rock; the mariners hasten away, and look on their strife with fear."

"Thou risest like the sun, on my soul, replied the son of Semo. Thine arm is mighty, O Torlath! and worthy of my wrath. Retire, ye men of Ullin, to Slimora's shady side. Behold the chief of Erin, in the day of his fame. Carril, tell to mighty Connal, if Cuthullin must fall, tell him I accused the winds, which roar on Togorma's waves. Never was he absent in battle, when the strife of my fame arose. Let his sword be before Cormac, like the beam of heaven. Let his counsel sound in Temora, in the day of danger!"

He rushed, in the sound of his arms, like the terrible spirit of Loda, when he comes, in the roar of a thousand storms, and scatters battles from his eyes. He sits on a cloud over Lochlin's seas. His mighty hand is on his sword. Winds lift his flaming locks! The waning moon half lights his dreadful face. His features blended in darkness arise to view. So terrible was Cuthullin in the day of his fame. Torlath fell by his hand. Lego's heroes mourned. They gather around the chief, like the clouds of the desert. A thousand swords rose at once; a thousand arrows flew; but he stood like a rock in the midst of a roaring sea. They fell around. He strode in blood. Dark Slimora echoed wide. The sons of Ullin came on. The battle spread over Lego. The chief of Erin overcame. He returned over the field with his fame. But pale he returned! The joy of his face was dark. He rolled his eyes in silence. The sword hung, unsheathed, in his hand. His spear bent at every step!

"Carril," said the chief in secret, "the strength of Cuthullin fails. My days are with the years that are past. No morning of mine shall arise. They shall seek me at Temora, but I shall not be found. Cormac will weep in his hall, and say, Where is Erin's chief? But my name is renowned! my fame in the song of bards. The youth will say, in secret, O let me die as Cuthullin died! Renown clothed him like a robe. The light of his fame is great. — Draw the arrow from my side. Lay Cuthullin beneath that oak. Place the shield of Caithbat near, that they may behold me amidst the arms of my fathers!"

"And is the son of Semo fallen?" said Carril with a sigh." Mournful are Tura's walls. Sorrow dwells at Dunsci. Thy spouse is left alone in her youth. The son of thy love is alone! He shall come to Bragla and ask her why she weeps! He shalt lift his eyes to the wall, and see his father's sword. Whose sword is that? he will say. The soul of his mother is sad. Who is that, like the hart of the desert, in the murmur of his course? His eyes look wildly round in search of his friend. Connal, son of Colgar, where hast thou been, when the mighty fell? Did the seas of Togorma roll around thee? Was the wind of the south in thy sails? The mighty have fallen in battle, and thou wast not there. Let none tell it in Selma, nor in Morven's woody land. Fingal will be sad, and the sons of the desert mourn!"

By the dark–rolling waves of Lego they raised the hero's tomb. Luath, at a distance, lies. The song of bards rose over the dead.

Blest be thy soul, son of Semo! Thou wert mighty in battle. Thy strength was like the strength of a stream; thy speed like the eagle's wing. Thy path in battle was terrible: the steps of death were behind thy sword. Blest be thy soul, son of Semo, car– borne chief of Dunsci! Thou hast not fallen by the sword of the mighty, neither was thy blood on the spear of the brave. The arrow came, like the sting of death in a blast: nor did the feeble hand, which drew the bow, perceive it. Peace to thy soul, in thy cave, chief of the isle of mist!

"The mighty are dispersed at Temora; there is none in Cormac's hall. The king mourns in his youth. He does not behold thy return. The sound of thy shield is ceased: his foes are gathering round. Soft be thy rest in thy cave, chief of Erin's wars! Bragla will not hope for thy return, or see thy sails in ocean's foam. Her steps are not on the shore: nor her ear open to the voice of thy rowers. She sits in the hall of shells. She sees the arms of him that is no more. Thine eyes are full of tears, daughter of car–borne Sorglan! Blest be thy soul in death, O chief of shady Tura!"

Togorma, i. e. "the island of blue waves," one of the Hebrides.

This is the song of the bards over Cuthullin's tomb.

THE BATTLE OF LORA.

ARGUMENT

Fingal, at his return from Ireland, after he had expelled Swaran from that kingdom, made a feast to all his heroes: he forgot to invite Ma–Ronnan and Aldo, two chiefs, who had not been along with him in his expedition. They resented his neglect; and went over to Erragon, king of Sora, a country of Scandinavia, the declared enemy of Fingal. The valor of Aldo soon gained him a great reputation in Sora; and Lorma, the beautiful wife of Erragon, fell in love with him. He found means to escape with her, and to come to Fingal, who resided then in Selma, on the western coast. Erragon invaded Scotland, and was slain in battle by Gaul the son of Morni, after he had rejected terms of peace offered him by Fingal. In this war Aldo fell, in a single combat, by the hands of his rival Erragon, and the unfortunate Lorma afterward died of grief.

THE POEMS OF OSSIAN

SON of the distant land, who dwellest in the secret cell; do I hear the sound of thy grove? or is it thy voice of songs? The torrent was loud in my ear; but I heard a tuneful voice. Dost thou praise the chiefs of thy land: or the spirits of the wind? But, lonely dweller of rocks! look thou on that heathy plain. Thou seest green tombs, with their rank, whistling grass, with their stones of mossy heads. Thou seest them, son of the rock, but Ossian's eyes have failed!

A mountain—stream comes roaring down, and sends its waters round a green hill. Four mossy stones, in the midst of withered grass, rear their heads on the top. Two trees which the storms have bent, spread their whistling branches around. This is thy dwelling, Erragon; this thy narrow house; the sound of thy shells has been long forgot in Sora. Thy shield is become dark in thy hall. Erragon, king of ships, chief of distant Sora! how hast thou fallen on our mountains? How is the mighty low? Son of the secret cell! dost thou delight in songs? Hear the battle of Lora. The sound of its steel is long since past. So thunder on the darkened hill roars and is no more. The sun returns with his silent beams. The glittering rocks, and the green heads of the mountains, smile.

The bay of Cona received our ships from Erin's rolling waves. Our white sheets hung loose to the masts. The boisterous winds roared behind the groves of Morven. The horn of the king is sounded; the deer start from their rocks. Our arrows flew in the woods. The feast of the hill is spread. Our joy was great on our rocks, for the fall of the terrible Swaran. Two heroes were forgot at our feast. The rage of their bosoms burned. They rolled their red eyes in secret. The sigh bursts from their breasts. They were seen to talk together, and to throw their spears on earth. They were two dark clouds in the midst of our joy; like pillars of mist on the settled sea: they glitter to the sun, but the mariners fear a storm.

"Raise my white sails," said Ma—Ronnan, "raise them to the winds of the west. Let us rush, O Aldo! through the foam of the northern wave. We are forgot at the feast: but our arms have been red in blood. Let us leave the hills of Fingal, and serve the king of Sora. His countenance is fierce. War darkens around his spear. Let us be renowned, O Aldo, in the battles of other lands!"

They took their swords, their shields of thongs. They rushed to Lumar's resounding bay. They came to Sora's haughty king, the chief of bounding steeds. Erragon had returned from the chase. His spear was red in blood. He bent his dark face to the ground; and

141

whistled as he went. He took the strangers to his feast: they fought and conquered in his wars.

Aldo returned with his fame towards Sora's lofty walls. From her tower looked the spouse of Erragon, the humid, rolling eyes of Lorma. Her yellow hair flies on the wind of ocean. Her white breast heaves, like snow on heath; when the gentle winds arise, and slowly move it in the light. She saw young Aldo, like the beam of Sora's setting sun. Her soft heart sighed. Tears filled her eyes. Her white arm supported her head. Three days she sat within the hall, and covered her grief with joy. On the fourth she fled with the hero, along the troubled sea. They came to Cona's mossy towers, to Fingal king of spears.

"Aldo of the heart of pride!" said Fingal, rising in wrath; "shall I defend thee from the rage of Sora's injured king? Who will now receive my people into their halls? Who will give the feast of strangers, since Aldo of the little soul has dishonored my name in Sora? Go to thy hills, thou feeble hand! Go: hide thee in thy caves. Mournful is the battle we must fight with Sora's gloomy king. Spirit of the noble Trenmor! when will Fingal cease to fight? I was born in the midst of battles, and my steps must move in blood to the tomb. But my hand did not injure the weak, my steel did not touch the feeble in arms. I behold thy tempests, O Morven! which will overturn my halls! when my children are dead in battle, and none remains to dwell in Selma. Then will the feeble come, but they will not know my tomb. My renown is only in song. My deeds shall be as a dream to future times!"

His people gathered around Erragon, as the storms round the ghosts of night; when he calls them from the top of Morven, and prepares to pour them on the land of the stranger. He came to the shore of Cona. He sent his bard to the king to demand the combat of thousands: or the land of many hills! Fingal sat in his hall with the friends of his youth around him. The young heroes were at the chase, far distant in the desert. The gray-haired chiefs talked of other times; of the actions of their youth; when the aged Nartmor came, the chief of streamy Lora.

"This is no time," said Nartmor, "to hear the songs of other years: Erragon frowns on the coast, and lifts ten thousand swords. Gloomy is the king among his chiefs! he is like the darkened moon amidst the meteors of night; when they sail along her skirts, and give the light that has failed o'er her orb." "Come," said Fingal, "from thy hall, come, daughter of my love: come from thy hall, Bosmina, maid of streamy Morven! Nartmor, take the steeds of the strangers. Attend the daughter of Fingal! Let her bid the king of Sora to our feast, to Selma's shaded wall. Offer him, O Bosmina! the peace of heroes, and the wealth of generous Aldo. Our youths are far distant. Age is on our trembling hands!"

She came to the host of Erragon, like a beam of light to a cloud. In her right hand was seen, a sparkling shell. In her left an arrow of gold. The first, the joyful mark of peace! The latter, the sign of war. Erragon brightened in her presence, as a rock before the sudden beams of the sun; when they issue from a broken cloud divided by the roaring wind!

"Son of the distant Sora," began the mildly–blushing maid," come to the feast of Morven's king, to Selma's shaded walls. Take the peace of heroes, O warrior! Let the dark sword rest by thy side. Choosest thou the wealth of kings? Then hear the words of generous Aldo. He gives to Erragon a hundred steeds, the children of the rein; a hundred maids from distant lands; a hundred hawks with fluttering wing, that fly across the sky. A hundred girdles shall also be thine, to bind high–bosomed maids. The friends of the births of heroes. The cure of the sons of toil. Ten shells, studded with gems, shall shine in Sora's towers: the bright water trembles on their stars, and seems to be sparkling wine. They gladdened once the kings of the world, in the midst of their echoing halls. These, O hero! shall be thine; or thy white bosomed spouse. Lorma shall roll her bright eyes in thy halls; though Fingal loves the generous Aldo: Fingal, who never injured a hero, though his arm is strong!"

"Soft voice of Cona!" replied the king, "tell him, he spreads his feast in vain. Let Fingal pour his spoils around me. Let him bend beneath my power. Let him give me the swords of his fathers: the shields of other times; that my children may behold them in my halls, and say, 'These are the arms of Fingal!'" "Never shall they behold them in thy halls," said the rising pride of the maid. "They are in the hands of heroes, who never yield in war. King of echoing Sora! the storm is gathering on our hills. Dost thou not foresee the fall of thy people, son of the distant land?"

She came to Selma's silent halls. The king beheld her downcast eyes. He rose from his place, in his strength. He shook his aged locks. He took the sounding mail of Trenmor. The dark– brown shield of his fathers. Darkness filled Selma's hall, when he stretched his hand to the spear: the ghosts of thousands were near, and foresaw the death of the people. Terrible joy rose in the face of the aged heroes. They rushed to meet the foe. Their thoughts are on the deeds of other years: and on the fame that rises from death!

Now at Trathal's ancient tomb the dogs of the chase appeared. Fingal knew that his young heroes followed. He stopped in the midst of his course. Oscar appeared the first; then Morni's son, and Nmi's race. Fercuth showed his gloomy form. Dermid spread his dark hair on wind. Ossian came the last. I hummed the song of other times. My spear supported my steps over the little streams. My thoughts were of mighty men. Fingal struck his bossy shield, and gave the dismal sign of war. A thousand swords at once, unsheathed, gleam on the waving heath. Three gray–haired sons of the song raise the tuneful, mournful voice. Deep and dark, with sounding steps, we rush, a gloomy ridge, along; like the shower of the storm when it pours on a narrow vale.

The king of Morven sat on his hill. The sunbeam of battle flew on the wind. The friends of his youth are near, with all their waving locks of age. Joy rose in the hero's eyes when he beheld his sons in war; when he saw us amidst the lightning of swords, mindful of the deeds of our fathers. Erragon came on, in his strength, like the roar of a winter stream. The battle falls around his steps: death dimly stalks along by his side.

"Who comes," said Fingal, "like the bounding roe!; like the hart of echoing Cona? His shield glitters on his side. The clang of his armor is mournful. He meets with Erragon in the strife. Behold the battle of the chiefs! It is like the contending of ghosts in a gloomy storm. But fallest thou, son of the hill, and is thy white bosom stained with blood? Weep, unhappy Lorma! Aldo is no more!" The king took the spear of his strength. He was sad for the fall at Aldo. He bent his deathful eyes on the foe: but Gaul met the king of Sora. Who can relate the light of the chiefs? The mighty stranger fell! "Sons of Cona!' Fingal cried aloud, "stop the hand of death. Mighty was he that is low. Much is he mourned in Sora! The stranger will come towards his hall, and wonder why it is so silent. The king is fallen, O stranger! The joy of his house is ceased. Listen to the sound of his woods! Perhaps his ghost is murmuring there! But he is far distant, on Morven, beneath the sword of a foreign foe." Such were the words of Fingal, when the bard raised the song of peace. We stopped our uplifted swords. We spared the feeble foe. We laid Erragon in a tomb. I raised the voice of grief. The clouds of night came rolling down. The ghost of Erragon appeared to some. His face was cloudy and dark; a half– formed sigh in his breast. "Blest be thy soul, O king of Sora! thine arm was terrible in war!"

Lorma sat in Aldo's hall. She sat at the light of a flaming oak. The night came down, but he did not return. The soul of Lorma is sad! "What detains thee, hunter of Cona? Thou didst promise to return. Has the deer been distant far? Do the dark winds sigh, round! thee, on the heath? I am in the land of strangers; who is my friend, but Aldo? Come from thy sounding hills, O my best beloved!"

Her eyes are turned towards the gate. She listens to the rustling blast. She thinks it is Aldo's tread. Joy rises in her face! But sorrow returns again, like a thin cloud on the moon. "Wilt thou not return, my love? Let me behold the face of the hill. The moon is in the east. Calm and bright is the breast of the lake! When shall I behold his dogs, returning from the chase? When shall I hear his voice, loud and distant on the wind? Come from thy sounding hills, hunter of woody Cona!" His thin ghost appeared, on a rock, like a watery beam of feeble light: when the moon rushes sudden from between two clouds, and the midnight shower is on the field. She followed the empty form over the heath. She knew that her hero fell. I heard her approaching cries on the wind, like the mournful voice of the breeze, when it sighs on the grass of the cave

She came. She found her hero! Her voice was heard no more. Silent she rolled her eyes. She was pale and wildly sad! Few were her days on Cona. She sunk into the tomb. Fingal commanded his bards; they sung over the death of Lorma. The daughters of Morven mourned her, for one day in the year, when the dark winds of autumn returned!

Son of the distant land! Thou dwellest in the field of fame! O let the song arise, at times, in praise of those who fell! Let their thin ghosts rejoice around thee; and the soul of Lorma come on a feeble beam; when thou liest down to rest, and the moon looks into thy cave. Then shalt thou see her lovely; but the tear is still on her cheek!

Comhal, the Father of Fingal, was slain in battle, against the tribe of Morni, the very day that Fingal was born; so that he may with propriety, be said to have been "born in the midst of battles."

Sanctified girdles, till very lately were kept in many families in the north of Scotland; they were bound about women in labor, and were supposed to alleviate their pains, and to accelerate the birth. They were impressed with several mystical figures, and the ceremony of binding them about the woman's waist, was accompanied with words and gestures, which showed the custom to have come originally from the Druids.

The kings of the world: the Roman emperors.

TEMORA.

AN EPIC POEM.

TEMORA — BOOK I.

ARGUMENT.

Cairbar, the son of Borbar–duthul, lord of Atha, in Connaught, the most Potent chief of the race of the Fir–bolg, having murdered, at Temora, the royal palace, Cormac, the son of Artho, the young king of Ireland, usurped the throne. Cormac was lineally descended from Conar, the son of Trenmor, the great– grandfather of Fingal, king of those Caledonians who inhabited the western coast of Scotland. Fingal resented the behavior of Cairbar, and resolved to pass over into Ireland with an army, to re–establish the royal family on the Irish throne. Early intelligence of his designs coming to Cairbar, he assembled some of his tribes in Ulster, and at the same time ordered his brother Cathmor to follow him speedily with an army from Temora. Such was the situation of affairs when the Caledonian invaders appeared on the coast of Ulster. The poem opens in the morning. Cairbar is represented as retired from the rest of the army, when one of his scouts brought him news of the landing of Fingal. He assembles a council of his chiefs. Foldath, the chief of Moma, haughtily despises the enemy; and is reprimanded warmly by Malthos. Cairbar, after hearing their debate, orders a feast to be prepared, to which, by his bard Olla, he invites Oscar, the son of Ossian; resolving to pick a quarrel with that hero, and so have some pretext for killing him. Oscar came to the feast; the quarrel happened; the followers of both fought, and Cairbar and Oscar fell by mutual wounds. The noise of the battle reached Fingal's army. The king came on to the relief of Oscar, and the Irish fell back to the army of Cathmor, who was advanced to the banks of the river Lubar, on the heath of Moi–lena. Fingal, after mourning over his grandson, ordered Ullin, the chief of his bards, to carry his body to Morven, to be there interred. Night coming on, Althan, the son of Conachar, relates to the king the particulars of the murder of Cormac. Fillan, the son of Fingal, is sent to observe the motions of Cathmor, by night, which concludes the action of the first day. The scene of this book is a plain, near the hill of Mora, which rose on the borders of the heath of Moi–lena in Ulster.

THE POEMS OF OSSIAN

THE blue waves of Erin roll in light. The mountains are covered with day. Trees shake their dusky heads in the breeze. Gray torrents pour their noisy streams. Two green hills, with aged oaks, surround a narrow plain. The blue course of a stream is there. On its banks stood Cairbar of Atha. His spear supports the king: the red eye of his fear is sad. Cormac rises in his soul, with all his ghastly wounds. The gray form of the youth appears in darkness. Blood pours from his airy side. Cairbar thrice threw his spear on earth. Thrice he stroked his beard. His steps are short. He often stops. He tosses his sinewy arms. He is like a cloud in the desert, varying its form to every blast. The valleys are sad around, and fear, by turns, the shower! The king at length resumed his soul. He took his pointed spear. He turned his eye to Moi−lena. The scouts of blue ocean came. They came with steps of fear, and often looked behind. Cairbar knew that the mighty were near. He called his gloomy chiefs.

The sounding steps of his warriors came. They drew at once their swords. There Morlath stood with darkened face. Hidalla's long hair sighs in the wind. Red−haired Cormar bends on his spear, and rolls his sidelong−looking eyes. Wild is the look of Malthos, from beneath two shaggy brows. Foldath stands, like an oozy rock, that covers its dark sides with foam. His spear is like Slimora's fir, that meets the wind of heaven. His shield is marked with the strokes of battle. His red eye despises danger. These, and a thousand other chiefs, surrounded the king of Erin, when the scout of ocean came, Mor−annal, from streamy Moi− lena, His eyes hang forward from his face. His lips are trembling pale!

"Do the chiefs of Erin stand," he said, "silent as the grove of evening? Stand they, like a silent wood, and Fingal on the coast? Fingal, who is terrible in battle, the king of streamy Morven!" "Hast thou seen the warrior?" said Cairbar with a sigh. "Are his heroes many on the coast? Lifts he the spear of battle? or comes the king in peace?" "In peace be comes not, king of Erin; I have seen his forward spear. It is a meteor of death. The blood of thousands is on its steel. He came first to the shore, strong in the gray hair of age. Full rose his sinewy limbs, as he strode in his might. That sword is by his side, which gives no second wound. His shield is terrible, like the bloody moon, ascending through a storm. Then came Ossian, king of songs. Then Morni's son, the first of men. Connal leaps forward on his spear. Dermid spreads his dark−brown locks. Fillan bends his bow, the young hunter of streamy Moruth. But who is that before them, like the terrible course of a stream? It is the son of Ossian, bright between his locks! His long hair falls on his back. His dark brows are half enclosed in steel. His sword hangs loose on his side. His spear glitters as he moves. I fled from his terrible eyes, king of high Temora!"

"Then fly, thou feeble man," said Foldath's gloomy wrath. "Fly to the gray streams of thy land, son of the little soul! Have not I seen that Oscar? I beheld the chief in war. He is of the mighty in danger: but there are others who lift the spear. Erin has many sons as brave, king of Temora of groves. Let Foldath meet him in his strength. Let me stop this mighty stream. My spear is covered with blood. My shield is like the wall of Tura!"

"Shall Foldath alone meet the foe?" replied the dark−browed Malthos? "Are they not on our coast, like the waters of many streams? Are not these the chiefs who vanquished Swaran, when the sons of green Erin fled? Shall Foldath meet their bravest hero? Foldath of the heart of pride! Take the strength of the people! and let Malthos come. My sword is red with slaughter, but who has heard my words?"

"Sons of green Erin," said Hidalla, "let not Fingal hear your words. The foe might rejoice, and his arm be strong in the land. Ye are brave, O warriors! Ye are tempests in war. Ye are like storms, which meet the rocks without fear, and overturn the woods! But let us move in our strength, slow as a gathered cloud! Then shall the mighty tremble; the spear shall fall from the hand of the valiant. We see the cloud of death, they will say, while shadows fly over their face. Fingal will mourn in his age. He shall behold his flying fame. The steps of his chiefs will cease in Morven. The moss of years shall grow in Selma!"

Cairbar heard their words in silence, like the cloud of a shower: it stands dark on Cromla, till the lightning bursts its side. The valley gleams with heaven's flame; the spirits of the storm rejoice. So stood the silent king of Temora; at length his words broke forth. "Spread the feast on Moi−lena. Let my hundred bards attend. Thou red−haired Olla, take the harp of the king. Go to Oscar, chief of swords. Bid Oscar to our joy. To−day we feast and hear the song; to−morrow break the spears! Tell him that I have raised the tomb of Cathol; that bards gave his friend to the winds. Tell him that Cairbar has heard of his fame, at the stream of resounding Carun. Cathmor, my brother, is not here. He is not here with his thousands, and our arms are weak. Cathmor is a foe to strife at the feast! His soul is bright as that sun! But Cairbar must fight with Oscar, chiefs of woody Temora, His words for Cathol were many! the wrath of Cairbar burns! He shall fall on Moi−lena. My fame shall rise in blood!"

Their faces brightened round with joy. They spread over Moi–lena. The feast of shells is prepared. The songs of bards arise. The chiefs of Selma heard their joy. We thought that mighty Cathmor came. Cathmor, the friend of strangers! the brother of red–haired Cairbar. Their souls were not the same. The light of heaven was in the bosom of Cathmor. His towers rose on the banks of Atha: seven paths led to his halls. Seven chiefs stood on the paths, and called the stranger to the feast! But Cathmor dwelt in the wood, to shun the voice of praise!

Olla came with his songs. Oscar went to Cairbar's feast. Three hundred warriors strode along Moi–lena of the streams. The gray dogs bounded on the heath: their howling reached afar. Fingal saw the departing hero. The soul of the king was sad. He dreaded Cairbar's gloomy thoughts, amidst the feast of shells. My son raised high the spear of Cormac. A hundred bards met him with songs. Cairbar concealed, with smiles, the death that was dark in his soul. The feast is spread. The shells resound. Joy brightens the face of the host. But it was like the parting beam of the sun, when he is to hide his red head in a storm!

Cairbar rises in his arms. Darkness gathers on his brow. The hundred harps cease at once. The clang of shields is heard. Far distant on the heath Olla raised a song of wo. My son knew the sign of death; and rising seized his spear. "Oscar," said the dark–red Cairbar, "I behold the spear of Erin. The spear of Temora glitters in thy hand, son of woody Morven! It was the pride of a hundred kings. The death of heroes of old. Yield it, son of Ossian, yield it to car–borne Cairbar!"

"Shall I yield," Oscar replied, "the gift of Erin's injured king; the gift of fair–haired Cormac, when Oscar scattered his foes? I came to Cormac's halls of joy, when Swaran fled from Fingal. Gladness rose in the face of youth. He gave the spear of Temora. Nor did he give it to the feeble: neither to the weak in soul. The darkness of thy face is no storm to me: nor are thine eyes the flame of death. Do I fear thy clanging shield? Tremble I at Olla's song? No Cairbar, frighten the feeble; Oscar is a rock!"

"Wilt thou not yield the spear?" replied the rising pride of Cairbar." Are thy words so mighty, because Fingal is near? Fingal with aged locks, from Morven's hundred groves! He has fought with little men. But he must vanish before Cairbar, like a thin pillar of mist before the winds of Atha!" — "Were he who fought with little men, near Atha's haughty chief, Atha's chief would yield green Erin to avoid his rage! Speak not of the mighty, O

Cairbar! Turn thy sword on me. Our strength is equal: but Fingal is renowned! the first of mortal men!"

Their people saw the darkening chiefs. Their crowding steps are heard. Their eyes roll in fire. A thousand swords are half unsheathed. Red–haired Olla raised the song of battle. The trembling joy of Oscar's soul arose: the wonted joy of his soul when Fingal's horn was heard. Dark as the swelling wave of ocean before the rising winds, when it bends its head near the coast, came on the host of Cairbar!

Daughter of Toscar! why that tear? He is not fallen yet. Many were the deaths of his arm before my hero fell!

Behold they fall before my son, like groves in the desert; when an angry ghost rushes through night, and takes their green heads in his hand! Morlath falls. Maronnan dies. Conachar trembles in his blood. Cairbar shrinks before Oscar's sword! He creeps in darkness behind a stone. He lifts the spear in secret, he pierces my Oscar's side! He falls forward on his shield, his knee sustains the chief. But still his spear is in his hand! See, gloomy Cairbar falls! The steel pierced his forehead, and divided his red hair behind. He lay like a shattered rock, which Cromla shakes from its shaggy side, when the green–valleyed Erin shakes its mountains from sea to sea!

But never more shall Oscar rise! He leans on his bossy shield. His spear is in his terrible hand. Erin's sons stand distant and dark. Their shouts arise, like crowded streams. Moi–lena echoes wide. Fingal heard the sound. He took the spear of Selma. His steps are before us on the heath. He spoke the words of wo. "I hear the noise of war. Young Oscar is alone. Rise, sons of Morven: join the hero's sword!"

Ossian rushed along the heath. Fillan bounded over Moi– lena. Fingal strode in his strength. The light of his shield is terrible. The sons of Erin saw it far distant. They trembled in their souls. They knew that the wrath of the king arose: and they foresaw their death. We first arrived. We fought. Erin's chiefs withstood our rage. But when the king came, in the sound of his course, what heart of steel could stand? Erin fled over Moi–lena. Death pursued their flight. We saw Oscar on his shield. We saw his blood around. Silence darkened on every face. Each turned his back and wept. The king strove to hide his tears. His gray beard whistled in the wind. He bends his head above the chief. His words are mixed with sighs.

"Art thou fallen, O Oscar! in the midst of thy course? the heart of the aged beats over thee! He sees thy coming wars! The wars which ought to come he sees! They are cut off from thy fame! When shall joy dwell at Selma? When shall grief depart from Morven? My sons fall by degrees: Fingal is the last of his race. My fame begins to pass away. Mine age will be without friends. I shall sit a gray cloud in my hall. I shall not hear the return of a son, in his sounding arms. Weep, ye heroes of Morven! never more shall Oscar rise!"

And they did weep, O Fingal! Dear was the hero to their souls. He went out to battle, and the foes vanished. He returned in peace, amidst their joy. No father mourned his son slain in youth: no brother his brother of love. They fell without tears, for the chief of the people is low! Bran is howling at his feet: gloomy Luath is sad; for he had often led them to the chase; to the bounding roe of the desert!

When Oscar saw his friends around, his heaving breast arose. "The groans," he said, "of aged chiefs; the howling of my dogs; the sudden bursts of the song of grief, have melted Oscar's soul. My soul, that never melted before. It was like the steel of my sword. Ossian, carry me to my hills! Raise the stones of my renown. Place the horn of a deer: place my sword by my side; The torrent hereafter may raise the earth: the hunter may find the steel, and say, 'This has been Oscar's sword, the pride of other years!'" "Fallest thou, son of my fame? shall I never see thee, Oscar? When others hear of their sons, shall I not hear of thee? The moss is on thy four gray stones. The mournful wind is there. The battle shall be fought without thee. Thou shalt not pursue the dark−brown hinds. When the warrior returns from battles, and tells of other lands; 'I have seen a tomb,' he will say, 'by the roaring stream, the dark dwelling of a chief. He fell by car−borne Oscar, the first of mortal men.' I, perhaps, shall hear his voice. A beam of joy will rise in my soul."

Night would have descended in sorrow, and morning returned in the shadow of grief. Our chiefs would have stood, like cold−dropping rocks on Moi−lena, and have forgot the war; did not the king disperse his grief, and raise his mighty voice. The chiefs, as new−wakened from dreams, lift up their heads around.

"How long on Moi−lena shall we weep? How long pour in Erin our tears? The mighty will not return. Oscar shall not rise in his strength. The valiant must fall in their day, and be no more known on their hills. Where are our fathers, O warriors! the chiefs of the times of old? They have set, like stars that have shone. We only hear the sound of their praise. But they were renowned in their years: the terror of other times. Thus shall we pass away, in the day of our fall. Then let us be renowned when we may; and leave our fame behind us, like the last beams of the sun, when he hides his red head in the west. The traveller mourns his absence, thinking of the flame of his beams. Ullin, my aged bard! take thou the ship of the king. Carry Oscar to Selma of harps. Let the daughters of Morven weep. We must fight in Erin, for the race of fallen Cormac. The days of my years begin to fail. I feel the weakness of my arm. My fathers bend from their clouds, to receive their gray-haired son. But before I go hence, one beam of fame shall rise. My days shall end, as my years began, in fame. My life shall be one stream of light to bards of other times!"

Ullin raised his white sails. The wind of the south came forth. He bounded on the waves towards Selma. I remained in my grief, but my words were not heard. The feast is spread on Moi- lena. A hundred heroes reared the tomb of Cairbar. No song is raised over the chief. His soul has been dark and bloody. The bards remembered the fall of Cormac! what could they say in Cairbar's praise?

Night came rolling down. The light of a hundred oaks arose. Fingal sat beneath a tree. Old Althan stood in the midst. He told the tale of fallen Cormac. Althan the son of Conachar, the friend of car-borne Cuthullin. He dwelt with Cormac in windy Temora, when Semo's son fell at Lego's stream. The tale of Althan was mournful. The tear was in his eye when he spoke.

"The setting sun was yellow on Dora. Gray evening began to descend. Temora's woods shook with the blast of the inconstant wind. A cloud gathered in the west. A red star looked from behind its edge. I stood in the wood alone. I saw a ghost on the darkening air! His stride extended from hill to hill. His shield was dim on his side. It was the son of Semo! I knew the warrior's face. But he passed away in his blast; and all was dark around! My soul was sad. I went to the hall of shells. A thousand lights arose. The hundred bards had strung the harp. Cormac stood in the midst, like the morning star, when it rejoices on the eastern hill, and its young beams are bathed in showers. Bright and silent is its progress aloft, but the cloud that shall hide it is near! The sword of Artho was in the hand of the king. He looked with joy on its polished studs; thrice he attempted to draw it, and thrice he failed; his yellow locks are spread on his shoulders! his cheeks of youth are red. I mourned over the beam of youth, for he was soon to set!

"'Althan!' He said with a smile, ' didst thou behold my father? Heavy is the sword of the king; surely his arm was strong. O that I were like him in battle, when the rage of his wrath arose! then would I have met, with Cuthullin, the car–borne son of Cantla! But years may come on, O Althan! and my arm be strong. Hast thou heard of Semo's son, the ruler of high Temora? he might have returned with his fame. He promised to return to–night. My bards wait him with songs. My feast is spread in the hall of kings.'

"I heard Cormac in silence. My tears began to flow. I hid them with my aged locks. The king perceived my grief. 'Son of Conachar!' he said, 'is the son of Semo low? Why bursts the sigh in secret? Why descends the tear? Comes the car–borne Torlath? Comes the sounds of red–haired Cairbar? They come! for I behold thy grief. Mossy Tura's chief is low! Shall I not rush to battle? But I cannot lift the spear! O had mine arm the strength of Cuthullin, soon would Cairbar fly; the fame of my fathers would be renewed; and the deeds of other times!'

"He took his bow. The tears flow down from both his sparkling eyes. Grief saddens round. The bards bend forward, from their hundred harps. The lone blast touched their trembling strings. The sound is sad and low! a voice is heard at a distance, as of one in grief. It was Carril of other times, who came from dark Slimora. He told of the fall of Cuthullin. He told of his mighty deeds. The people were scattered round his tomb. Their arms lay on the ground. They had forgot the war, for he their sire, was seen no more!

"'But who,' said the soft–voiced Carril, 'who come like bounding roes? Their stature is like young trees in the valley, growing in a shower! Soft and ruddy are their cheeks! Fearless souls look forth from their eyes? Who but the sons of Usnoth, chief of streamy Etha? The people rise on every side, like the strength of an half–extinguished fire, when the winds come, sudden, from the desert, on their rustling wings. Sudden glows the dark brow of the hill; the passing mariner lags, on his winds. The sound of Caithbat's shield was heard. The warriors saw Cuthullin in Nathos. So rolled his sparkling eyes! his steps were such on the heath. Battles are fought at Lego. The sword of Nathos prevails. Soon shalt thou behold him in thy halls, king of Temora of groves!'

"'Soon may I behold the chief!' replied the blue–eyed king. But my soul is sad for Cuthullin His voice was pleasant in mine ear. Often have we moved, on Dora, to the chase of the dark– brown hinds. His bow was unerring on the hills. He spoke of mighty men. He told of the deeds of my fathers. I felt my rising joy. But sit thou at thy feast, O

Carril! I have often heard thy voice. Sing in praise of Cuthullin. Sing of Nathos of Etha!'

"Day rose on Temora, with all the beams of the east. Crathin came to the hall, the son of old Gell ma. 'I behold,' he said, 'a cloud in the desert, king of Erin! a cloud it seemed at first, but now a crowd of men! One strides before them in his strength. His red hair flies in the wind. His shield glitters to the beam of the east. His spear is in his hand.' — 'Call him to the feast of Temora,' replied the brightening king. 'My hall is in the house of strangers, son of generous Gell ma! It is perhaps the chief of Etha, coming in all his renown. Hail, mighty stranger! art thou of the friends of Cormac? But, Carril, he is dark and unlovely. He draws his sword. Is that the son of Usnoth, bard of the times of old?'

"' It is not the son of Usnoth!' said Carril. 'It is Cairbar, thy foe.' 'Why comest thou in thy arms to Temora? chief of the gloomy brow. Let not thy sword rise against Cormac! 'Whither dost thou turn thy speed?' he passed on in darkness.. He seized the hand of the king. Cormac foresaw his death; the rage of his eyes arose. 'Retire, thou chief of Atha! Nathos comes with war. Thou art bold in Cormac's hall, for his arm is weak.' The sword entered the side of the king. He fell in the halls of his father. His fair hair is in the dust. His blood is smoking round.

"'Art thou fallen in thy halls?' said Carril, 'O son of noble Artho! The shield of Cuthullin was not near. Nor the spear of thy father. Mournful are the mountains of Erin, for the chief of the people is low! Blest be thy soul, O Cormac! Thou art darkened in thy youth!'"

"His words came to the ears of Cairbar. He closed us in the midst of darkness. He feared to stretch his sword to the bards, though his soul was dark. Long we pined alone! At length the noble Cathmor came. He heard our voice from the cave. He turned the eye of his wrath on Cairbar.

"'Brother of Cathmor,' he said, 'how long wilt thou pain my soul? Thy heart is a rock. Thy thoughts are dark and bloody! But thou art the brother of Cathmor; and Cathmor shall shine in thy war. But my soul is not like thine; thou feeble hand in fight! The light of my bosom is stained with thy deeds. Bards will not sing of my renown; they may say, "Cathmor was brave, but he fought for gloomy Cairbar. "They will pass over my tomb in silence. My fame shall not be heard. Cairbar! loose the bards. They are the sons of future times. Their voice shall be heard in other years; after the kings of Temora have failed. We came forth at the words of the chief. We saw him in his strength. He was like thy youth,

O Fingal! when thou first didst lift the spear. His face was like the plain of the sun, when it is bright. No darkness travelled over his brow. But he came with his thousands to aid the red−haired Cairbar. Now he comes to revenge his death, O king of woody Morven!'

"Let Cathmor come," replied the king," I love a foe so great. His soul is bright. His arm is strong. His battles are full of fame. But the little soul is a vapor that hovers round the marshy lake. It never rises on the green hill, lest the winds should meet it there. Its dwelling is in the cave: it sends forth the dart of death! Our young heroes, O warriors! are like the renown of our fathers. They fight in youth. They fall. Their names are in song. Fingal is amid his darkening years. He must not fall, as an aged oak, across a secret stream. Near it are the steps of the hunter, as it lies beneath the wind. 'How has that tree fallen?' he says, and, whistling, strides along. Raise the song of' joy, ye bards of Morven! Let our souls forget the past. The red stars look on us from the clouds, and silently descend. Soon shall the gray beam of the morning rise, and show us the foes of Cormac. Fillan! my son, take thou the spear of the king. Go to Mora's dark−brown side. Let thine eyes travel over the heath. Observe the foes of Fingal; observe the course of generous Cathmor. I hear a distant sound, like falling rocks in the desert. But strike thou thy shield, at times, that they may not come through night, and the fame of Morven cease. I begin to be alone, my son. I dread the fall of my renown!"

The voice of bards arose. The king leaned on the shield of Trenmor. Sleep descended on his eyes. His future battles arose in his dreams. The host are sleeping around. Dark−haired Fillan observes the foe. His steps are on the distant hill. We hear, at time; his clanging shield.

Mor−annal here alludes to the particular appearance of Fingal's spear. If a man upon his first landing in a strange country, kept the point of his spear forward, it denoted, in those days, that he came in a hostile manner, and accordingly he was treated as an enemy; if he kept the point behind him, it was a token of friendship, and ht was immediately invited to the feast, according to the hospitality of the times.

The clang of shields: when a chief was determined to kill a person already in his power, it was usual to signify that his death was intended, by the pound of a shield struck with the blunt end of a spear: at the same time that a bard at a distance raised the death−song.

The lone blast touched their trembling strings: that prophetic sound mentioned in other poems, which the harps of the bards emitted before the death of a person worthy and renowned.

TEMORA — BOOK II

ARGUMENT.

This book opens, we may suppose, about midnight, with a soliloquy of Ossian, who had retired from the rest of the army, to mourn for his son Oscar. Upon hearing the noise of Cathmor's army approaching, he went to find out his brother Fillan, who kept the watch on the hill of Mora, in the front of Fingal's army. In the conversation of the brothers, the episode of Conar, the son of Trenmor, who was the first king of Ireland, is introduced, which lays open the origin of the contests between the Gael and the Fir-bolg, the two nations who first possessed themselves of that island. Ossian kindles a fire on Mora: upon which Cathmor desisted from the design he had formed of surprising the army of the Caledonians. He calls a council of his chiefs: reprimands Foldath for advising a night attack, as the Irish were so much superior in number to the enemy. The bard Fonar introduces the story of Crothar, the ancestor of the king, which throws further light on the history of Ireland, and the original pretensions of the family of Atha to the throne of that kingdom. The Irish chiefs lie down to rest, and Cathmor himself undertakes the watch. In his circuit round the army he is met by Ossian. The interview of the two heroes is described. Cathmor obtains a promise from Ossian to order a funeral elegy to be sung over the grave of Cairbar: it being the opinion of the times, that the souls of the dead could not be happy till their elegies were sung by a bard. Morning comes. Cathmor and Ossian part; and the latter, casually meeting with Carril the son of Kinfena, sends that bard, with a funeral song, to the tomb of Cairbar.

FATHER of heroes! O Trenmor! High dweller of eddying winds! where the dark-red thunder marks the troubled clouds! Open thou thy stormy halls. Let the bards of old be near. Let them draw near with songs and their half viewless harps. No dweller of misty valley comes! No hunter unknown at his streams! It is the car-borne Oscar, from the field of war. Sudden is thy change, my son, from what thou wert on dark Moi-lena! The blast folds thee in its skirt, and rustles through the sky! Dost thou not behold thy father, at the stream of night? The chiefs of Morven sleep far distant. They have lost no son! But ye

156

have lost a hero, chiefs of resounding Morven! Who could equal his strength, when battle rolled against his side, like the darkness of crowded waters? Why this cloud on Ossian's soul? It ought to burn in danger. Erin is near with her host. The king of Selma is alone. Alone thou shalt not be, my father, while I can lift the spear!

I rose in all my arms. I rose and listened to the wind. The shield of Fillan is not heard. I tremble for the son of Fingal. "Why should the foe come by night? Why should the dark−haired warrior fall?" Distant, sullen murmurs rise; like the noise of the lake of Lego, when its waters shrink, in the days of frost, and all its bursting ice resounds. The people of Lara look to heaven, and foresee the storm! My steps are forward on the heath. The spear of Oscar is in my hand? Red stars looked from high. I gleamed along the night.

I saw Fillan silent before me, bending forward from Mora's rock. He heard the shout of the foe. The joy of his soul arose. He heard my sounding tread, and turned his lifted spear. "Comest thou, son of night, in peace? Or dost thou meet my wrath? The foes of Fingal are mine. Speak, or fear my steel. I stand not, in vain, the shield of Morven's race." "Never mayest thou stand in vain, son of blue−eyed Clatho! Fingal begins to be alone. Darkness gathers on the last of his days. Yet he has two sons who ought to shine in war. Who ought to be two beams of light, near the steps of his departure."

"Son of Fingal," replied the youth, "it is not long since I raised the spear. Few are the marks of my sword in war. But Fillan's soul is fire! The chiefs of Bolga crowd around the shield of generous Cathmor. Their gathering is on the heath. Shall my steps approach their host? I yielded to Oscar alone in the strife of the race of Cona!"

"Fillan, thou shalt not approach their host; nor fall before thy fame is known. My name is heard in song; when needful, I advance. From the skirts of night I shall view them over all their gleaming tribes. Why, Fillan, didst thou speak of Oscar? Why awake my sigh! I must forget the warrior, till the storm is rolled away. Sadness ought not to dwell in danger, nor the tear in the eye of war. Our fathers forgot their fallen sons, till the noise of arms was past. Then sorrow returned to the tomb, and the song of bards arose. The memory of those who fell quickly followed the departure of war: when the tumult of battle is past, the soul in silence melts away for the dead.

"Conar was the brother of Trathal, first of mortal men. His battles were on every coast. A thousand streams rolled down the blood of. his foes. His fame filled green Erin, like a

157

pleasant gale. The nations gathered in Ullin, and they blessed the king; the king of the race of their fathers, from the land of Selma.

"The chiefs of the south were gathered, in the darkness of their pride. In the horrid cave of Moma they mixed their secret words. Thither often, they said, the spirits of their fathers came; showing their pale forms from the chinky rocks; reminding them of the honor of Bolga. 'Why should Conar reign,' they said, 'the son of resounding Morven?'

"They came forth, like the streams of the desert, with the roar of their hundred tribes. Cona was a rock before them: broken, they rolled on every side. But often they returned, and the sons of Selma fell. The king stood, among the tombs of his warriors. He darkly bent his mournful face. His soul was rolled into itself: and he had marked the place where he was to fall: when Trathal came, in his strength, his brother from cloudy Morven. Nor did he come alone. Colgar was at his side: Colgar the son of the king and of white–bosomed Solin–corma.

"As Trenmor, clothed with meteors, descends from the halls of thunder, pouring the dark storm before him over the troubled sea: so Colgar descended to battle, and wasted the echoing field. His father rejoiced over the hero: but an arrow came! His tomb was raised without a tear. The king was to revenge his son. He lightened forward in battle, till Bolga yielded at her streams!

"When peace returned to the land: when his blue waves bore the king to Morven: then he remembered his son, and poured the silent tear. Thrice did the bards, at the cave of Furmono, call the soul of Colgar. They called him to the hills of his land. He heard them in his mist. Trathal placed his sword in the cave, that the spirit of his son might rejoice."

"Colgar, son of Trathal," said Fillan, "thou wert renowned in youth! but the king hath not marked my sword, bright streaming on the field. I go forth with the crowd. I return without my fame. But the foe approaches, Ossian! I hear their murmur on the heath. The sound of their steps is like thunder, in the bosom of the ground, when the rocking hills shake their groves, and not a blast pours from the darkened sky!"

Ossian turned sudden on his spear. He raised the flame of an oak on high. I spread it large on Mora's wind. Cathmor stopt in his course. Gleaming he stood, like a rock, on whose sides are the wandering blasts; which seize its echoing streams, and clothe them with ice.

So stood the friend of strangers! The winds lift his heavy locks. Thou art the tallest of the race of Erin, king of streamy Atha!

"First of bards" said Cathmor, "Fonar, call the chiefs of Erin. Call red-haired Cormar: dark-browed Malthos: the sidelong- looking gloom of Maronnan. Let the pride of Foldath appear. The red-rolling eye of Turlotho. Nor let Hidalla be forgot; his voice, in danger, is the sound of a shower, when it falls in the blasted vale, near Atha's falling stream. Pleasant is its sound on the plain, whilst broken thunder travels over the sky!"

They came in their clanging arms. They bent forward to his voice, as if a spirit of their fathers spoke from a cloud of night. Dreadful shone they to the light, like the fall of the stream of Bruno, when the meteor lights it, before the nightly stranger. Shuddering he stops in his journey, and looks up for the beam of the morn!

"Why delights Foldath," said the king, "to pour the blood of foes by night? Fails his arm in battle, in the beams of day? Few are the foes before us; why should we clothe us in shades? The valiant delight to shine in the battles of their land! Thy counsel was in vain, chief of Moma! The eyes of Morven do not sleep. They are watchful as eagles on their mossy rocks. Let each collect beneath his cloud the strength of his roaring tribe. To-morrow I move, in light, to meet the foes of Bolga! Mighty was he that is low, the race of Borbar-duthul!"

"Not unmarked," said Foldath, "were my steps be. fare thy race. In light, I met the foes of Cairbar. The warrior praised my deeds. But his stone was raised without a tear! No bard sung over Erin's king. Shall his foes rejoice along their mossy hills? No they must not rejoice! He was the friend of Foldath. Our words were mixed, in secret, in Moma's silent cave; whilst thou, a boy in the field, pursued'st the thistle's beard. With Moma's sons I shall rush abroad, and find the foe on his dusky hills. Fingal shall die without his song, the gray-haired king of Selma."

" Dost thou think, thou feeble man," replied Cathmor, half enraged: "Dost thou think Fingal can fail, without his fame, in Erin? Could the bards be silent at the tomb of Selma's king; the song would burst in secret! the spirit of the king would rejoice! It is when thou shalt fall, that the bard shall forget the song. Thou art dark, chief of Moma, though thine arm is a tempest in war. Do I forget the king of Erin, in his narrow house? My soul is not lost to Cairbar, the brother of my love! I marked the bright beams of joy which travelled over his cloudy mind, when I returned, with fame, to Atha of the streams."

Tall they removed, beneath the words of the king. Each to his own dark tribe; where, humming, they rolled on the heath, faint–glittering to the stars: like waves in a rocky bay, before the nightly wind. Beneath an oak lay the chief of Atha. His shield, a dusky round, hung high. Near him, against a rock, leaned the fair stranger of Inis–huna: that beam of light, with wandering locks, from Lumon of the roes. At a distance rose the voice of Fonar, with the deeds of the days of old. The song fails, at times, in Lubar's growing roar.

"Crothar," began the bard, first dwelt at Atha's mossy stream! A thousand oaks, from the mountains, formed his echoing hail. The gathering of the people was there, around the feast of the blue–eyed king. But who, among his chiefs, was like the stately Crothar? Warriors kindled in his presence. The young sigh of the virgins rose. In Alnecma was the warrior honored: the first of the race of Bolga.

"He pursued the chase in Ullin: on the moss–covered top of Drumardo. From the wood looked the daughter of Cathmin, the blue–rolling eye of Con–l ma. Her sigh rose in secret. She bent her head, amidst her wandering locks. The moon looked in, at night, and saw the white tossing of her arms; for she thought of the mighty Crothar in the season of dreams.

"Three days feasted Crothar with Cathmin. On the fourth they awaked the hinds. Con–l ma moved to the chase, with all her lovely steps. She met Crothar in the narrow path. The bow fell at once from her hand. She turned her face away, and half hid it with her locks. The love of Crothar rose. He brought the white–bosomed maid to Atha. Bards raised the song in her presence. Joy dwelt round the daughter of Cathmin.

"The pride of Turloch rose, a youth who loved the white– handed Con–l ma. He came, with battle, to Alnecma; to Atha of the roes. Cormul went forth to the strife, the brother of car–borne Crothar. He went forth, but he fell. The sigh of his people rose. Silent and tall across the stream, came the darkening strength of Crothar: he rolled the foe from Alnecma. He returned midst the joy of Con–l ma.

"Battle on battle comes. Blood is poured on blood. The tombs of the valiant rise. Erin's clouds arc hung round with ghosts. The chiefs of the South gathered round the echoing shield of Crothar. He came, with death to the paths of the foe. The virgins wept, by the streams of Ullin. They looked the mist of the hill: no hunter descended from its folds. Silence darkened in the land. Blasts sighed lonely on grassy tombs.

"Descending like the eagle of heaven, with all his rustling winds, when he forsakes the blast with joy, the son of Trenmor came; Conar, arm of death, from Morven of the groves, lie poured his might along green Erin. Death dimly strode behind his sword. The sons of Bolga fled from his course, as from a stream, that, bursting from the stormy desert, rolls the fields together, with all their echoing woods Crothar met him in battle: but Alnecma's warriors fled. The king of Atha slowly retired, in the grief of his soul. He afterward shone in the south; but dim as the sun of autumn, when he visits, in his robes of mist, Lara of dark streams. 'The withered grass is covered with dew; the field, though bright, is sad."

"Why wakes the bard before me," said Cathmor, "the memory of those who fled? Has some ghost, from his dusky cloud, bent forward to thine ear; to frighten Cathmor from the field, with the tales of old? Dwellers of the skirts of night, your voice is but a blast to me; which takes the gray thistle's head, and strews its beard on streams. Within my bosom is a voice. Others hear it not. His soul forbids the king of Erin to shrink back from war."

Abashed, the bard sinks back on night; retired, lie bends above a stream. His thoughts are on the days of Atha, when Cathmor heard his song with joy. His tears came rolling down. The winds are in his beard. Erin sleeps around. No sleep comes down on Cathmor's eyes. Dark, in his soul, he saw the spirit of low–laid Cairbar. He saw him, without his song, rolled in a blast of night. He rose. His steps were round the host. He struck, at times, his echoing shield. The sound reached Ossian's ear on Mora's mossy brow.

"Fillan," I said, "the foes advance. I hear the shield of war. Stand thou in the narrow path. Ossian shall mark their course. if over my fall the host should pour; then be thy buckler heard. Awake the king on his heath, lest his fame should fly away." I strode in all my rattling arms; wide bounding over a stream that darkly winded in the field, before the king of Atha. Green Atha's king with lifted spear, came forward on my course. Now would we have mixed in horrid, fray, like two contending ghosts, that bending forward from two clouds, send forth the roaring winds; did not Ossian behold, on high, the helmet of Erin's kings. The eagle's wing spread above it, rustling in the breeze. A red star looked through the plumes. I stopt the lifted spear.

"The helmet of kings is before me! Who art thou, son of night? Shall Ossian's spear be renowned, when thou art lowly laid?" At once he dropt the gleaming lance. Growing before me seemed the form. He stretched his hand in night. He spoke the words of kings.

"Friend of the spirits of heroes, do I meet thee thus in shades? I have wished for thy stately steps in Atha, in the days of joy. Why should my spear now arise?' The sun must behold us, Ossian, when we bend, gleaming in the strife. Future warriors shall mark the place, and shuddering think of other years. They shall mark it, like the haunt of ghosts, pleasant and dreadful to the soul ."

"Shall it then be forgot," I said, "where we meet in peace? Is the remembrance of battles always pleasant to the soul? Do not we behold, with joy, the place where our fathers feasted? But our eyes are full of tears, on the fields of their war. This stone shall rise with all its moss and speak to other years. 'Here Cathmor and Ossian met; the warriors met in peace!' When thou, O stone, shalt fail: when Lubar's stream shall roll away; then shall the traveller come and bend here, perhaps, in rest. When the darkened moon is rolled over his head, our shadowy forms may come, and, mixing with his dreams, remind him of his place. But why turnest thou so dark away; son of Borbar–duthul?"

"Not forgot, son of Fingal, shall we ascend these winds. Our deeds are streams of light, before the eyes of bards. But darkness is rolled on Atha: the king is low without his song; still there was a beam towards Cathmor, from his stormy soul; like the moon in a cloud, amidst the dark–red course of thunder."

"Son of Erin," I replied, "my wrath dwells not in his earth. My hatred flies on eagle wings, from the foe that is low. He shall hear the song of bards. Cairbar shall rejoice on his winds."

Cathmor's swelling soul arose. He took the dagger from his side, and placed it gleaming in my hand. He placed it in my hand, with sighs, and silent strode away. Mine eyes followed his departure. He dimly gleamed, like the form of a ghost, which meets a traveller by night, on the dark–skirted heath. His words are dark, like songs of old: with morning strides the unfinished shade away!

Who comes from Luba's vale? from the skirts of the morning mist? The drops of heaven are on his head. His steps are in the paths of the sad. It is Carril of other times. He comes from Tura's silent cave. I behold it dark in the rock, through the thin folds of mist. There, perhaps, Cuthullin sits, on the blast which bends its trees. Pleasant is the song of the morning from the bard of Erin.

"The waves crowd away," said Carril." They crowd away for fear. They hear the sound of thy coming forth, O sun! Terrible is thy beauty, son of heaven, when death is descending on thy locks: when thou rollest thy vapors before thee, over the blasted host. But pleasant is thy beam to the hunter, sitting by the rock in a storm, when thou showest thyself from the parted cloud, and brightenest his dewy locks he looks down on the streamy vale, and beholds the de. scent of roes! How long shalt thou rise on war, and roll, a bloody shield, through heaven? I see the death of heroes, dark wandering over thy face!"

"Why wander the words of Carril?" I said. "Does the son of heaven mourn? lie is unstained in his course, ever rejoicing in his fire. Roll on, thou careless light. Thou too, perhaps, must fall. Thy darkening hour may seize thee, struggling as thou rollest through thy sky. But pleasant is the voice of the bard: pleasant to Ossian's soul! It is like the shower of the morning, when it comes through the rustling vale, on which the sun looks through mist, just rising from his rocks. But this is no time, O bard! to sit down, at the strife of song. Fingal is in arms on the vale. Thou seest the flaming shield of the king. His face darkens between his locks. He beholds the wide rolling of Erin. Does not Carril behold that tomb, beside the roaring stream? Three stones lift their gray heads, beneath a bending oak. A king is lowly laid! Give thou his soul to the wind. He is the brother of Cathmor! Open his airy hall! Let thy song be a stream of joy to Cairbar's darkened ghost!"

TEMORA — BOOK III.

ARGUMENT.

Morning coming on, Fingal, after a speech to his people, devolved the command on Gaul, the son of Morni; it being the custom of the times, that the king should not engage, till the necessity of affairs required his superior valor and conduct. The king and Ossian retire to the hill of Cormul, which overlooked the field of battle. The bards sing the war–song.

THE POEMS OF OSSIAN

The general conflict is described. Gaul, the son of Morni, distinguishes himself; kills Tur—lathon, chief of Moruth, and other chiefs of lesser name. On the other hand, Foldath, who commanded the Irish army (for Cathmor, after the example of Fingal, kept himself from battle,) fights gallantly; kills Connal, chief of Dun—lora, and advances to engage Gaul himself. Gaul, in the mean time, being wounded in the hand, by a random arrow, is covered by Fillan the son of Fingal, who performs prodigies of valor. Night comes on. The horn of Fingal recalls his army. The bards meet them with a congratulatory song, in which the praises of Gaul and Fillan are particularly celebrated. The chiefs sit down at a feast; Fingal misses Connal. The episode of Connal and Duth—caron is introduced; which throws further light on the ancient history of Ire land. Carril is despatched to raise the tomb of Connal. The action of this book takes up the second day from the opening of the poem.

"Who is that at blue—streaming Lubar? Who, by the bending hill of roes? Tall he leans on an oak torn from high, by nightly winds. Who but Comhal's son, brightening in the last of his fields? His gray hair is on the breeze. He half unsheathes the sword of Luno. His eyes are turned to Moi—lena, to the dark moving of foes. Dost thou hear the voice of the king? it is like the bursting of a stream in the desert, when it comes, between its echoing rocks, to the blasted field of the sun!

Wide—skirted comes down the foe! Sons of woody Selma, arise! Be ye like the rocks of our land, in whose brown sides are the rolling of streams. A beam of joy comes on my soul. I see the foe mighty before me. It is when he is feeble, that the sighs of Fingal are heard: lest death should come without renown, and darkness dwell on his tomb. Who shall lead the war, against the host of Alnecma? It is only when danger grows, that my sword shalt shine. Such was the custom, heretofore, of Trenmor the ruler of winds! and thus descended to battle the blue—shielded Trathal!"

The chiefs bend towards the king. Each darkly seems to claim the war. They tell, by halves, their mighty deeds. They turn their eyes on Erin. But far before the rest the son of Morni stands. Silent he stands, for who had not heard of the battles of Gaul They rose within his soul. His hand, in secret, seized the sword. The sword which he brought from Strumon, when the strength of Morni failed. On his spear leans Fillan of Selma, in the wandering of his locks. Thrice he raises his eyes to Fingal: his voice thrice fails him as he speaks. My brother could not boast of battles: at once he strides away. Bent over a distant stream he stands: the tear hangs in his eye. He strikes, at times, the thistle's head, with his inverted spear. Nor is he unseen of Fingal. Sidelong he beholds his son. He beholds him with bursting joy; and turns, amid his crowded soul. In silence turns the king towards Mora of woods. He hides the big tear with his locks. At length his voice is heard.

"First of the sons of Morni! Thou rock that defiest the storm! Lead thou my battle for the race of low−laid Cormac. No boy's staff is thy spear: no harmless beam of light thy sword. Son of Morni of steeds, behold the foe! Destroy! Fillan, observe the chief! He is not calm in strife: nor burns he, heedless in battle. My son, observe the chief! He is strong as Lubar's stream, but never foams and roars. High on cloudy Mora, Fingal shall behold the war. Stand, Ossian, near thy father, by the falling stream. Raise the voice, O bards! Selma, move beneath the sound. It is my latter field. Clothe it over with light."

As the sudden rising of winds; or distant rolling of troubled seas, when some dark ghost in wrath heaves the billows over an isle: an isle the seat of mist on the deep, for many dark−brown years! So terrible is the sound of the host, wide moving over the field. Gaul is tall before them. The streams glitter within his strides. The bards raise the song by his side. He strikes his shield between. On the skirts of the blast the tuneful voices rise.

"On Crona," said the bards, "there bursts a stream by night. It swells in its own dark course, till morning's early beam. Then comes it white from the hill, with the rocks and their hundred groves. Far be my steps from Crona. Death is tumbling there. Be ye a stream from Mora, sons of cloudy Morven!

"Who rises, from his car, on Clutha? The hills are troubled before the king! The dark woods echo round, and lighten at his steel. See him amidst the foe, like Colgach's sportful ghost: when he scatters the clouds and rides the eddying winds! It is Morni of bounding steeds! Be like thy father, O Gaul!

"Selma is opened wide. Bards take the trembling harps. Ten youths bear the oak of the feast. A distant sunbeam marks the hill. The dusky waves of the blast fly over the fields of grass. Why art thou silent, O Selma? The king returns with all his fame. Did not the battle roar? yet peaceful is his brow! It roared, and Fingal overcame. Be like thy father, O Fillan!"

They move beneath the song. High wave their arms, as rushy fields beneath autumnal winds. On Mora stands the king in arms. Mist flies round his buckler abroad; as aloft it hung on a bough, on Cormul's mossy rock. In silence I stood by Fingal, and turned my eyes on Cromla's wood: lest I should behold the host, and rush amid my swelling soul. My foot is forward on the heath. I glittered, tall in steel: like the falling stream of Tromo, which nightly winds bind over with ice. The boy sees it on high gleaming to the early beam: towards it he turns his ear, wonders why it is so silent.

Nor bent over a stream is Cathmor, like a youth in a peaceful field. Wide he drew forward the war, a dark and troubled wave. But when he beheld Fingal on Mora, his generous pride arose. "Shall the chief of Atha fight, and no king in the field? Foldath, lead my people forth, thou art a beam of fire."

Forth issues Foldath of Moma, like a cloud, the robe of ghosts. He drew his sword, a flame from his side. He bade the battle move. The tribes, like ridgy waves, dark pour their strength around. Haughty is his stride before them. His red eye rolls in wrath. He calls Cormul, chief of Dun–ratho; and his words were heard.

"Cormul, thou beholdest that path. It winds green behind the foe. Place thy people there; lest Selma should escape from my sword. Bards of green–valleyed Erin, let no voice of yours arise. The sons of Morven must fall without song. They are the foes of Cairbar. Hereafter shall the traveller meet their dark, thick mist, on Lena, where it wanders with their ghosts, beside the reedy lake. Never shall they rise, without song, to the dwelling of winds."

Cormul darkened as he went. Behind him rushed his tribe. They sunk beyond the rock. Gaul spoke to Fillan of Selma; as his eye pursued the course of the dark–eyed chief of Dun–ratho. "Thou beholdest the steps of Cormul! Let thine arm be strong! When he is low, son of Fingal, remember Gaul in war. Here I fall forward into baffle, amid the ridge of shields!"

The sign of death ascends: the dreadful sound of Morni's shield. Gaul pours his voice between. Fingal rises on Mora. He saw them from wing to wing, bending at once in strife. Gleaming on his own dark hill, stood Cathmor, of streamy Atha. The kings were like two spirits of heaven, standing each on his gloomy cloud: when they pour abroad the winds, and lift the roaring seas. The blue tumbling of waves is before them, marked with the paths of whales. They themselves are calm and bright. The gale lifts slowly their locks of mist.

What beam of light hangs high in air? What beam but Morni's dreadful sword? Death is strewed on thy paths, O Gaul! Thou foldest them together in thy rage. Like a young oak falls Tur–lathon, with his branches round him. His high–bosomed spouse stretches her white arms, in dreams, to the returning chief, as she sleeps by gurgling Moruth, in her disordered locks. It is his ghost, Oichoma. The chief is lowly laid. Hearken not to the winds for Tur–lathon's echoing shield. It is pierced, by his streams. Its sound is passed away.

Not peaceful is the hand of Foldath. He winds his course in blood. Connal met him in fight. They mixed their clanging steel. Why should mine eyes behold them? Connal, thy locks are gray! Thou wert the friend of strangers, at the moss–covered rock of Dun–Ion. When the skies were rolled together: then thy feast was spread. The stranger heard the winds without; and rejoiced at thy burning oak. Why, son of Duth–caron, art thou laid in blood? the blasted tree bends above thee. Thy shield lies broken near. Thy blood mixes with the stream, thou breaker of the shields!

Ossian took the spear, in his wrath. But Gaul rushed forward on Foldath. The feeble pass by his side: his rage is turned on Moma's chief. Now they had raised their deathful spears: unseen an arrow came. it pierced the hand of Gaul. His steel fell sounding to earth. Young Fillan came, with Cormul's shield! lie stretched it large before the chief. Foldath sent his shouts abroad, and kindled all the field: as a blast that lifts the wide–winged flame over Lumon's echoing groves.

"Son of blue–eyed Clatho," said Gaul, "O Fillan! thou art a beam from heaven; that, coming on the troubled deep, binds up the tempest's wing. Cormul is fallen before thee. Early art thou in the fame of thy fathers. Rush not too far, my hero. I cannot lift the spear to aid. I stand harmless in battle: but my voice shall be poured abroad. The sons of Selma shall hear, and remember my former deeds."

His terrible voice rose on the wind. The host bends forward in fight. Often had they heard him at Strumon, when he called them to the chase of the hinds. He stands tall amid the war, as an oak in the skins of a storm, which now is clothed on high, in mist: then shows its broad waving head. The musing hunter lifts his eye, from his own rushy field!

My soul pursues thee, O Fillan! through the path of thy fame. Thou rollest the foe before thee. Now Foldath, perhaps, may fly: but night comes down with its clouds. Cathmor's horn is heard on high. The sons of Selma hear the voice of Fingal, from Mora's gathered mist. The bards pour their song, like den, on the returning war.

"Who comes from Strumon," they said, "amid her wandering locks? She is mournful in her steps, and lifts her blue eyes towards Erin. Why art thou sad, Evir–choma? Who is like thy chief in renown? He descended dreadful to battle; he returns, like a light from a cloud. He raised the sword in wrath: they shrunk before blue–shielded Gaul!

"Joy, like the rustling gale, comes on the soul of the king. He remembers the battles of old; the days wherein his fathers fought. The days of old return on Fingal's mind, as he beholds the renown of his sons. As the sun rejoices, from his cloud, over the tree his beams have raised, as it shades its lonely head on the heath; so joyful is the king over Fillan!

"As the rolling of thunder on hills when Lara's fields are still and dark, such are the steps of Selma, pleasant and dreadful to the ear. They return with their sound, like eagles to their dark– browed rock, after the prey is torn on the field, the dun sons of the bounding hind. Your fathers rejoice from their clouds, sons of streamy Selma!"

Such was the nightly voice of bards, on Mora of the hinds. A flame rose, from a hundred oaks, which winds had torn from Cormul's steep. The feast is spread in the midst; around sat the gleaming chiefs. Fingal is there in his strength. The eagle wing of his helmet sounds. The rustling blasts of the west unequal rush through night. Long looks the king in silence round; at length his words are heard.

"My soul feels a want in our joy. I behold a breach among my friends. The head of one tree is low. The squally wind pours in on Selma. Where is the chief of Dun–lora? Ought Connal to be forgot at the feast? When did he forget the stranger, in the midst of his echoing hall? Ye are silent in my presence! Connal is then no more! Joy meet thee, O warrior! like a stream of light. Swift be thy course to thy fathers, along the roaring winds. Ossian, thy soul is fire; kindle the memory of the king. Awake the, battles of Connal, when first he shone in war. The locks of Connal were gray. His days of youth were mixed with mine.. In one day Duth– caron first strung bows against the roes of Dun–lora."

"Many," I said, "are our paths to battle in green valleyed Erin. Often did our sails arise, over tho blue tumbling waves; when we came in other days, to aid the race of Cona. The strife roared once in Alnecma, at the foam–covered streams of Duth– ula. With Cormac descended to battle Duth–caron, from cloudy Selma. Nor descended Duth–caron alone; his son was by his side, the long–haired youth of Connal, lifting the first of his spears. Thou didst command them, O Fingal! to aid the king of Erin.

"Like the bursting strength of ocean, the sons of Bolga rushed to war. Colc–ulla was before them, the chief of blue stream Atha. The battle was mixed on the plain. Cormac shone in his own strife, bright as the forms of his fathers. But, far before the rest, Duth–caron hewed down the foe. Nor slept the arm of Connal by his father's side. Colc–ulla prevailed on the plain: like scattered mist fled the people of Cormac.

"Then rose the sword of Duth–caron, and the steel of broad– shielded Connal. They shaded their flying friends, like two rocks with their heads of pine. Night came down on Duth–ula; silent strode the chiefs over the field. A mountain–stream roared across the path, nor could Duth–caron bound over its course. 'Why stands my father?' said Connal, 'I hear the rushing foe.'

"'Fly, Connal,' he said. 'Thy father's strength begins to fail. I come wounded from battle. Here let me rest in night.' 'But thou shalt not remain alone,' said Connal's bursting sigh. 'My shield is an eagle's wing to cover the king of Dun–lora.' He bends dark above his father. The mighty Duth–caron dies!

"Day rose, and night returned. No lonely ban appeared, deep musing on the heath: and could Connal leave the tomb of his father, till lie should receive his fame? He bent the bow against the roes of Duth–ula. He spread the lonely feast. Seven nights he laid his head on the tomb, and saw his father in his dreams. lie saw him rolled, dark in a blast, like the vapor of reedy Lego. At length the steps of Colgan came, the bard of high Temora. Duth–caron received his fame and brightened, as he rose on the wind."

"Pleasant to the ear," said Fingal, "is the praise of the kings of men; when their bows are strong in battle; when they soften at the sight of the sad. Thus let my name be renowned, when the bards shall lighten my rising soul. Carril, son of Kinfena! take the bards, and raise a tomb. To–night let Connal dwell within his narrow house. Let not the soul of the valiant wander on the winds. Faint glimmers the moon at Moi–lena, through the broad– headed groves of the hill! Raise stones, beneath its beam, to all the fallen in war. Though no chiefs were they, yet their hands were strong in fight. They were my rock in danger:

the mountain from which I spread my eagle wings. Thence am I renowned. Carril, forget not the low!"

Loud, at once, from the hundred bards, rose the song of the tomb. Carril strode before them; they are the murmur of streams behind his steps. Silence dwells in the vales of Moi−lena, where each, with its owl: dark rib, is winding between the hills. I heard the voice of the bards, lessening, as they moved along. I leaned forward from my shield, and felt the kindling of my soul. Half formed, the words of my song burst forth upon the wind. So hears a tree, on the vale, the voice of spring around. It pours its green leaves to the sun. it shakes its lonely head. The hum of the mountain bee is near it; the hunter sees it with joy, from the blasted heath.

Young Fillan at a distance stood. His helmet lay glittering on the ground. His dark hair is loose to the blast. A beam of light is Clatho's son! He heard the words of the king with joy. He leaned forward on his spear.

"My son," said car−borne Fingal, "I saw thy deeds, and my soul was glad." "The fame of our fathers," I said, "bursts from its gathering cloud. Thou art brave, son of Clatho! but headlong in the strife. So did not Fingal advance, though he never feared a foe. Let thy people be a ridge behind. They are thy strength in the field. Then shalt thou be long renowned, and behold the tombs of the old. The memory of the past returns, my deeds in other years: when first I descended from ocean on the green−valleyed isle."

We bend towards the voice of the king. The moon looks abroad from her cloud. The gray−skirted mist is near: the dwelling of the ghosts!

The southern parts of Ireland went, for some time, under the name of Bolga, from the Fir−bolg or Belgae of Britain, who settled a colony there. "Bolg" signifies a "quiver," from which proceeds "Fir−bolg," i. e., "bowmen:" so called from their using bows more than any of the neighboring nations.

Bruno was a place of worship, (Fing. b. 6.) in Craca, which is supposed to be one of the isles of Shetland

By "the stranger of Inis−huna," is meant Sul−malla. — B iv.

Alnecma, or Alnecmacht, was the ancient name of Connaught. Ullin is still the Irish name of the province of Ulster

TEMORA — BOOK IV

ARGUMENT

The second night continues. Fingal relates, at the feast, his own first expedition into Ireland, and his marriage with Ros–cranna, the daughter of Cormac, king of that island. The Irish chiefs convene in the presence of Cathmor. The situation of the king described. The story of Sul–malla, the daughter of Conmor, king of Inis–huna, who, in the disguise of a young warrior, hath followed Cathmor to the war. The sullen behavior of Foldath, who had commanded in the battle of the preceding day, renews the difference between him and Malthos: but Cathmor, interposing, ends it. The chiefs feast, and hear the song of Fonar the bard. Cathmor returns to rest, at a distance from the army. The ghost of his brother Cairbar appears to him in a dream; and obscurely foretells the issue of the war. The soliloquy of the king. He discovers Sul–malla. Morning comes. Her soliloquy closes the book.

"BENEATH an oak," said the king, "I sat on Selma's streamy rock, when Connal rose, from the sea, with the broken spear of Duth–caron. Far distant stood the youth. He turned away his eyes. He remembered the steps of his father, on his own green hill. I darkened in my place. Dusky thoughts flew over my soul. The kings of Erin rose before me. I half unsheathed the sword. Slowly approached the chiefs. They lifted up their silent eyes. Like a ridge of clouds, they wait for the bursting forth of my voice. My voice was, to them, a wind from heaven, to roll the mist away.

"I bade my white sails to rise, before the roar of Cona's wind. Three hundred youths looked, from their waves, on Fingal's bossy shield. High on the mast it hung, and marked the dark– blue sea. But when night came down, I struck, at times, the warning boss: I struck, and looked on high, for fiery–haired Ul– erin. Nor absent was the star of heaven. It travelled red between the clouds. I pursued the lovely beam, on the faint– gleaming deep. With morning, Erin rose in mist. We came into the bay of Moi–lena, where its blue waters tumbled, in the bosom of echoing woods. Here Cormac, in his secret halls, avoids the strength of Colc–ulla. Nor he alone, avoids the foe. The blue eye of Ros–cranna is there: Ros–cranna, white–handed maid, the daughter of the king!

"Gray, on his pointless spear, came forth the aged steps of Cormac. He smiled from his waving locks; but grief was in his soul. He saw us few before him, and his sigh arose. 'I see the arms of Trenmor,' he said; 'and these are the steps of the king! Fingal! thou art a beam of light to Cormac's darkened soul! Early is thy fame, my son: but strong are the foes of Erin. They are like the roar of streams in the land, son of car–borne Comhal!' 'Yet they may be rolled away,' I said, in my rising soul. 'We are not of the race of the feeble, king of blue–shielded hosts! Why should fear come amongst us, like a ghost of night? The soul of the valiant grows when foes increase in the field. Roll no darkness, king of Erin, on the young in war!'

"The bursting tears of the king came down. He seized my hand in silence. 'Race of the daring Trenmor!' at length he said, 'I roll no cloud before thee. Thou burnest in the fire of thy fathers. I behold thy fame. It marks thy course in battle, like a stream of light. But wait the coming of Cairbar; my so must join thy sword. He calls the sons of Erin from all their distant streams.'

"We came to the hall of the king, where it rose in the midst of rocks, on whose dark sides were the marks of streams of old. Broad oaks bend around with their moss. The thick birch is waving near. Half hid, in her shadowy grove, Ros–cranna raises the song. Her white hands move on the harp. I beheld her blues rolling eyes. She was like a spirit of heaven half folded in the skirt of a cloud!

Three days we feasted at Moi–lena. She rises bright in my troubled soul. Cormac beheld me dark. He gave the white– bosomed maid. She comes with bending eye, amid the wandering of her heavy locks. She came! Straight the battle roared. Colc–ulla appeared: I took my spear. My sword rose, with my people against the ridgy foe. Alnecma fled. Colc–ulla fell. Fingal returned with fame.

"Renowned is he, O Fillan, who fights in the strength of his host. The bard pursues his steps through the land of the foe. But he who fights alone, few are his deeds to other times! He shines to–day, a mighty light. To–morrow he is low. One song contains his fame. His name is one dark field. He is forgot; but where his tomb sends forth the tufted grass."

Such are the words of Fingal, on Mora of the roes. Three bards, from the rock of Cormul, pour down the pleasing song. Sleep descends in the sound, on the broad–skirted host. Carril returned with the bards, from the tomb of Dunlora's chief. The voice of morning shall not come to the dusky bed of Duth–caron. No more shalt thou hear the tread of roes around thy narrow house!

As roll the troubled clouds, around a meteor of night, when they brighten their sides with its light along the heaving sea; so gathers Erin around the gleaming form of Cathmor. He, tall in the midst, careless lifts, at times, his spear: as swells, or falls the sound of Fonar's distant harp. Near him leaned, against a rock, Sul–malla of blue eyes, the white–bosomed daughter of Conmor, king of Inis–huna. To his aid came blue–shielded Cathmor, and rolled his foes away. Sul–malla beheld him stately in the hail of feasts. Nor careless rolled the eyes of Cathmor on the long–haired maid!

"The third day arose, when Fithil came, from Erin of the streams. He told of the lifting up of the shield in Selma: he told of the danger of Cairbar. Cathmor raised the sail at Cluba; but the winds were in other lands. Three days he remained on the coast, and turned his eyes on Conmor's halls. He remembered the daughter of strangers, and his sigh arose. Now when the winds awaked the wave: from the hill came a youth in arms; to lift the sword with Cathmor, in his echoing fields. It was the white– armed Sul–malla. Secret she dwelt beneath her helmet. Her steps were in the path of the king: on him her blue eyes rolled with joy, when he lay by his rolling streams: But Cathmor thought that on Lumon she still pursued the roes. He thought, that fair on a rock, she stretched her white hand to the wind; to feel its course from Erin, the green dwelling of her love. He had promised to return, with his white–bosomed sails. The maid is near thee, O Cathmor: leaning on her rock.

The tall forms of the chiefs stand around; all but dark– browed Foldath. He leaned against a distant tree, rolled into his haughty soul. His bushy hair whistles in the wind. At times, bursts the hum of a song. He struck the tree at length, in wrath; and rushed before the king! Calm and stately, to the beam of the oak, arose the form of young Hidalla. His hair falls round his blushing cheek, in the wreaths of waving light. Soft was his voice in Clonra, in the valley of his fathers. Soft was his voice when he touched the harp, in the hall near his roaring stream!

"King of Erin," said Hidalla, "now is the time to feast. Bid the voice of bards arise. Bid them roll the night away. The soul returns, from song, more terrible to war. Darkness settles on Erin. From hill to hill bend the skirted clouds. Far and gray, on the heath, the dreadful strides of ghosts are seen: the ghosts of those who fell bend forward to their song. Bid, O Cathmor! the harps to rise, to brighten the dead, on their wandering blasts."

"Be all the dead forgot," said Foldath's bursting wrath. "Did not I fail in the field? Shall I then hear the song? Yet was not my course harmless in war. Blood was a stream around my steps. But the feeble were behind me. 'The foe has escaped from my sword. In Conra's vale touch thou the harp. Let Dura answer to the voice of Hidalla. Let some maid look, from the wood, on thy long yellow locks. Fly from Lubar's echoing plain. This is the field of heroes!"

"King of Erin," Malthos said, "it is thine to lead in war. Thou art a fire to our eyes, on the dark–brown field. Like a blast thou hast passed over hosts. Thou hast laid them low in blood. But who has heard thy words returning from the field? The wrathful delight in death; their remembrance rests on the wounds of their spear. Strife is folded in their thoughts: their words are ever heard. Thy course, chief of Moma, was like a troubled stream. The dead were rolled on thy path: but others also lift the spear. We were not feeble behind thee: but the foe was strong."

Cathmor beheld the rising rage and bending forward of either chief: for, half unsheathed, they held their swords, and rolled their silent eyes. Now would they have mixed in horrid fray, had not the wrath of Cathmor burned. He drew his sword: it gleamed through night, to the high–flaming oak! "Sons of pride," said the king," allay your swelling souls. Retire in night. Why should my rage arise? Should I contend with both in arms! It is no time for strife! Retire, ye clouds, at my feast. Awake my soul no more."

They sunk from the king on either side; like two columns of morning mist, when the sun rises, between them, on his glittering rocks. Dark is their rolling on either side: each towards its reedy pool!

Silent sat the chiefs at the feast. They look, at times, on Atha's king, where he strode, on his rock, amid his settling soul. The host lie along the field. Sleep descends on Moi–lena. The voice of Fonar ascends alone, beneath his distant tree. It ascends in the praise of Cathmor, son of Larthon of Lumon. But Cathmor did not hear his praise. He lay at the

174

roar of a stream. The rustling breeze of night flew over his whistling locks.

His brother came to his dreams, half seen from his low– hung cloud. Joy rose darkly in his face. He had heard the song of Carril . A blast sustained his dark–skirted cloud: which he seized in the bosom of night, as he rose, with his fame, towards his airy hail. Half mixed with the noise of the stream, he poured his feeble words.

"Joy meet the soul of Cathmor. His voice was heard on Moi– lena. The bard gave his song to Cairbar. He travels on the wind. My form is in my father's hall, like the gliding of a terrible light, which darts across the desert, in a stormy night. No bard shall be wanting at thy tomb when thou art lowly laid. The sons of song love the valiant. Cathmor, thy name is a pleasant gale. The mournful sounds arise! On Lubar's field there is a voice! Louder still, ye shadowy ghosts! The dead were full of fame! Shrilly swells the feeble sound. The rougher blast alone is heard! Aid soon is Cathmor low!" Rolled into himself he flew, wide on the bosom of winds. The old oak felt his departure, and shook its whistling head. Cathmor starts from rest. He takes his deathful spear. He lifts his eyes around. He sees but dark–skirted night.

"It was the voice of the king," he said. "But now his form is gone. Unmarked is your path in the air, ye children of the night. Often, like a reflected beam, are ye seen in the desert wild: but ye retire in your blasts, before our steps approach. Go, then, ye feeble race! Knowledge with you there is none! Your joys are weak, and like the dreams of our rest, or the light winged thought, that flies across the soul. Shall Cathmor soon be low? Darkly laid in his narrow house! Where no morning comes, with her half–opened eyes? Away, thou shade! to fight is mine! All further thought away! I rush forth on eagles' wings, to seize my beam of flame. In the lonely vale of streams, abides the narrow soul. Years roll on, seasons return, but he is still unknown. In a blast comes cloudy death, and lays his gray head low. His ghost is folded in the vapor of the fenny field. Its course is never on hills, nor mossy vales of wind. So shall not Cathmor depart. No boy in the field was he, who only marks the bed of roes, upon the echoing hills. My issuing forth was with kings. My joy in dreadful plains: where broken hosts are rolled away, like seas before the wind."

So spoke the king of Alnecma, brightening in his rising soul. Valor, like a pleasant flame, is gleaming within his breast. Stately is his stride on the heath! The beam of east is poured around. He saw his gray host on the field, wide spreading their ridges in light. He rejoiced, like a spirit of heaven, whose steps came forth on the seas, when he beholds them peaceful round, and all the winds are laid. But soon he awakes the waves, and rolls them large to some echoing shore.

On the rushy bank of a stream slept the daughter of Inis– huna. The helmet had fallen from her head. Her dreams were in the lands of her fathers. There morning is on the field. Gray streams leap down from the rocks. The breezes, in shadowy waves, fly over the rushy fields. There is the sound that prepares for the chase. There the moving of warriors from the hall. But tall above the rest is seen the hero of streamy Atha. He bends his eye of love on Sul–malla, from his stately steps. She turns, with pride, her face away, and careless bends the bow.

Such were the dreams of the maid when Cathmor of Atha came. He saw her fair face before him, in the midst of her wandering locks. He knew the maid of Lumon. What should Cathmor do? His sighs arise. His tears come down. But straight he turns away. "This is no time, king of Atha, to awake thy secret soul. The battle is rolled before thee like a troubled stream."

He struck that warning boss, wherein dwelt the voice of war. Erin rose around him, like the sound of eagle wing. Sul– malla started from sleep, in her disordered locks. She seized the helmet from earth. She trembled in her place. "Why should they know in Erin of the daughter of Inis–huna?" She remembered the race of kings. The pride of her soul arose! Her steps are behind a rock, by the blue–winding stream of a vale; where dwelt the dark– brown hind ere yet the war arose, thither came the voice of Cathmor, at times, to Sul–malla's ear. Her soul is darkly sad. She pours her words on wind.

"The dreams of Inis–huna departed. They are dispersed from my soul. I hear not the chase in my land. I am concealed in the skirt of war. I look forth from my cloud. No beam appears to light my path. I behold my warriors low; for the broad–shielded king is near. He that overcomes in danger, Fingal, from Selma of spears! Spirit of departed Conmor! are thy steps on the bosom of winds? Comest thou, at times, to other lands, father of sad Sul– malla? Thou dost come! I have heard thy voice at night; while yet I rose on the wave to Erin of the streams. The ghosts of fathers, they say, call away the souls of their race, while they behold them lonely in the midst of wo. Call me, my father, away! When Cathmor is low on earth, then shall Sul–malla be lonely in the midst of wo!

Ul–erin, "the guide to Ireland," was a star known by that name in the days of Fingal

The song of Carril: the funeral elegy at the tomb of Cairbar.

He struck that warning boss: in order to understand this passage, it is necessary to look to the description of Cathmor's shield in the seventh book. This shield had seven principal bosses, the sound of each of which, when struck with a spear, conveyed a particular order from the king to his tribes. The sound of one of them, as here, was the signal for the army to assemble.

TEMORA — BOOK V

ARGUMENT.

The poet, after a short address to the harp of Cona, describes the arrangement of both armies on either side of the river Lubar. Fingal gives the command to Fillan; but at the same time orders Gaul, the son of Morni, who had been wounded in the hand in the preceding battle, to assist him with his counsel. The army of the Fir–bolg is commanded by Foldath. The general onset is described. the great actions of Fillan. He kills Rothmar and Culmin. But when Fillan conquers in one wing, Foldath presses hard on the other. He wounds Dermid, the son of Duthno, and puts the whole wing to flight. Dermid deliberates with himself. and, at last, resolves to put a stop to the progress of Foldath, by engaging him in single combat. When the two chiefs were approaching towards one another, Fillan came suddenly to the relief of Dermid; engaged Foldath, and killed him. The behavior of Malthos towards the fallen Foldath. Fillan puts the whole army, of the Fir–bolg to flight. The book closes with an address to Clatho, the mother of that hero.

THOU dweller between the shields that hang, on high, in Ossian's hall! Descend from thy place, O harp, and let me hear thy voice! Son of Alpin, strike the string. Thou must awake the soul of the bard. The murmur of Lora's stream has rolled the tale away. I stand in the cloud of years. Few are its openings towards the' past; and when the vision comes, it is but dim and dark. I hear thee, harp of Selma! my soul returns like a breeze, which the sun brings back to the vale, where dwelt the lazy mist.

Lubar is bright before me in the windings of its vale. On either side, on their hills, arise the tall forms of the kings. Their people are poured around them, bending forward to their words: as if their fathers spoke, descending from the winds. But they themselves are like two rocks in the midst; each with its dark head of pines, when they are seen in the desert, above low-sailing mist. High on their face are streams which spread their foam on blasts of wind!

Beneath the voice of Cathmor pours Erin, like the sound of flame. Wide they come down to Lubar. Before them is the stride of Foldath. But Cathmor retires to his hill, beneath his bending oak. The tumbling of a stream is near the king. He lifts, at times, his gleaming spear. It is a flame to his people, in the midst of war. Near him stands the daughter of Conmor, leaning on a rock. She did not rejoice at the strife. Her soul delighted not in blood. A valley spreads green behind the hill, with its three, blue streams. The sun is there in silence. The dun mountain roes come down. On these are turned the eyes of Sul-malla in her thoughtful mood.

Fingal beholds Cathmor, on high, the son of Borbar- duthul! he beholds the deep rolling of Erin, on the darkened plain. He strikes that warning boss, which bids the people to obey, when he sends his chief before them, to the field of renown. Wide rise their spears to the sun. Their echoing shields reply around. Fear, like a vapor, winds not among the host: for he, the king, is near, the strength of streamy Selma. Gladness brightens the hero. We hear his words with joy.

"Like the coming forth of winds, is the sound of Selma's sons! They are mountain waters, determined in their course. Hence is Fingal renowned. Hence is his name in other lands. He was not a lonely beam in danger: for your steps were always near! But never was Fingal a dreadful form, in your presence, darkened into wrath. My voice was no thunder to your ears. Mine eyes sent forth no death. When the haughty appeared, I beheld them not. They were forgot at my feasts. Like mist they melted away. A young beam is before you! Few are his paths to war! They are few, but he is valiant. Defend my dark-haired son. Bring Fillan back with joy. Hereafter he may stand alone. His form is like his fathers. His soul is a flame of their fire. Son of car-borne Morni, move behind the youth. Let thy voice reach his ear, from the skirts of war. Not unobserved rolls battle before thee, breaker of the shields."

The king strode, at once, away to Cormul's lofty rock. Intermitting darts the light from his shield, as slow the king of heroes moves. Sidelong rolls his eye o'er the heath, as forming advance the lines. Graceful fly his half-gray locks round his kingly features, now lightened with dreadful joy. Wholly mighty is the chief! Behind him dark and slow I moved. Straight came forward the strength of Gaul. His shield hung loose on its thong. He spoke, in haste, to Ossian. "Bind, son of Fingal, this shield! Bind it high to the side of Gaul. The foe may behold it, and think I lift the spear. If I should fall, let my tomb be hid in the field; for fall I must without fame. Mine arm cannot lift the steel. Let not Evir−choma hear it, to blush between her locks. Fillan, the mighty behold us! Let us not forget the strife. Why should they come from their hills, to aid our flying field!"

He strode onward, with the sound of his shield. My voice pursued him as he went. "Can the son of Morni fall, without his fame in Erin? But the deeds of the mighty are forgot by themselves. They rush carless over the fields of renown. Their words are never heard!" I rejoiced over the steps of the chief. I strode to the rock of the king, where he sat, in his wandering locks, amid the mountain wind!

In two dark ridges bend the host towards each other, at Lubar Here Foldath rises a pillar of darkness: there brightens the youth of Fillan. Each, with his spear in the stream, sent forth the voice of war. Gaul struck, the shield of Selma. At once they plunge in battle! Steel pours its gleam on steel: like the fall of streams shone the field, when they mix their foam together, from two dark−browed rocks! Behold he comes, the son of fame! He lays the people low! Deaths sit on blasts around him! Warriors strew thy paths, O Fillan!

Rothmar, the shield of warriors, stood between two chinky rocks. Two oaks, which winds had bent from high, spread their branches on either side. He rolls his darkening eyes on Fillan, and, silent, shades his friends. Fingal saw the approaching fight. The hero's soul arose. But as the stone of Loda falls, shook, at once, from rocking Drumanard, when spirits heave the earth in their wrath; so fell blue−shielded Rothmar.

Near are the steps of Culmin; the youth came, bursting into tears. Wrathful he cut the wind, ere yet he mixed his strokes with Fillan. He had first bent the bow with Rothmar, at the rock of his own blue streams. There they had marked the place of the roe, as the sunbeam flew over the fern. Why, son of Cul−allin! why, Culmin, dost thou rush on that beam of light? It is a fire that consumes. Son of Cul−allin, retire. Your fathers were not equal in the glittering strife of the field. The mother of Culmin remains in the hall. She looks forth on blue−rolling Strutha. A whirlwind rises, on the stream, dark−eddying round the ghost of her son. His dogs are howling in their place. His shield is bloody in the hall. "Art thou fallen, my fair−haired son, in Erin's dismal war?"

As a roe, pierced in secret, lies panting, by her wonted streams; the hunter surveys her feet of wind! He remembers her stately bounding before. So lay the son of Cul–allin beneath the eye of Fillan. His hair is rolled in a little stream. His blood wanders on his shield. Still his hand holds the sword, that failed him in the midst of danger. "Thou art fallen," said Fillan, "ere yet thy fame was heard. Thy father sent thee to war. He expects to hear of thy deeds. He is gray, perhaps, at his streams. His eyes are towards Moi–lena. But thou shalt not return with the spoil of the fallen foe!"

Fillan pours the flight of Erin before him, over the resounding heath. But, man on man, fell Morven before the dark– red rage of Foldath: for, far on the field, he poured the roar of half his tribes. Dermid stands before him in wrath. The sons of Selma gathered around. But his shield is cleft by Foldath. His people fly over the heath.

Then said the foe in his pride, "They have fled. My fame begins! Go, Malthos, go bid Cathmor guard the dark rolling of ocean; that Fingal may not escape from my sword. He must lie on earth. Beside some fen shall his tomb be seen. It shall rise without a song. His ghost shall hover, in mist, over the reedy pool."

Malthos heard, with darkening doubt. He rolled his silent eyes. He knew the pride of Foldath. He looked up to Fingal on his hills; then darkly turning, in doubtful mood, he plunged his sword in war.

In Clono's narrow vale, where bend two trees above the stream, dark, in his grief, stood Duthno's silent son. The blood pours from the side of Dermid. His shield is broken near. His spear leans against a stone. Why, Dermid, why so sad? "I hear the roar of battle. My people are alone. My steps are slow on the heath and no shield is mine. Shall he then prevail? It is then after Dermid is low! I will call thee forth, O Foldath, and meet thee yet in fight."

He took his spear, with dreadful joy. The son of Morni came. "Stay, son of Duthno, stay thy speed. Thy steps are marked with blood. No bossy shield is thine. Why shouldst thou fall unarmed?" — "Son of Morni, give thou thy shield. It has often rolled back the war! I shall stop the chief in his course. Son of Morni, behold that stone! It lifts its gray head through grass. There dwells a chief of the race of Dermid. Place me there in night."

He slowly rose against the hill. He saw the troubled field: the gleaming ridges of battle, disjointed and broken around. As distant fires, on heath by night, now seem as lost in smoke: now rearing their red streams on the hill, as blow or cease the winds; so met the intermitting war the eye of broad−shielded Dermid. Through the host are the strides of Foldath, like some dark ship on wintry waves, when she issues from between two isles to sport on resounding ocean!

Dermid with rage beholds his course. He strives to rush along. But he fails amid his steps; and the big tear comes down. He sounds his father's horn. He thrice strikes his bossy shield. He calls thrice the name of Foldath, from his roaring tribes. Foldath, with joy, beholds the chief. He lifts aloft his bloody spear. As a rock is marked with streams, that fell troubled down its side in a storm; so streaked with wandering blood, is the dark chief of Moma! The host on either side withdraw from the contending kings. They raise, at once, their gleaming points. Rushing comes Fillan of Selma. Three paces back Foldath withdraws, dazzled with that beam of light, which came, as issuing from a cloud, to save the wounded chief. Growing in his pride he stands. He calls forth all his steel.

As meet two broad−winged eagles, in their sounding strife, in winds: so rush the two chiefs, on Moi−lena, into gloomy fight. By turns are the steps of the kings [Fingal and Cathmor] forward on their rocks above; for now the dusky war seems to descend on their swords. Cathmor feels the joy of warriors!, on his mossy hill: their joy in secret, when dangers rise to match their souls. His eye is not turned on Lubar, but on Selma's dreadful king. He beholds him, on Mora, rising in his arms.

Foldath falls on his shield. The spear of Fillan pierced the king. Nor looks the youth on the fallen, but onward rolls the war. The hundred voices of death arise. "Stay, son of Fingal, stay thy speed. Beholdest thou not that gleaming form, a dreadful sign of death? Awaken not the king of Erin. Return, son of blue−eyed Clatho."

Malthos beholds Foldath low. He darkly stands above the chief. Hatred is rolled from his soul. He seems a rock in a desert, on whose dark side are the trickling of waters; when the slow− sailing mist has left it, and all its trees are blasted with winds. He spoke to the dying hero about the narrow house. "Whether shall thy gray stones rise in Ullin, or in Moma's woody land; where the sun looks, in secret, on the blue streams of Dalrutho? Them are the steps of thy daughter, blue−eyed Dardu−lena!"

"Rememberest thou her," said Foldath, "because no son is mine; no youth to roll the battle before him, in revenge of me? Malthos, I am revenged. I was not peaceful in the field. Raise the tombs of those I have slain, around my narrow house. Often shall I forsake the blast, to rejoice above their graves; when I behold them spread around, with their long–whistling grass."

His soul rushed to the vale of Moma, to Dardu–lena's dreams, where she slept, by Dalrutho's stream, returning from the chase of the hinds. Her bow is near the maid, unstrung. The breezes fold her long hair on her breasts. Clothed in the beauty of youth, the love of heroes lay. Dark bending, from the skirts of the wood, her wounded father seemed to come. He appears, at times, then hid himself in mist. Bursting into tears she arose. She knew that the chief was low. To her came a beam from his soul, when folded in its storms. Thou wert the last of his race, O blue–eyed Dardu–lena.

Wide spreading over echoing Lubar, the flight of Bolga is rolled along. Fillan hangs forward on their steps. He strews, with dead, the heath. Fingal rejoices over his son. Blue–shielded Cathmor rose.

Son of Alpin, bring the harp. Give Fillan's praise to the wind. Raise high his praise in mine ear, while yet he shines in war.

"Leave, blue–eyed Clatho, leave thy hail! Behold that early beam of thine! The host is withered in its course. No further look, it is dark. Light trembling from the harp, strike, virgins, strike the sound. No hunter he descends from the dewy haunt of the bounding roe. He bends not his bow on the wind; nor sends his gray arrow abroad.

"Deep folded in red war! See battle roll against his side. Striding amid the ridgy strife, he pours the death of thousands forth. Fillan is like a spirit of heaven, hat descends from the skirt of winds. The troubled ocean feels his steps, as he strides from wave to wave. His path kindles behind him. Islands shake their heads on the heaving seas! Leave, blue–eyed Clatho, leave thy hall!"

By "the stone of Loda" is meant a place of worship among the Scandinavians.

The poet metaphorically calls Fillan a beam of light.

Dogs were thought to be sensible of the death of their master, let it happen at ever so great a distance. It was also the opinion of the times, that the arms, which warriors left at home, became bloody when they themselves fell in battle.

TEMORA — BOOK VI.

ARGUMENT

This book opens with a speech of Fingal, who sees Cathmor descending to the assistance of his flying army. The king despatches Ossian to the relief of Fillan. He himself retires behind the rock of Cormul, to avoid the sight of the engagement between his son and Cathmor. Ossian advances. The descent of Cathmor described. He rallies the army, renews the battle, and, before Ossian could arrive, engages Fillan himself. Upon the approach of Ossian, the combat between the two heroes ceases. Ossian and Cathmor prepare to fight, but night coming on pre vents them. Ossian returns to the place where Cathmor and Fillan fought. He finds Fillan mortally wounded, and leaning against a rock. Their discourse. Fillan dies, his body is laid, by Ossian, in a neighboring cave. The Caledonian army return to Fingal. He questions them about his son, and understanding that he was killed, retires, in silence, to the rock of Cormul. Upon the retreat of the army of Fingal, the Fir−bolg advance. Cathmor finds Bran, one of the dogs of Fingal, lying on the shield of Fillan, before the entrance of the cave, where the body of that hero lay. His reflection thereupon. He returns, in a melancholy mood, to his army. Malthos endeavors to comfort him, by the example of his father, Borbar−duthul. Cathmor retires to rest. The song of Sul−malla concludes the book, which ends about the middle of the third night from the opening of the poem.

"Cathmor rises on his hill! Shall Fingal take the sword of Luna? But what shall become of thy fame, son of white−bosomed Clatho? Turn not thine eyes from Fingal, fair daughter of Inis− tore. I shall not quench thy early beam. It shines along my soul. Rise, wood−skirted Mora, rise between the war and me! Why should Fingal behold the strife, lest his dark −haired warrior should fall? Amidst the song, O Carril, pour the sound of the trembling harp! Here are the voices of rocks! and there the bright tumbling of waters. Father of Oscar! lift the spear! defend the young in arms. Conceal thy steps from Fillan. He must not know that I doubt his steel. No cloud of mine shall rise, my son, upon thy soul of fire!"

He sunk behind his rock, amid the sound of Carril's song. Brightening in my growing soul, I took the spear of Temora. I saw, along Moi—lena, the wild tumbling of battle; the strife of death, in gleaming rows, disjointed and broken round. Fillan is a beam of fire. From wing to wing is his wasteful course. The ridges of war melt before him. They are rolled, in smoke, from the fields!

Now is the coming forth of Cathmor, in the armor of kings! Dark waves the eagle's wing, above his helmet of fire. Unconcerned are his steps, as if they were to the chase of Erin. He raises, at times, his terrible voice. Erin, abashed, gathers round. Their souls return back, like a stream. They wonder at the steps of their fear. He rose, like the beam of the morning, on a haunted heath: the traveller looks back, with bending eye, on the field of dreadful forms! Sudden from the rock of Moi—lena, are Sul—malla's trembling steps. An oak takes the spear from her hand. Half bent she looses the lance. But then are her eyes on the king, from amid her wandering locks! No friendly strife is before thee! No light contending of bows, as when the youth of Inis—huna come forth beneath the eye of Conmor!

As the rock of Runo, which takes the passing clouds as they fly, seems growing, in gathered darkness, over the streamy heath; so seems the chief of Atha taller, as gather his people around. As different blasts fly over the sea, each behind its dark— blue wave; so Cathmor's words, on every side, pour his warriors forth. Nor silent on his hill is Fillan. He mixes his words with his echoing shield. An eagle be seemed, with sounding wings, calling the wind to his rock, when he sees the coming forth of the roes, on Lutha's rushy field!

Now they bend forward in battle. Death's hundred voices arise. The kings, on either side, were like fires on the souls of the host. Ossian bounded along. High rocks and trees rush tall between the war and me. But I hear the noise of steel, between my clanging arms. Rising, gleaming on the hill, I behold the backward steps of hosts: their backward steps on either side, and wildly—looking eyes. The chiefs were met in dreadful fight! The two blue—shielded kings! Tall and dark, through gleams of steel, are seen the striving heroes! I rush. My fears for Fillan fly, burning, across my soul!

I come. Nor Cathmor flies; nor yet comes on; he sidelong stalks along. An icy rock, cold, tall, he seems. I call forth all my steel. Silent awhile we stride, on either side of a rushing stream: then, sudden turning, all at once, we raise our pointed spears. We raise our spears, but night comes down. It is dark and silent round; but where the distant steps of hosts are sounding over the heath.

I come to the place where Fillan fought. Nor voice nor sound is there. A broken helmet lies on earth, a buckler cleft in twain. Where, Fillan, where art thou, young chief of echoing Morven? He hears me, leaning on a rock, which bends its gray head over the stream. He hears; but sullen, dark he stands. At length. I saw the hero.

"Why standest thou, robed in darkness, son of woody Selma! Bright is thy path, my brother in this dark–brown field! Long has been thy strife in battle! Now the horn of Fingal is heard. Ascend to the cloud of thy father, to his hill of feasts. In the evening mists he sits, and hears the sound of Carril's harp. Carry joy to the aged, young breaker of the shields!"

"Can the vanquished carry joy? Ossian, no shield is mine! It lies broken on the field. The eagle–wing of my helmet is torn. It is when foes fly before them, that fathers delight in their sons. But their sighs burst forth, in secret, when their young warriors yield. No: Fillan shall not behold the king! Why should the hero mourn?"

"Son of blue–eyed Clatho! O Fillan, awake not my soul! Wert thou not a burning fire before him? Shall he not rejoice? Such fame belongs not to Ossian; yet is the king still a sun to me. He looks on my steps with joy. Shadows never rise on his face. Ascend, O Fillan, to Mora! His feast is spread in the folds of mist."

"Ossian! give me that broken shield: those feathers that are rolled in the wind. Place them near to Fillan, that less of his fame may fall. Ossian, I begin to fail. Lay me in that hollow rock. Raise no stone above, lest one should ask about my fame. I am fallen in the first of my fields, fallen without renown. Let thy voice alone send joy to my flying soul. Why should the bard know where dwells the lost beam of Clatho?"

"Is thy spirit on the eddying winds, O Fillan, young breaker of shields. Joy pursue my hero, through his folded clouds. The forms of thy fathers, O Fillan, bend to receive their son! I behold the spreading of their fire on Mora: the blue–rolling of their wreaths. Joy meet thee, my brother! But we are dark and sad! I behold the foe round the aged. I behold the wasting away of his fame. Thou art left alone in the field, O gray–haired king of Selma!"

I laid him in the hollow rock, at the roar of the nightly stream. One red star looked in on the hero. Winds lift, at times, his locks. I listen. No sound is heard. The warrior slept! as lightning on a cloud, a thought came rushing along my soul. My eyes roll in fire: my stride was in the clang of steel. "I will find thee, king of Erin! in the gathering of thy thousands find thee. Why should that cloud escape, that quenched our early beam? Kindle your meteors on your hills, my fathers. Light my daring steps. I will consume in wrath. — But should not I return? The king is without a son, gray–haired among his foes! His arm is not as in the days of old. His fame grows dim in Erin. Let me not behold him, laid low in his latter field — But can I return to the king? Will he not ask about his son?" Thou oughtest to defend young Fillan." — Ossian will meet the foe! Green Erin, thy sounding tread is pleasant to my ear. I rush on thy ridgy host, to shun the eyes of Fingal. I hear the voice of the king, on Mora's misty top! He calls his two sons! I come, my father, in my grief. I come like an eagle, which the flame of night met in the desert, and spoiled of half his wings!

Distant, round the king, on Mora, the broken ridges of Morven are rolled. They turned their eyes: each darkly bends, on his own ashen spear. Silent stood the king in the midst. Thought on thought rolled over his soul: as waves on a secret mountain lake, each with its back of foam. He looked; no son appeared, with his long–beaming spear. The sighs rose, crowding, from his soul; but he concealed his grief. At length I stood beneath an oak. No voice of mine was heard.! What could I say to Fingal in this hour of wo? His words rose, at length, in the midst: the people shrunk backward as he spoke.

"Where is the son of Selma; he who led in war? I behold not his steps, among my people, returning from the field. Fell the young bounding roe, who was so stately on my hills? He fell! for ye are silent. The shield of war is cleft in twain. Let his armor be near to Fingal; and the sword of dark–brown Luno. I am waked on my hills; with morning I descend to war!"

High on Cormul's rock, an oak is flaming to the wind. The gray skirts of mist are rolled around; thither strode the king in his wrath. Distant from the host he always lay, when battle burnt within his soul. On two spears hung his shield on high; the gleaming sign of death! that shield, which he was wont to strike, by night, before he rushed to war. It was then his warriors knew when the king was to lead in strife; for never was his buckler heard, till the wrath of Fingal arose. Unequal were his steps on high, as ho shone on the beam of the oak; he was dreadful as the form of the spirit of night, when he clothes, on

186

his wild gestures with mist, and, issuing forth, on the troubled ocean, mounts the car of winds.

Nor settled, from the storm, is Erin's sea of war! they glitter, beneath the moon, and, low humming, still roll on the field. Alone are the steps of Cathmor, before them on the heath: he hangs forward, with all his arms, on Morven's flying host. Now had he come to the mossy cave, where Fillan lay in night. One tree was bent above! the stream, which glittered over the rock. There shone to the moon the broken shield of Clatho's son; and near it, on grass, lay hairy–footed Bran. He had missed the chief on Mora, and searched him along the wind. He thought that the blue–eyed hunter slept; he lay upon his shield. No blast came over the heath unknown to bounding Bran.

Cathmor saw the white–breasted dog; he saw the broken shield. Darkness is blown back on his soul; he remembers the falling away of the people. They came, a stream; are rolled away; another race succeeds. But some mark the fields, as they pass, with their own mighty names. The heath, through dark brown years, is theirs; some blue stream winds to their fame. Of these be the chief of Atha, when he lays him down on earth. Often may the voice of future times meet Cathmor in the air; when he strides from wind to wind, or folds himself in the wing of a storm.

Green Erin gathered round the king to hear the voice of his power. Their joyful faces bend unequal, forward, in the light of the oak. They who were terrible, were removed; Lubar winds again in their host. Cathmor was that beam from heaven, which shone when his people were dark. He was honored in the midst. Their souls arose with ardor around! The king alone no gladness showed; no stranger he to war!

"Why is the king so sad?" said Malthos, eagle–eyed. "Remains there a foe at Lubar t Lives there among them who can lift the spear? Not so peaceful was thy father, Borbar–duthul, king of spears. His rage was a fire that always burned: his joy over fallen foes was great. Three days feasted the gray–haired hero, when he heard that Calmar fell: Calmar who aided the race of Ullin, from Lara of the streams. Often did he feel, with his hands, the steel which they said had pierced his foe. He felt it with his hands, for Borbar–duthul's eyes had failed. Yet was the king a sun to his friends; a gale to lift their branches round. Joy was around him in his halls: he loved the sons of Bolga. His name remains in Atha, like the awful memory of ghosts whose presence was terrible; but they blew the storm away. Now let the voices of Erin raise the soul of the king; he that shone when war was dark, and laid the mighty low. Fonar, from that gray– browed rock pour the tale of other times: pour it on wide–skirted Erin, as it settles round.

"To me," said Cathmor, "no song shall rise; nor Fonar sit on the rock of Lubar. The mighty there are laid low. Disturb not their rushing ghosts. Far, Malthos, far remove the sound of Erin's song. I rejoice not over the foe, when he ceases to lift the spear. With morning we pour our strength abroad. Fingal is wakened on his echoing hill."

Like waves, blown back by sudden winds, Erin retired, at the voice of the king. Deep, rolled into the field of night, they spread their humming tribes. Beneath his own tree, at intervals, each bard sat down with his harp. They raised the song, and touched the string: each to the chief he loved. Before a burning oak Sul–malla touched, at times, the harp. She touched the harp, and heard, between, the breezes in her hair. In darkness near lay the king of Atha, beneath an aged tree. The beam of the oak was turned from him; he saw the maid, but was not seen. His soul poured forth, in secret, when he beheld her fearful eye. "But battle is before thee, son of Borbar–duthul."

Amidst the harp, at intervals, she listened whether the warrior slept. Her soul was up; she longed, in secret, to pour her own sad song. The field is silent. On their wings the blasts of night retire. The bards had ceased; and meteors came, red– winding with their ghosts. The sky grew dark: the forms of the dead were blended with the clouds. But heedless bends the daughter of Conmor over the decaying flame. Thou wert alone in her soul, car–borne chief of Atha. She raised the voice of the song, and touched the harp between.

"Clun–galo came; she missed the maid. Where art thou, beam of light? Hunters from the mossy rock, saw ye the blue–eyed fair? Are her steps on grassy Lumon; near the bed of roes? Ah, me! I behold her bow in the hail. Where art thou, beam of light?

"Cease, love of Conmor, cease! I hear thee not on the ridgy heath. My eye is turned to the king, whose path is terrible in war. He for whom my soul is up, in the season of my rest. Deep– bosomed in war he stands; he beholds me not from his cloud. Why, sun of Sul–malla, dost thou not look forth? I dwell in darkness here: wide over me flies the shadowy mist. Filled with dew are my locks: look thou from thy cloud, O sun of Sul–malla's soul!"

"I will consume in wrath —" Here the sentence is designedly left unfinished. The sense is, that he was resolved, like a destroying fire, to consume Cathmor, who had killed his brother. In the midst of this resolution, the situation of Fingal suggests itself to him in a very strong light. He resolves to return to assist the king in prosecuting the war. But then his shame for not defending his brother recurs to him. He is determined again to go and find out Cathmor. We may consider him as in the act of advancing towards the enemy, when the horn of Fingal sounded on Mora, and called back his people to his presence.

The voices of Erin: A poetical expression for the bards of Ireland.

Clun–galo: the wife of Conmor, king of Inis–huna, and the mother of Sul–malla. She is here represented as missing her daughter, after she had fled with Cathmor.

TEMORA — BOOK VII.

ARGUMENT.

This book begins about the middle of the third night from the opening of the poem. The poet describes a kind of mist, which rose by night from the Lake of Lego, and was the usual residence of the souls of the dead, during the interval between their decease and the funeral song. The appearance of the ghost of Fillan above the cave where his body lay. His voice comes to Fingal on the rock of Cormul. The king strikes the shield of Trenmor, which was an infallible sign of his appearing in arms himself. The extraordinary effect of the sound of the shield. Sul–malla, starting from sleep, awakes Cathmor. Their affecting discourse. She insists with him to sue for peace; he resolves to continue the war. He directs her to retire to the neighboring valley of Lona, which was the residence of an old Druid, until the battle of the next day should be over. He awakes his army with the sound of his shield. The shield described. Fonar, the bard, at the desire of Cathmor, relates the first settlement of the Fir–bolg in Ireland, under their leader Larthon. Morning comes. Sul–malla retires to the valley of Lona. A lyric song concludes the book.

From the wood–skirted waters of Lego ascend, at times, gray–bosomed mists; when the gates of the west are closed, on the sun's eagle eye. Wide, over Lara's stream, is poured the vapor dark and deep: the moon, like a dim shield, lay swimming through its folds. With this, clothe the spirits of old their sudden gestures on the wind, when they stride, from blast to blast, along the dusky night. Often, blended with the gale, to some warrior's grave, they roll the mist a gray dwelling to his ghost, until the songs arise.

A sound came from the desert; it was Conar, king of Inis– fail. He poured his mist on the grave of Fillan, at blue–winding Lubar. Dark and mournful sat the ghost, in his gray ridge of smoke. The blast, at times, rolled him together; but the form returned again. It returned with bending eyes, and dark winding of locks of mist.

It was dark. The sleeping host were still in the skirts of night. The flame decayed, on the hill of Fingal; the king lay lonely on his shield. His eyes were half clothed in sleep: the voice of Fillan came. "Sleeps the husband of Clatho? Dwells the father of the fallen in rest? Am I forgot in the folds of darkness; lonely in the season of night?"

"Why dost thou mix," said the king, "with the dreams of my father? Can I forget thee, my son, or thy path of fire in the field? Not such come the deeds of the valiant on the soul of Fingal. They are not a beam of lightning, which is seen and is then no more. I remember thee, O Fillan! and my wrath begins to rise."

The king took his deathful spear, and struck the deeply– sounding shield: his shield, that hung high in night, the dismal sign of war. Ghosts fled on every side, and rolled their gathered forms on the wind. Thrice from the winding vales arose the voice of deaths. The harps of the bards, untouched, sound mournful over the hill.

He struck again the shield; battles rose in the dreams of his host. The wide–tumbling strife is gleaming over their souls. Blue–shielded kings descended to war. Backward–looking armies fly; and mighty deeds are half hid in the bright gleams of steel.

But when the third sound arose, deer started from the clefts of their rocks. The screams of fowl are heard in the desert, as each flew frightened on his blast. The sons of Selma half rose and half assumed their spears. But silence rolled back on the host: they knew the shield of the king. Sleep returned to their eyes; the field was dark and still.

No sleep was thine in darkness, blue–eyed daughter of Conmor! Sul–malla heard the dreadful shield, and rose, amid the night. Her steps are towards the king of Atha. "Can danger shake his daring soul?" In doubt, she stands with bending eyes. Heaven burns with all its stars.

Again the shield resounds! She rushed. She stopt. Her voice half rose. It failed. She saw him, amidst his arms, that gleamed to heaven's fire. She saw him dim in his locks, that rose to nightly wind. Away, for fear, she turned her steps. "Why should the king of Erin awake? Thou art not a dream to his rest, daughter of Inis–huna."

More dreadful rings the shield. Sul–malla starts. Her helmet fails. Loud echoes Lubar's rock, as over it rolls the steel. Bursting from the dreams of night, Cathmor half rose beneath his tree. He saw the form of the maid above him, on the rock. A red star, with twinkling beams, looked through her floating hair.

"Who comes through night to Cathmor in the season of his dreams? Bring'st thou aught of war? Who art thou, son of night? Stand'st thou before me, a form of the times of old? a voice from the fold of a cloud, to warn me of the danger of Erin?"

"Nor lonely scout am I, nor voice from folded cloud," she said, "but I warn thee of the danger of Erin. Dost thou hear that sound? It is not the feeble, king of Atha, that rolls his signs on night."

"Let the warrior roll his signs," he replied, "To Cathmor they are the sounds of harps. My joy is great, voice of night, and burns over all my thoughts. This is the music of kings, on lonely hills, by night; when they light their daring souls, the sons of mighty deeds! The feeble dwell alone, in the valley of the breeze; where mists lift their morning skirts, from the blue–winding streams."

"Not feeble, king of men, were they, the fathers of my race. They dwelt in the folds of battle, in their distant lands. Yet delights not my soul in the signs of death! Lie, who never yields, comes forth: O send the bard of peace!"

Like a dropping rock in the desert, stood Cathmor in his tears. Her voice came, a breeze on his soul, and waked the memory of her land; where she dwelt by her peaceful streams, before he came to the war of Conmor.

"Daughter of strangers," he said, (she trembling turned away,) "long have I marked thee in thy steel, young pine of Inis– huna. But my soul, I said, is folded in a storm. Why should that beam arise, till my steps return in peace? Have I been pale in thy presence, as thou bid'st me to fear the king? The time of danger, O maid, is the season of my soul; for then it swells a mighty stream, and rolls me on the foe.

"Beneath the moss—covered rock of Lona, near his own loud stream; gray in his locks of age, dwells Clonmal king of harps. Above him is his echoing tree, and the dun bounding of roes. The noise of our strife reaches his ear, as he bends in the thoughts of years. There let thy rest be, Sul—malla, until our battle cease. Until I return, in my arms, from the skirts of the evening mist, that rises on Lona, round the dwelling of my love."

A light fell on the soul of the maid: it rose kindled before the king. She turned her face to Cathmor, from amidst her waving locks. "Sooner shall the eagle of heaven be torn from the stream of his roaring wind, when he sees the dun prey before him, the young sons of the bounding roe, than thou, O Cathmor, be turned from the strife of renown. Soon may I see thee, warrior, from the skirts of the evening mist, when it is rolled around me, on Lona of the streams. While yet thou art distant far, strike, Cathmor, strike the shield, that joy may return to my darkened soul, as I lean on the mossy rock. But if thou shouldst fall, I am in the land of strangers; O send thy voice from thy cloud, to the midst of Inis—huna!"

"Young branch of green—headed Lumon, why dost thou shake in the storm? Often has Cathmor returned, from darkly rolling wars. The darts of death are but hail to me; they have often rattled along my shield. I have risen brightened from battle, like a meteor from a stormy cloud. Return not, fair beam, from thy vale, when the roar of battle grows. Then might the foe escape, as from my fathers of old.

"They told to Son—mor, of Clunar, who was slain by Cormac in fight. Three days darkened Son—mor, over his brother's fall. His spouse beheld the silent king and foresaw his steps in war. She prepared the bow, in secret, to attend her blue—shielded hero. To her dwelt darkness at Atha, when he was not there. From their hundred streams, by night, poured down the sons of Alnecma. They had heard the shield of the king, and their rage arose. In clanging arms, they moved along towards Ullin of the groves. Son—mor struck his shield, at times the leader of the war.

"Far behind followed Sul—allin, over the streamy hills. She was a light on the mountain, when they crossed the vale below. Her steps were stately on the vale, when they rose on the mossy hill. She feared to approach the king, who left her in echoing Atha. But when the roar of battle rose; when host was rolled on host, when Son—mor burnt, like the fire of heaven in clouds, with her spreading hair came Sul—allin, for she trembled for her king.

192

He stopt the rushing strife to save the love of heroes. The foe fled by night; Clunar slept without his blood; the blood which ought to be poured upon the warrior's tomb.

"Nor rose the rage of Son–mor, but his days were silent and dark. Sul–allin wandered by her gray stream. with her tearful eyes. Often did she look on the hero, when he was folded in his thoughts. But she shrunk from his eyes, and turned her lone steps away. Battles rose, like a tempest, and drove the mist from his soul. He beheld with joy her steps in the hall, and the white rising of her hands on the harp."

In his arms strode the chief of Atha, to where his shield hung, high, in night: high on a mossy bough over Lubar's streamy roar. Seven bosses rose on the shield; the seven voices of the king, which his warriors received, from the wind, and marked over all the tribes.

On each boss is placed a star of night: Canmathon with beams unshorn; Col–derna rising from a cloud; U–leicho robed in mist; and the soft beam of Cathlin glittering on a rock. Smiling, on its own blue wave, Rel–durath half sinks its western light. The red eye of Berthin looks, through a grove, on the hunter, as he returns, by night, with the spoils of the bounding roe. Wide, in the midst, rose the cloudless beams of Ton–thna, that star, which looked by night on the course of the sea–tossed Larthon: Larthon, the first of Bolga's race, who travelled on the winds. White–bosomed spread the sails of the king, towards streamy Inis–fail; dun night was rolled before him, with its skirts of mist. Unconstant blew the winds, and rolled him from wave to wave. Then rose the fiery–haired Ton–thna, and smiled from her parted cloud. Larthon blessed the well–known beam, as it faint gleamed on the deep.

Beneath the spear of Cathmor rose that voice which awakes the bards. They came, dark winding from every side: each with the sound of his harp. Before him rejoiced the king, as the traveller, in the day of the sun; when he hears, far rolling around, the murmur of mossy streams: streams that burst in the desert from the rock of roes.

"Why," said Fonar, "hear we the voice of the king in the season of his rest? Were the dim forms of thy fathers bending in thy dreams? Perhaps they stand on that cloud, and wait for Fonar's song; often they come to the fields where their sons are to lift the spear. Or shall our voice arise for him who lifts the spear no more; he that consumed the field, from Moma of the groves?"

"Not forgot is that cloud in war, bard of other times. High shall his tomb rise, on Moi-lena, the dwelling of renown. But, now, roll back my soul to the times of my fathers: to the years when first they rose, on Inis-huna's waves. Nor alone pleasant to Cathmor is the remembrance of wood-covered Lumon. Lumon of the streams, the dwelling of white-bosomed maids."

"Lumon of the streams, thou risest on Fonar's soul! Thy sun is on thy side, on the rocks of thy bending trees. The dun roe is seen from thy furze; the deer lifts its branchy head; for he sees, at times, the hound on the half-covered heath. Slow, on the vale, are the steps of maids; the white-armed daughters of the bow: they lift their blue eyes to the hill, from amidst their wandering locks. Not there is the stride of Larthon, chief of Inis-huna. He mounts the wave on his own dark oak, in Cluba's ridgy bay. That oak which he cut from Lumon, to bound along the sea. The maids turn their eyes away, lest the king should be lowly laid; for never had they seen a ship, dark rider of the wave!

"Now he dares to call the winds, and to mix with the mist of ocean. Blue Inis-fail rose, in smoke; but dark-skirted night came down. The sons of Bolga feared. The fiery-haired Ton-thna rose. Culbin's bay received the ship, in the bosom of its echoing woods. There issued a stream from Duthuma's horrid cave; where spirits gleamed, at times, with their half finished forms.

"Dreams descended on Larthon: he saw seven spirits of his fathers. He heard their half-formed words, and dimly beheld the times to come. He beheld the kings of Atha, the sons of future days. They led their hosts along the field, like ridges of mist, which winds pour in autumn, over Atha of the groves.

Larthon raised the hall of Semla, to the music of the harp. He went forth to the roes of Erin, to their wonted streams. Nor did he forget green-headed Lumon; he often bounded over his seas, to where white-handed Flathal looked from the hill of roes. Lumon of the foamy streams, thou risest on Fonar's soul!"

Mourning pours from the east. The misty heads of the mountains rise. Valleys show, on every side, the gray winding of the streams. His host heard the shield of Cathmor: at once they rose around; like a crowded sea, when first it feels the wings of the wind, The waves know not whither to roll; they lift their troubled heads.

Sad and slow retired Sul—malla to Lona of the streams. She went, and often turned; her blue eyes rolled in tears. But when she came to the rock, that darkly covered Lona's vale, she looked, from her bursting soul, on the king; and sunk, at once, behind.

Son of Alpin, strike the string. Is there aught of joy in the harp? Pour it then on the soul of Ossian: it is folded in mist. I hear thee, O bard! in my night. But cease the lightly—trembling sound. The joy of grief belongs to Ossian, amidst his dark—brown years.

Green thorn of the hill of ghosts, that shakest thy head to nightly winds! I hear no sound in thee, is there no spirit's windy skirt now rustling in thy leaves? Often are the steps of the dead, in the dark—eddying blasts; when the moon, a dun shield, from the east is rolled along the sky.

Ullin, Carril, and Ryno, voices of the days of old! Let me hear you, while yet it is dark, to please and awake my soul. I hear you not, ye sons of song; in what hall of the clouds is your rest? Do you touch the shadowy harp, robed with morning mist, where the rustling sun comes forth from his green—headed waves?

Lumon: A hill in Inis—huna, near the residence of Sul—malla.

TEMORA — BOOK VIII

ARGUMENT.

The fourth morning from the opening of the poem comes on Fingal, still continuing in the place to which he had retired on the preceding sight, is seen, at intervals, through the mist which covered the rock of Cormul. The descent of the king is described. He orders Gaul, Dermid, and Carril the bard, to go to the valley of China, and conduct from thence the Caledonian army, Ferad— artho, the son of Cairbar, the only person remaining of the family of Conar, the first king of Ireland. The king makes the command of the army, and prepares for battle. Marching towards the enemy, he comes to the cave of Lubar, where the body of Fillan lay. Upon seeing his dog, Bran, who lay at the entrance of the cave, his grief returns. Cathmor arranges the Irish army in order of battle. The appearance of that hero. The general conflict is described. The actions of Fingal and Cathmor. A storm. The total rout of the Fir—bolg. The two kings engage, in a column of mist, on the banks of Lubar, Their attitude and conference after the combat. The death of Cathmor. Fingal resigns the spear of Trenmor to Ossian. The ceremonies observed on that occasion. The spirit of Cathmor, in the mean time, appears to Sul—malla, in the valley of Lona. Her sorrow. Evening comes on. A feast is prepared. The coming of Ferad—artho is announced by the songs of a hundred bards. The poem closes with a speech of Fingal.

As when the wintry winds have seized the waves of the mountain lake, have seized them in stormy night, and clothed them over with ice; white to the hunter's early eye, the billows still seem to roll. He turns his ear to the sound of each unequal ridge. But each is silent, gleaming, strewn with boughs, and tufts of grass, which shake and whistle to the wind, over their gray seats of frost. So silent shone to the morning the ridges of Morven's host, as each warrior looked up from his helmet towards the hill of the king; the cloud—covered hill of Fingal, where he strode in the folds of mist. At times is the hero seen, greatly dim in all his arms. From thought to thought tolled the war, along his mighty soul.

Now is the coming forth of the king. First appeared the sword of Luno; the spear half issuing from a cloud, the shield still dim in mist. But when the stride of the king came abroad, with all his gray dewy locks in the wind; then rose the shouts of his host over every moving tribe. They gathered, gleaming round, with all their echoing shields. So rise the green seas round a spirit, that comes down from the squally wind. The traveller hears the sound afar, and lifts his head over the rock. He looks on the troubled bay, and thinks he dimly sees the form. The waves sport, unwieldy, round, with all their backs of foam.

Far distant stood the son of Morni, Duthno's race, and Cona's bard. We stood far distant; each beneath his tree. We shunned the eyes of the king: we had not conquered in the field. A little stream rolled at my feet: I touched its light wave, with my spear. I touched it with my spear: nor there was the soul of Ossian. It darkly rose, from thought to thought, and sent abroad the sigh.

"Son of Morni," said the king, "Dermid, hunter of roes! why are ye dark, like two rocks, each with its trickling waters? No wrath gathers on Fingal's soul, against the chiefs of men. Ye are my strength in battle; the kindling of my joy in peace. My early voice has been a pleasant gale to your years, when Fillan prepared the bow. The son of Fingal is not here, nor yet the chase of the bounding roes. But why should the breakers of shields stand, darkened, far way?"

Tall they strode towards the king: they saw him turned to Morn's wind. His, tears came down for his blue−eyed son, no slept in the cave of streams. But he brightened before them, and spoke to the broad−shielded kings.

"Crommal, with woody rocks, and misty top, the field of winds, pours forth, to the sight, blue Lubar's streamy roar. Behind it rolls clear−winding Lavath, in the still vale of deer. A cave is dark in a rock; above it strong−winged eagles dwell; broad− headed oaks, before it, sound in Cluna's wind. Within, in his locks of youth, is Ferad−artho, blue−eyed king, the son of broad− shielded Cairbar, from Ullin of the roes. He listens to the voice of Condan, as gray he bends in feeble light. He listens, for his foes dwell in the echoing halls of Temora. He comes, at times, abroad in the skirts of mist, to pierce the bounding roes. When the sun looks on the field, nor by the rock, nor stream, is he! He shuns the race of Bolga, who dwell in his father's hall. Tell him, that Fingal lifts the spear, and that his foes, perhaps, may fail.

"Lift up, O Gaul, the shield before him. Stretch, Dermid, Temora's spear. Be thy voice in his ear, O Carril, with the deeds of his fathers. Lead him to green Moi−lena, to the dusky field of ghosts; for there, I fall forward, in battle, in the folds of war. Before dun night descends, come to high Dunmora's top. Look, from the gray skirts of mist, on Lena of the streams. If there my standard shall float on wind, over Lubar's gleaming stream, then has not Fingal failed in the last of his fields."

Such were his words; nor aught replied the silent striding kings. They looked sidelong on Erin's host, and darkened as they went. Never before had they left the king, in the midst of the stormy field. Behind them, touching at times his harp, the gray− haired Carril moved. He foresaw the fall, of the people, and mournful was the sound! It was like a breeze that comes, by fits, over Lego's reedy lake; when sleep half descends on the hunter, within his mossy cave.

"Why bends the bard of Cona," said Fingal, "over his secret stream? Is this a time for sorrow, father of low−laid Oscar? Be the warriors remembered in peace; when echoing shields are heard no more. Bend, then, in grief, over the flood, where blows the mountain breeze. Let them pass on thy soul, the blue−eyed dwellers of the tomb. But Erin rolls to war; wide tumbling, rough, aid dark. Lift, Ossian, lift the shield. I am alone, my son

THE POEMS OF OSSIAN

As comes the sudden voice of winds to the becalmed ship of Inis–huna, and drives it large, along the deep, dark rider of the wave; so the voice of Fingal sent Ossian, tall along the heath. He lifted high his shining shield, in the dusky wing of war; like the broad, blank moon, in the skirt of a cloud, before the storms. arise.

Loud, from moss–covered Mora, poured down, at once, the broad–winged war. Fingal led his people forth, king of Morven of streams. On high spreads the eagle's wing. His gray hair is poured on his shoulders broad. In thunder are his mighty strides. He often stood, and saw, behind, the wide–gleaming rolling of armor. A rock he seemed, gray over with ice, whose woods are high in wind. Bright streams leapt from its head, and spread their foam on blasts.

Now he came to Lubar's cave, where Fillan darkly slept. Bran still lay on the broken shield: the eagle–wing is strewed by the winds. Bright, from withered furze, looked forth the hero's spear. Then grief stirred the soul of the king, like whirlwinds blackening on a lake. He turned his sudden step, and leaned on his bending spear.

White–breasted Bran came bounding with joy to the known path of Fingal. He came, and looked towards the cave, where the blue–eyed hunter lay, for he was wont to stride, with morning, to the dewy bed of the roe. It was then the tears of the king came down and all his soul was dark. But as the rising wind rolls away the storm of rain, and leaves the white streams to the sun, and high hills with their heads of grass; so the returning war brightened the mind of Fingal. He bounded, on his spear, over Lubar, and struck his echoing shield. His ridgy host bend forward, at once, with all their pointed steel.

Nor Erin heard, with fear, the sound: wide they come rolling along. Dark Malthos, in the wing of war, looks forward from shaggy brows. Next rose that beam of light, Hidalla! then the sidelong–looking gloom of Maronnan. Blue–shielded Clonar lifts the spear: Cormar shakes his bushy locks on the wind. Slowly, from behind a rock, rose the bright form of Atha. First appeared his two–pointed spears, then the half of his burnished shield: like the rising of a nightly meteor, over the valley of ghosts. But when ha shone all abroad, the hosts plunged, at once, into strife. The gleaming waves of steel are poured on either side.

As meet two troubled seas, with the rolling of all their waves, when they feel the wings of contending winds, in the rock– sided firth of Lumon; along the echoing hills in the dim course of ghosts: from the blast fall the torn groves on the deep, amidst the foamy path of whales. So mixed the hosts! Now Fingal; now Cathmor came abroad. The dark tumbling of death is before them: the gleam of broken steel is rolled on their steps, as, loud, the high–bounding kings hewed down the ridge of shields.

Maronnan fell, by Fingal, laid large across a stream. The waters gathered by his side, and leapt gray over his bossy shield. Clonar is pierced by Cathmor; nor yet lay the chief on earth. An oak seized his hair in his fall. His helmet rolled on the ground. By its thong, hung his broad shield; over it wandered his streaming blood. Tla–min shall weep, in the hall, and strike her heaving breast. Nor did Ossian forget the spear, in the wing of his war. He strewed the field with dead. Young Hidallan came. "Soft voice of streamy Clonra! why dost thou lift the steel? O that we met in the strife of song, in thine own rushy vale!" Malthos beheld him low, and darkened as he rushed along. On either side of a stream, we bent in the echoing strife. Heaven comes rolling down; around burst the voices of squally winds. Hills are clothed, at times, in fire. Thunder rolls in wreaths of mist. In darkness shrunk the foe: Morven's warriors stood aghast. Still I bent over the stream, amidst my whistling locks.

Then rose the voice of Fingal, and the sound of the flying foe. I saw the king, at times, in lightning, darkly striding in his might. I struck my echoing shield, and hung forward on the steps of Alnecma; the foe is rolled before me, like a wreath of smoke.

The sun looked forth from his cloud. The hundred streams of Moi–lena shone. Slow rose the blue columns of mist, against the glittering hill. Where are the mighty kings? Nor by that stream, nor wood, are they! I hear the clang of arms! Their strife is in the bosom of that mist. Such is the contending of spirits in a nightly cloud, when they strive for the wintry wings of winds, and the rolling of the foam–covered waves.

I rushed along. The gray mist rose. Tall, gleaming, they stood at Lubar. Cathmor leaned against a rock. His half–fallen shield received the stream, that leapt from the moss above. Towards him is the stride of Fingal: he saw the hero's blood. His sword fell slowly to his side. He spoke, amidst his darkening joy.

"Yields the race of Borbar–duthul? Or still does he lift the spear? Not unheard is thy name, at Atha, in the green dwelling of strangers. It has come, like the breeze of his desert, to the ear of Fingal. Come o my hill of feasts: the mighty fail, at times. No fire am

199

I to low–laid foes; I rejoice not over the fall of the brave. To close the wound is mine: I have known the herbs of the hills. I seized their fair heads, on high, as they waved by their secret streams. Thou art dark and silent, king of Atha of strangers!"

"By Atha of the stream," he said, "there rises a mossy rock. On its head is the wandering of boughs, within the course of winds. Dark, in its face, is a cave, with its own loud rill. There have I heard the tread of strangers, when they passed to my hall of shells. Joy rose, like a flame, on my soul; I blest the echoing rock. Here be my dwelling, in darkness; in my grassy vale. From this I shall mount the breeze, that pursues my thistle's beard; or look down on blue–winding Atha, from its wandering mist."

"Why speaks the king of the tomb? Ossian, the warrior has failed! Joy meet thy soul, like a stream, Cathmor friend of strangers! My son, I hear the call of years; they take my spear as they pass along. Why does not Fingal, they seem to say, rest within his hall? Dost thou always delight in blood? In the tears of the sad? No; ye dark–rolling years, Fingal delights not in blood. Tears are wintry streams that waste away my soul. But when I lie down to rest, then comes the mighty voice of war. It awakes me in my hall and calls forth all my steel. It shall call it forth no more; Ossian, take thou thy father's spear. Lift it, in battle, when the proud arise.

"My fathers, Ossian, trace my steps; my deeds are pleasant to their eyes. Wherever I come forth to battle, on my field, are their columns of mist. But mine arm rescued the feeble! the haughty found my rage was fire. Never over the fallen did mine eye rejoice. For this, my fathers shall meet me, at the gates of their airy halls, tall, with robes of light, with mildly–kindled eyes. But to the proud in arms, they are darkened moons in heaven, which send the fire of night red wandering over their face.

"Father of heroes, Trenmor, dweller of eddying winds, I give thy spear to Ossian: let thine eye rejoice. Thee have I seen, at times, bright from between thy clouds; so appear to my son, when he is to lift the spear: then shall he remember thy mighty deeds, though thou art now but a blast."

He gave the spear to my hand, and raised at once a stone on high, to speak to future times, with its gray head of moss. Beneath he placed a sword in earth, and one bright boss from his shield. Dark in thought awhile he bends: his words at length came forth.

"When thou, O stone, shalt moulder down, and lose thee in the moss of years, then shall the traveller come, and whistling pass away. Thou knowest not, feeble man, that fame once shone on Moi−lena. Here Fingal resigned his spear, after the last of his fields. Pass away, thou empty shade! in thy voice there is no renown. Thou dwellest by some peaceful stream; yet a few years, and thou art gone. No one remembers thee, thou dweller of thick mist! But Fingal shall be clothed with fame, a beam of light to other times; for he went forth, with echoing steel, to save the weak in arms."

Brightening, in his fame, the king strode to Lubar's sounding oak, where it bent, from its rock, over the bright tumbling stream. Beneath it is a narrow plain, and the sound of the fount of the rock. Here the standard of Morven poured its wreaths on the wind, to mark the way of Ferad−artho from his secret vale. Bright, from his parted west, the son of heaven looked abroad. The hero saw his people, and heard their shouts of joy. In broken ridges round, they glittered to the beam. The king rejoiced, as a hunter in his own green vale, when, after the storm is rolled away, he sees the gleaning sides of the rocks. The green thorn shakes its head in their face; from their top look forward the roes.

Gray, at his mossy cave, is bent the aged form of Clonmal. The eyes of the bard had failed. He leaned forward on his staff. Bright in her locks, before him, Sul−malla listened to the tale; the tale of the kings of Atha, in the days of old. The noise of battle had ceased in his Sir: he stopt and raised the secret sigh. The spirits of the dead, they said, often lightened along his soul. He saw the king of Atha low, beneath his bending tree.

"Why art thou dark?" said the maid." The strife of arms is past. Soon shall he come to thy cave, over thy winding streams. The sun looks from the rocks of the west. The mists of the lake arise. Gray they spread on that hill, the rushy dwelling of roes. From the mist shall my king appear! Behold, he comes in his arms. Come to the cave of Clonmal, O my best beloved!"

It was the spirit of Cathmor, stalking, large, a gleaming form. He sunk by the hollow stream, that roared between the hills. "It was but the hunter," she said," who searches for the bed of the roe. His steps are not forth to war; his spouse expects him with night. He shall, whistling, return with the spoils of the dark− brown hinds." Her eyes were turned to the bill; again the stately form came down. She rose in the midst of joy. He retired again in mist. Gradual vanish his limbs of smoke, and mix with the mountain wind. Then she knew that he fell! "King of Erin, art thou low!" Let Ossian forget her grief; it wastes the

201

soul of age.

Evening came down on Moi–lena. Gray rolled the streams of the land. Loud came forth the voice of Fingal: the beam of oaks arose. The people gathered round with gladness, with gladness blended with shades. They sidelong looked to the king, and beheld his unfinished joy. Pleasant from the way of the desert, the voice of music came. It seemed, at first, the noise of a stream, far distant on its rocks. Slow it rolled along the hill, like the ruffled wing of a breeze, when it takes the tufted beard of the rocks, in the still season of night. It was the voice of Condon, mixed with Carril's trembling harp. They came, with blue–eyed Ferad–artho, to Mora of the streams.

Sudden bursts the song from our bards, on Lena: the host struck their shields midst the sound. Gladness rose brightening on the king, like the beam of a cloudy day, when it rises on the green hill, before the roar of winds. He struck the bossy shield of kings; at once they cease around. The people lean forward, from their spears, towards the voice of their land.

"Sons of Morven, spread the feast; send the night away in song. Ye have shone around me, and the dark storm is past. My people are the windy rocks, from which I spread my eagle wings, when I rush forth to renown, and seize it on its field. Ossian, thou hast the spear of Fingal; it is not the staff of a boy with which he strews the thistles round, young wanderer of the field. No: it is the lance of the mighty, with which they stretched forth their hands to death. Look to thy fathers, my son; they are awful beams. With morning lead Ferad–artho forth to the echoing halls of Temora. Remind him of the kings of Erin: the stately forms of old. Let not the fallen be forgot: they were mighty in the field. Let Carril pour his song, that the kings may rejoice in their mist. To morrow I spread my sails to Selma's shaded walls: where streamy Duth–ula winds through the seats of roes."

CONLATH AND CUTHONA.

ARGUMENT.

Conlath was the youngest of Morni's sons, and brother to the celebrated Gaul. He was in love with Cuthona, the daughter of Rumar, when Toscar, the son of Kenfena, accompanied by Fercuth his friend, arrived from Ireland, at Mora, where Conlath dwelt.

He was hospitably received, and according to the custom of the times, feasted three days with Conlath. On the fourth he set sail, and coasting the island of waves, one of the Hebrides, be saw Cuthona hunting, fell in love with her, and carried her away, by force, in his ship. He was forced, by stress of weather, into I– thona, a desert isle. In the mean time Conlath hearing of the rape, sailed after him, and found him on the point of sailing for the coast of Ireland. They fought: and they and their followers fell by mutual wounds. Cuthona did not long survive: for she died of grief the third day after. Fingal hearing of their unfortunate death, sent Stormal the son of Moran to bury them, but forgot to send a bard to sing the funeral song over their tombs. The ghost of Conlath comes long after to Ossian, to entreat him to transmit to posterity, his and Cuthona's fame. For it was the opinion of the times, that the souls of the deceased were not happy, till their elegies were composed by a bard.

Did not Ossian hear a voice? or is it the sound of days that are no more? Often does the memory of former times come, like the evening sun, on my soul. The noise of the chase is renewed. In thought, I lift the spear. But Ossian did hear a voice! Who art thou, son of night? The children of the feeble are asleep. The midnight wind is in my hall. Perhaps it is the shield of Fingal that echoes to the blast. It hangs in Ossian's hall. He feels it sometimes with his hands. Yes, I hear thee, my friend! Long has thy voice been absent from mine ear! What brings thee, on thy cloud, to Ossian, son of generous Morni! Are the friends of the aged near thee? Where is Oscar, son of fame? He was often near thee, O Conlath, when the sound of battle arose.

Ghost of Conlath: Sleeps the sweet voice of Cona, in the midst of his rustling hall? Sleeps Ossian in his hall, and his friends without their fame? The sea rolls round dark I–thona. Our tombs are not seen in our isle. How long shall our fame be unheard, son of resounding Selma?

Ossian: O that mine eyes could behold thee! Thou sittest, dim on thy cloud! Art thou like the mist of Lano? An half– extinguished meteor of fire? Of what are the skirts of thy robe? Of what is thine airy bow? He is gone on his blast like the shade of a wandering cloud. Come from thy wall, O harp! Let me hear thy sound. Let the light of memory rise on I–thona! Let me behold again my, friends! And Ossian does behold his friends, on the dark–blue isle. The cave of Thona appears, with its mossy rocks and bending trees. A stream roars at its mouth. Toscar bends over its course. Fercuth is sad by his side. Cuthona sits at a distance and weeps. Does the wind of the waves deceive me? Or do I hear them speak?

Toscar: The night was stormy. From their hills the groaning oaks came down. The sea darkly tumbled beneath the blast. The roaring waves climbed against our rocks. The lightning came often and showed the blasted fern. Fercuth! I saw the ghost who embroiled the night. Silent he stood, on that bank. His robe of mist flew on the wind. I could behold his tears. An aged man he seemed, and full of thought!

Fercuth: It was thy father, O Toscar. He foresees some death among his race. Such was his appearance on Cromla before the great Maronnan fell. Erin of hills of grass! how pleasant are thy vales! Silence is near thy blue streams. The sun is on thy fields. Soft is the sound of the harp in Sel ma. Lovely the cry of th hunter on Cromla. But we are in dark I–thona, surrounded by the storm. The billows lift their white heads above our rocks. We tremble amidst the night.

Toscar: Whither is the soul of battle fled, Fercuth, with locks of age? I have seen thee undaunted in danger: thine eyes burning with joy in the light. Whither is the soul of battle fled? Our fathers never feared. Go; view the settling sea: the stormy wind is laid. The billows still tremble on the deep. They seem to fear the blast. Go; view the settling sea. Morning is gray on our rocks. The sun will look soon from his east; in all his pride of light! I lifted up my sails with joy before the halls of generous Conlath. My course was by a desert isle: where Cuthona pursued the deer. I saw her, like that beam of the sun that issues from the cloud. Her hair was on her heaving breast. She, bending forward, drew the bow. Her white arm seemed, behind her, like the snow of Cromla. Come to my soul, I said, huntress of the desert isle! But she wastes her time in tears. She thinks of the generous Conlath. Where can I find thy peace, Cuthona, lovely maid?

Cuthona: A distant steep bends over the sea, with aged trees and mossy rocks. The billow rolls at its feet. On its side is the dwelling of roes. The people call it Mora. There the towers of my love arise. There Conlath looks over the sea for his only love. The daughters of the chase returned. He beheld their downcast eyes. "Where is the daughter of Rumar?" But they answered not. My peace dwells on Mora, son of the distant land!

Toscar: Cuthona shall return to her peace: to the towers of generous Conlath. He is the friend of Toscar! I have feasted in his halls! Rise, ye gentle breezes of Erin. Stretch my sails towards Mora's shores. Cuthona shall rest on Mora; but the days of Toscar must be sad. I shall sit in my cave in the field of the sun. The blast will rustle in my trees, I shall think it is Cuthona's voice. But she is distant far, in the halls of the mighty Conlath!

Cuthona: Ha! what cloud is that? It carries the ghost of my fathers. I see the skirts of their robes, like gray and watery mist. When shall I fall, O Rumar? Sad Cuthona foresees her death. Will not Conlath behold me, before I enter the narrow house?

Ossian: He shall behold thee, O maid! He comes along the heaving sea. The death of Toscar is dark on his spear. A wound is in his side! He is pale at the cave of Thona. He shows his ghastly wound. Where art thou with thy tears, Cuthona? The chief of Mora dies. The vision grows dim on my mind. I behold the chiefs no more! But, O ye bards of future times, remember the fall of Conlath with tears. He fell before his day. Sadness darkened in his hall. His mother looked to his shield on the wall, and it was bloody. She knew that her hero fell. Her sorrow was heard on Mora. Art thou pale on thy rock, Cuthona, beside the fallen chiefs? Night comes, and day returns, but none appears to raise their tomb. Thou frightenest the screaming fowls away. Thy tears for ever flow. Thou art pale as a watery cloud, that rises from a lake.

The sons of green Selma came. They found Cuthona cold. They raised a tomb over the heroes. She rests at the side of Conlath! Come not to my dreams, O Conlath! Thou hast received thy fame. Be thy voice far distant from my hail; that sleep may descend at night. O that I could forget my friends; till my footsteps should cease to be seen; till I come among them with joy! and lay my aged limbs in the narrow house!

BERRATHON.

ARGUMENT.

Fingal, in his voyage to Lochlin, whither he had been invited by Starno, the father of Agandecca, touched at Berrathon an island of Scandinavia, where he was kindly entertained by Larthmor, the petty king of the place, who was a vassal of the supreme kings of Lochlin. The hospitality of Larthmor gained him Fingal's friendship, which that hero manifested, after the imprisonment of Larthmor by his own son, by sending Ossian and Toscar, the father of Malvina, so often mentioned, to rescue Larthmor, and to punish the unnatural behavior of Uthal. Uthal was handsome, and, by the ladies, much admired.

THE POEMS OF OSSIAN

Nina–thoma, the beautiful daughter of Tor–thoma, a neighboring prince, fell in love and fled with him. He proved inconstant; for another lady, whose name is not mentioned, gaining his affections, he confined Nina–thoma to a desert island, near the coast of Berrathon. She was relieved by Ossian, who, in company with Toscar, landing on Berrathon, defeated the forces of Uthal, and killed him in single combat. Nina–thoma, whose love not all the bad behavior of Uthal could erase, hearing of his death, died of grief. In the mean time Larthmor is restored, and Ossian and Toscar return in triumph to Fingal.

The poem opens with an elegy on the death of Malvina, the daughter of Toscar, and closes with the presages of Ossian's death.

BEND thy blue course, O stream! round the narrow plain of Lutha. Let the green woods hang over it, from their hills; the sun look on it at noon. The thistle is there on its rock, and shakes its beard to the wind. The flower hangs its heavy head, waving, at times, to the gale. "Why dost thou awake me, O gale?" it seems to say: "I am covered with the drops of heaven. The time of my fading is near, the blast that shall scatter my leaves. To-morrow shall the traveller come; he that saw me in my beauty shall come. His eyes will search the field, but they will not find me." So shall they search in vain for the voice of Cona, after it has failed in the field. The hunter shall come forth in the morning, and thee vote a of my harp shall not be heard. "Where is the son of car–borne Fingal?" The tear will be on his cheek! Then come thou, O Malvina! with all thy music, come! Lay Ossian in the plain of Lutha: let his tomb rise in the lovely field.

Malvina! where art thou, with thy songs; with the soft sound of thy steps? Son of Alpin, art thou near? where is the daughter of Toscar? "I passed, O son of Fingal, by Torlutha's mossy walls. The smoke of the hall was ceased. Silence was among the trees of the hill. The voice of the chase was over. I saw the daughters of the bow. I asked about Malvina, but they answered not. They turned their faces away: thin darkness covered their beauty. They were like stars, on a rainy hill, by night, each looking faintly through the mist!"

Pleasant be thy rest, O lovely beam! soon hast thou set on our hills! The steps of thy departure were stately, like the moon, on the blue–trembling wave. But thou hast left us in darkness, first of the maids of Lutha! We sit, at the rock, and there is no voice; no light but the meteor of fire! Soon hast thou set, O Malvina, daughter of generous Toscar! But thou risest, like the beam of the east, among the spirits of thy friends, where they sit, in their stormy halls, the chambers of the thunder! A cloud hovers over Cona. Its blue curling sides are high. The winds are beneath it, with their wings. Within it is the dwelling of Fingal. There the hero sits in darkness. His airy spear is in his hand. His shield, half covered with clouds, is like the darkened moon; when one half still remains in the wave, and the other looks sickly on the field!

His friends sit round the king, on mist! They hear the songs of Ullin; he strikes the half−viewless harp. He raises the feeble voice. The lesser heroes, with a thousand meteors, light the airy hall. Malvina rises in the midst: a blush is on her cheek. She beholds the unknown faces of her fathers. She turns aside her humid eyes. "An thou come so soon," said Fingal, "daughter of generous Toscar! Sadness dwells in the halls of Lutha. My aged son is sad! I hear the breeze of Cona, that was wont to lift thy heavy locks. It comes to the hall, but thou art not there. Its voice is mournful among the arms of thy fathers! Go, with thy rustling wing, O breeze! sigh on Malvina's tomb. It rises yonder beneath the rock, at the blue stream of Lutha. The maids are departed to their place. Thou alone, O breeze, mournest there!"

But who comes from the dusky west, supported on a cloud? A smile is on his gray, watery face. His locks of mist fly on wind. He bends forward on his airy spear. It is thy father, Malvina! "Why shinest thou, so soon, on our clouds," he says, "O lovely light of Lutha? But thou wert sad, my daughter. Thy friends had passed away. The sons of little men were in the hail. None remained of the heroes, but Ossian, king of spears!"

And dost thou remember Ossian, car−borne Toscar, son of Conloch? The battles of our youth were many. Our swords went together to the field. They saw us coming like two falling rocks. The sons of the stranger fled. "There come the warriors of Cona!" they said. "Their steps are in the paths of the flying!" Draw near, son of Alpin, to the song of the aged. The deeds of other times are in my soul. My memory beams on the days that are past: on the days of mighty Toscar, when our path was in the deep. Draw near, son of Alpin, to the last sound of the voice of Cona!

The king of Morven commanded. I raised my sails to the wind. Toscar, chief of Lutha, stood at my side: I rose on the dark− blue wave. Our course was to sea−surrounded Berrathon, the isle of many storms. There dwelt, with his locks of age, the stately strength of Larthmor. Larthmor, who spread the feast of shells to Fingal, when he went to Starno's halls, in the days of Agandecca. But when the chief was old, the pride of his son arose;

the pride of fair—haired Uthal, the love of a thousand maids. He bound the aged Larthmor, and dwelt in his sounding halls!

Long pined the king in his cave, beside his rolling sea. Day did not come to his dwelling: nor the burning oak by night. But the wind of ocean was there, and the parting beam of the moon. The red star looked on the king, when it trembled on the western wave. Snitho came to Selma's hall; Snitho, the friend of Larthmor's youth. He told of the king of Berrathon: the wrath of Fingal arose. Thrice he assumed the spear, resolved to stretch his hand to Uthal. But the memory of his deeds rose before the king. He sent his son and Toscar. Our joy was great on the rolling sea. We often half unsheathed our swords. For never before had we fought alone, in battles of the spear.

Night came down on the ocean. The winds departed on their wings. Cold and pale is the moon. The red stars lift their heads on high. Our course is slow along the coast of Berrathon. The white waves tumble on the rocks. "What voice is that," said Toscar, "which comes between the sounds of the waves? It is soft hut mournful, like the voice of departed bards. But I behold a maid. She sits on the rock alone. Her head bends on her arms of snow. Her dark hair is in the wind. Hear, son of Fingal, her song; it is smooth as the gliding stream. We came to the silent bay, and heard the maid of night.

"How long will ye roll round me, blue—tumbling waters of ocean? My dwelling was not always in caves, nor beneath the whistling tree. The feast was spread in Tor—thoma's hall. My father delighted in my voice. The youths beheld me in the steps of my loveliness. They blessed the dark—haired Nina—thoma. It was then thou didst come, O Uthal! like the sun in heaven! The souls of the virgins are thine, son of generous Larthmor! But why dost thou leave me alone, in the midst of roaring waters? Was my soul dark with thy death? Did my while hand lift the sword? Why then hast thou left me alone, king of high Fin—thormo?"

The tear started from my eye, when I heard the voice of the maid. I stood before her in my arms. I spoke the words of peace! "Lovely dweller of the cave! what sigh is in thy breast? Shall Ossian lift his sword in thy presence, the destruction of thy foes? Daughter of Tor—thoma, rise! I have heard the words of thy grief. The race of Morven are around thee, who never injured the weak. Come to our dark bosomed ship, thou brighter than the setting moon! Our course is to the rocky Berrathon, to the echoing walls of Fin—thormo." She came in her beauty; she came with all her lovely steps. Silent joy brightened in her face; as when the shadows fly from the field of spring; the blue stream is rolling in brightness, and the green bush bends over its course!

The morning rose with its beams. We came to Rothma's bay. A boar rushed from the wood: my spear pierced his side, and he fell. I rejoiced over the blood. I foresaw my growing fame. But now the sound of Uthal's train came, from the high Fin−thormo. They spread over the heath to the chase of the boar. Himself comes slowly on, in the pride of his strength. He lifts two pointed spears. On his side is the hero's sword. Three youths carry his polished bows. The bounding of five dogs is before him. His heroes move on, at a distance, admiring the steps of the king. Stately was the son of Larthmor! but his soul was dark! Dark as the troubled face of the moon, when it foretells the storms.

We rose on the heath before the king. He stopped in the midst of his course. His heroes gathered around. A. gray−haired bard advanced. "Whence are the sons of the strangers?" began the bard of song. "The children of the unhappy come to Berrathon: to the sword of car−borne Uthal. He spreads no feast in his hall. The blood of strangers is on his streams. If from Selma's walls ye come, from the mossy walls of Fingal, choose three youths to go to your king to tell of the fall of his people. Perhaps the hero may come and pour his blood on Uthal's sword. So shall the fame of Fin−thormo arise; like the growing tree of the vale!"

"Never, will it rise, O bard!" I said, in the pride of my wrath. "He would shrink from the presence of Fingal, whose eyes are the flames of death. The son of Comhal comes, and kings vanish before him. They are rolled together, like mist, by the breath of his rage. Shall three tell to Fingal, that his people fell? Yes! they may tell it, bard! but his people shall fall with fame!"

I stood in the darkness of my strength. Toscar drew his sword at my side. The foe came on like a stream. The mingled sound of death arose. Man took man; shield met shield; steel mixed its beams with steel. Darts hiss through air. Spears ring on mails. Swords on broken bucklers bound. All the noise of an aged grove beneath the roaring wind, when a thousand ghosts break the trees by night, such was the din of arms! But Uthal fell beneath my sword. The sons of Berrathon fled. It was then I saw him in his beauty, and the tear hung in my eye! "Thou art fallen, young tree, I said, with all thy beauty round thee. Thou art fallen on thy plains, and the field is bare. The winds come from the desert! there is no sound in thy leaves! Lovely art thou in death, son of car−borne Larthmor"

Nina—thoma sat on the shore. She heard the sound of battle. She turned her red eyes on Lethmal, the gray—haired bard of Selma. He alone had remained on the coast with the daughter of Tor—thoma. "Son of the times of old!" she said, "I hear the noise of death. Thy friends have met with Uthal, and the chief is low! O that I had remained on the rock, enclosed with the tumbling waves? Then would my soul be sad, but his death would not reach my ear. Art thou fallen on the heath, O son of high Fin— thormo? Thou didst leave me on a rock, but my soul was full of thee. Son of high Fin—thormo! art thou fallen on thy heath?"

She rose pale in her tears. She saw the bloody shield of Uthal. She saw it in Ossian's hand. Her steps were distracted on the heath. She flew. She found him. She fell. Her soul came forth in a sigh. Her hair is spread on her face. My bursting tears descend. A tomb arose on the unhappy. My song of wo was heard. "Rest, hapless children of youth! Rest at the noise of that mossy stream! The virgins will see your tomb, at the chase, and turn away their weeping eyes. Your fame will be in song. The voice of the harp will be heard in your praise. The daughters of Selma shall hear it: your renown shall be in other lands. Rest, children of youth, at the noise of the mossy stream!"

Two days we remained on the coast. The heroes of Berrathon convened. We brought Larthmor to his halls. The feast of shells is spread. The joy of the aged was great. He looked to the arms of his fathers; the arms which he left in his hall, when the pride of Uthal rose. We were renowned before Larthmor. He blessed the chiefs of Morven. He knew not that his son was low, the stately strength of Uthal! They had told, that he had retired to the woods, with the tears of grief. They had told it, but he was silent in the tomb of Rothma's heath.

On the fourth day we raised our sails, to the roar of the northern wind. Larthmor came to the coast. His bards exalted the song. The joy of the king was great; he looked to Rothma's gloomy heath. He saw the tomb of his son. The memory of Uthal rose. "Who of my heroes," he said, "lies there? he seems to have been of the kings of men. Was he renowned in my halls before the pride of Uthal rose? Ye are silent, sons of Berrathon! is the king of heroes low? My heart melts for thee, O Uthal! though thy hand was against thy father. O that I had remained in the cave! that my son had dwelt in Fin—thormo! I might have heard the tread of his feet, when he went to the chase of the boar. I might have heard his voice on the blast of my cave. Then would my soul be glad; but now darkness dwells in my halls."

Such were my deeds, son of Alpin, when the arm of my youth was strong. Such the actions of Toscar, the car–borne son of Conloch. But Toscar is on his flying cloud. I am alone at Lutha. My voice is like the last sound of the wind, when it forsakes the woods. But Ossian shall not be long alone. He sees the mist that shall receive his ghost. He beholds the mist that shall form his robe, when he appears on his hills. The Sons of feeble men shall behold me, and admire the stature of the chiefs of old. They shall creep to their caves. They shall look to the sky with fear: for my steps shall be in the clouds. Darkness shall roll on my side.

Lead, son of Alpin, lead the aged to his woods. The winds begin to rise. The dark wave of the lake resounds. Bends there not a tree from Mora with its branches bare? It bends, son of Alpin, in the rustling blast. My harp hangs on a blasted branch. The sound of its strings is mournful. Does the wind touch thee, O harp, or is it some passing ghost? It is the hand of Malvina! Bring me the harp, son of Alpin. Another song shall rise. My soul shall depart in the sound. My fathers shall hear it in their airy hail. Their dim faces shall hang, with joy, from their clouds; and their hands receive their son. The aged oak bends over the stream. It sighs with all its moss. The withered fern whistles near, and mixes, as it waves, with Ossian's hair.

"Strike the harp, and raise the song: be near, with all your wings, ye winds. Bear the mournful sound away to Fingal's airy hail. Bear it to Fingal's hall, that he may hear the voice of his son: the voice of him that praised the mighty!

"The blast of north opens thy gates, O king! I behold thee sitting on mist dimly gleaming in all thine arms. Thy form now is not the terror of the valiant. It is like a watery cloud, when we see the stars behind it with their weeping eyes. Thy shield is the aged moon: thy sword a vapor half kindled with fire. Dim and feeble is the chief who travelled in brightness be fore! But thy steps are on the winds of the desert. The storms are darkening in thy hand. Thou takest the sun in thy wrath, and hidest him in thy clouds. The sons of little men are afraid. A thousand showers descend. But when thou comest forth in thy mildness, the gale of the morning is near thy course. The sun laughs in his blue fields. The gray stream winds in its vale. The bushes shake their green heads in the wind. The roes bound towards the desert.

"There is a murmur in the heath! the stormy winds abate! I hear the voice of Fingal. Long has it been absent from mine ear! 'Come, Ossian, come away, he says. Fingal has received his fame. We passed away, like flames that have shone for a season. Our departure was in renown. Though the plains of our battles are dark and silent; our fame is in the four gray stones. The voice of Ossian has been heard. The harp has been strung in Selma. 'Come, Ossian, come away,' he says; 'come, fly with thy fathers on clouds.' I come, I come, thou king of men! The life of Ossian fails. I begin to vanish on Cona. My steps are not seen in Selma. Beside the stone of Mora I shall fall asleep. The winds whistling in my gray hair, shall not awaken me. Depart on thy wings, O wind, thou canst not disturb the rest of the bard. The night is long, but his eyes are heavy. Depart, thou rustling blast.

"But why art thou sad, son of Fingal? Why grows the cloud of thy soul? The chiefs of other times are departed. They have gone without their fame. The sons of future years shall pass away. Another race shall arise. The people are like the waves of ocean; like the leaves of woody Morven, they pass away in the rustling blast, and other leaves lift their green heads on high.

"Did thy beauty last, O Ryno? Stood the strength of car– borne Oscar! Fingal himself departed! The hails of his fathers forgot his steps. Shalt thou then remain, thou aged bard? when the mighty have failed? But my fame shall remain, and grow like the oak of Morven; which lifts its broad head to the storm, and rejoices in the course of the wind?"

The maids: that is, the young virgins who sung the funeral elegy over her tomb.

THE END

Printed in the United Kingdom
by Lightning Source UK Ltd.
113346UKS00002B/37